WESTWATER LOST AND FOUND

Westwater
LOST AND FOUND

EXPANDED EDITION

Mike Milligan

UTAH STATE UNIVERSITY PRESS
Logan

© 2024 by University Press of Colorado

Published by Utah State University Press
An imprint of University Press of Colorado
1580 North Logan Street, Suite 660
PMB 39883
Denver, Colorado 80203-1942

All rights reserved
Printed in the United States of America

 The University Press of Colorado is a proud member of Association of University Presses.

The University Press of Colorado is a cooperative publishing enterprise supported, in part, by Adams State University, Colorado State University, Fort Lewis College, Metropolitan State University of Denver, University of Alaska Fairbanks, University of Colorado, University of Denver, University of Northern Colorado, University of Wyoming, Utah State University, and Western Colorado University.

This paper meets the requirements of the ANSI/NISO Z39.48-1992 (Permanence of Paper).

ISBN: 978-1-64642-544-0 (hardcover)
ISBN: 978-1-64642-608-9 (paperback)
ISBN: 978-1-64642-545-7 (ebook)
https://doi.org/10.7330/9781646425457

Library of Congress Cataloging-in-Publication Data

Names: Milligan, Mike, author. | Kolb, E. L. (Ellsworth Leonardson), 1876–1960. Through the Grand Canyon from Wyoming to Mexico.
Title: Westwater lost and found : expanded edition / Mike Milligan.
Description: Logan : Utah State University Press, [2023] | Includes bibliographical references and index.
Identifiers: LCCN 2023037688 (print) | LCCN 2023037689 (ebook) | ISBN 9781646425440 (hardcover) | ISBN 9781646426089 (paperback) | ISBN 9781646425457 (ebook)
Subjects: LCSH: Westwater (Utah)—History. | Westwater (Utah)—Description and travel. | Colorado River (Colo.-Mexico)—History. | Colorado River (Colo.-Mexico)—Description and travel.
Classification: LCC F834.W477 M55 2023 (print) | LCC F834.W477 (ebook) | DDC 917.92/5—dc23/eng/20231108
LC record available at https://lccn.loc.gov/2023037688
LC ebook record available at https://lccn.loc.gov/2023037689

Cover photograph courtesy of Ross Henshaw, 2005.

*To my mother Pauline's children and grandchildren.
May they learn of her through her children.*

CONTENTS

List of Figures ix
Foreword by Roy Webb xv
Acknowledgments xix
"Life's Depths": A Poem xxv

Introduction 3

1 Westwater Camp: Water, Wood, and Grass 15

2 The Outlaw Brothers 40

3 Those Darn Woman's Shoes Found in Westwater's Cave 57

4 Dentists' Sabbatical on the Grand River in 1897 65

5 Ellsworth Kolb: Losing His Boyhood 79

6 Fellows and Torrence: Overcoming the Narrows 109

Epilogue 138

Appendix A: Frederick Kreutzfeldt (Creutzfeldt)—
Partial Journal Notes from 1853 149

Appendix B: Westwater Camp and Water Stop Chronology 159

Appendix C: Dr. James E. Miller's Letter to Frederick
S. Dellenbaugh, November 2, 1906 165

Appendix D: Robert Brewster Stanton's letter to
Dr. James E. Miller, May 11, 1909 169

Appendix E: Ellsworth L. Kolb's Newspaper Accounting of Section
Three of Black Canyon of the Gunnison River 171

*Appendix F: Ellsworth L. Kolb's 1918 Manuscript of
the Grand and Gunnison Rivers*   175

Appendix G: Colorado River Sites—Westwater Area   217

Notes   241

Bibliography   261

Index   275

FIGURES

0.1. Three Spanish Crosses located in the vicinity of Big Hole. *5*
1.1. Westwater launch site looking upstream in the direction of Ruby Canyon. *16*
1.2. A small Westwater railroad town existed in the vicinity of where the parked van is. *18*
1.3. A 1916 photo by Westwater resident Beatrix Simpson of a farm and Westwater Ranch in the distance. *20*
1.4. General Edward R. S. Canby. *21*
1.5. Map of Westwater area by Hayden Survey, 1875–1876. *22*
1.6. Map of three primary branches of the Old Spanish Trail. *23*
1.7. Antoine Robidoux inscription found along an early trapper trail entering into the Book Cliffs that led to the Salt Lake, Green River, and Rendezvous areas. *26*
1.8. North Branch of the Old Spanish Trail. *31*
1.9. Undated stereo image of Westwater where Westwater Creek drains into the Colorado River. *34*
1.10. Cisco Desert images near Green River, Utah. *37*
1.11. Whitewater enthusiasts at Westwater Canyon launch site. *38*
2.1. Outlaw Cave, in the middle of Westwater Canyon along the Colorado River. *41*
2.2. Dee Holladay at Outlaw Cave. *44*
2.3. Outlaw Grave. *45*
2.4. Train Robbery wood engraving. *47*
2.5. Gunnison Sheriff Cyrus W. (Doc) Shores (1834–1944). *49*
2.6. Outlaw Cave. *53*
2.7. Decommissioned Post Office at Cisco, Utah. *55*
3.1. Outlaw Cave interior view. *58*
3.2. Tabletop that includes woman's shoe found in Outlaw Cave. *61*

FIGURES

4.1. Galloway-style Cataract boat used on the Stone expedition in 1909. *66*
4.2. Robert Brewster Stanton (1846–1922) and Frederick Samuel Dellenbaugh (1853–1935). *68*
4.3. Dr. James Edwin Miller DDS (1857–1945). *69*
4.4. Westwater Canyon at the head of Skull Rapid. *74*
4.5. Big Drop 3, often called "Satan's Gut," at lowest recorded level of 2,700 cfs during week of July 1, 2002. *77*
4.6. Cataract Canyon, also known as the "Graveyard of the Colorado River," which offers some of the largest whitewater in the United States. *77*
5.1. Ellsworth Leonardson Kolb. *80*
5.2. July 26, 1916, L–R Ellsworth Kolb, John W. Shields, Nathan B. Stern, and Julius F. Stone pose with equipment along the Gunnison River near Cimarron, Colorado. *82*
5.3. Kolb Brothers in the Grand Canyon. *85*
5.4. Black Canyon of the Gunnison National Park taken upstream from the Narrows overlook on the North Rim. *91*
5.5. Bert Loper at Pierce Ferry in 1939. *95*
5.6. Ellsworth Kolb filming Shoshone Falls above Glenwood Springs. *96*
5.7. Westwater Station, 1902. *97*
5.8. Kolb and Loper camp above the Big Whirlpool aka Room of Doom in Westwater Canyon. *99*
5.9. Portage of one of the boats in the Black Canyon of the Gunnison River in Section Three. *101*
5.10. Between 1910 and 1924, Ellsworth Kolb next to biplane. *103*
5.11. Ellsworth Kolb, Gulf of California in 1913. *108*
6.1. The Black Canyon of the Gunnison National Park at Painted Wall taken from Chasm View on the North Rim. *111*
6.2. Utah juniper found on South Rim of the Black Canyon of the Gunnison National Park at Dragon Point overlook. *113*
6.3. Will Torrence and Abraham Lincoln Fellows. *116*
6.4. A. L. Fellows using an inflatable mattress when swimming in the Gunnison River in 1901. *117*
6.5. Carrying the boat around rapids in the Black Canyon in 1900. *118*
6.6. Milo Wynne aka Captain Black's second edition standard list of rapids and drops between East Portal and Chukar Trail in the Black Canyon of the Gunnison National Park. *120*

Figures | xi

6.7. Modified NPS map of the Black Canyon of the Gunnison National Park. *121*
6.8. The Narrows taken from the Narrows overlook. *123*
6.9. Black Canyon rapids at the Narrows. *124*
6.10. New Generation Rapid and Painted Wall taken from SOB Gulch by Milo Wynne aka Captain Black (2016). *126*
6.11. Buried Gunnison River, taken from the South Rim Chasm View overlook. *127*
6.12. A. L. Fellows in the Black Canyon of the Gunnison River looking up from transit point #44 at Torrence Falls in 1902. *128*
6.13. Great Falls Rapid as seen from the South Rim's Painted Wall overlook. *129*
6.14. Tom Janney kayaks Next or New Generation Rapid while Janson Stingl looks on. *132*
6.15. Walter Kirschbaum kayaking through a rapid on the Colorado River in the Grand Canyon in August 1960. *134*
6.16. Tom Janney kayaking 18' waterfall below the Narrows in the Black Canyon of the Gunnison National Park. *135*
7.1. Grand Canyon, with Jack Brennan, Don Harris, and Bert Loper scouting a rapid in 1939. *143*
7.2. Author and Westwater ranger Bob Brennan at the Three Spanish Crosses inscription in Westwater Canyon, April 26, 2022. *147*
13.1. Waterfall at Lake Fork of the Gunnison River. *177*
13.2. A swollen Gunnison River near Cimarron, Colorado. *181*
13.3. Crew from 1916, L–R Ellsworth Kolb, Julius F. Stone, John W. Shields, and Nathan B. (N. B.) Stern, pose along the Gunnison River at Cimmaron, Colorado. *182*
13.4. Julius F. Stone, John W. Shields, and N. B. Stern at the great pile of driftwood in the Black Canyon of the Gunnison River. *187*
13.5. Nearly boulder-dammed Gunnison River probably found in Section 2. *190*
13.6. Inflatable canoe defeated on the Gunnison River. *191*
13.7. Westwater Canyon, "The canyon is very picturesque and reminded us in a way of the Grand Canyon of Arizona." *192*
13.8. "Entrance to Westwater Canyon, Utah. One man rows; the other lies on the deck, hanging to the bulkheads." *193*
13.9. Kolb and Loper boat through the Gunnison Tunnel. *194*
13.10. Two new boats arrived for Ellsworth Kolb and Bert Loper to begin the third section of the Black Canyon in 1916. *196*

xii | FIGURES

13.11. Bert Loper helping portage boats around Flat Rock Falls, Black Canyon. *197*
13.12. Bert Loper working with dynamite to dislodge boat from rocks on the Gunnison River. *198*
13.13. Bert Loper looking downstream at the Narrows of the Gunnison River in the Black Canyon. *199*
13.14. Portage amid snow below the Narrows on the Gunnison River. *201*
13.15. Snow and ice cover what Ellsworth Kolb described as a twelve-foot waterfall. *204*
13.16. Painted Wall as seen from the North Rim of the Black Canyon near SOB Gulch. *205*
13.17. Large rapid located at the bottom of SOB Gulch currently known as either New or Next Generation Rapid. *205*
13.18. Back of photo reading, "only place where ice helped." *206*
13.19. Portaging boat at top of Torrence Falls in the Black Canyon of Gunnison. *208*
13.20. Ellsworth Kolb and Bert Loper with Peterborough canoe used on the Grand River and the second section of the Gunnison River. *211*
13.21. Loper and Kolb portaging boat around Shoshone Falls on Grand River above Glenwood Springs. *213*
13.22. Frank E. Dean and Bert Loper filming Whirlpool Rapid aka Skull Rapid while cowboy watches the event. *214*
13.23. Ellsworth Kolb photo at Whirlpool, today known as the Room of Doom in Westwater Canyon. *215*
14.1. Modified BLM map of Westwater highlighting additional historical sites. *218*
14.2. General location along bank where Charles Brock dugout was located; Captain Wilson E. Davis's photo from approximate time of the killings, and 1915 photo from San Quentin State Prison. *220*
14.3. Harvey Edward Herbert's home near the confluence of Bitter Creek with the Colorado River. *222*
14.4. Westwater water tank. *223*
14.5. The road to Westwater Launch is part of the Old Salt Lake Wagon Road; van parked in vicinity of former Westwater railroad station and tank. *223*
14.6. Elwood Clark Malin and stepson Jesse Hunt at Westwater. *225*
14.7. Old Wagon found at Westwater Ranch. *226*
14.8. Miners' Cabin, fireplace, and motor used by placer miners near Wild Horse Camp. *228*

14.9. Remains of Duplex Miners' Cabins.   *229*
14.10. Quadruped Petroglyph at Little Hole.   *230*
14.11. Little Dolores waterfall.   *231*
14.12. Outlaw Cave collage.   *232*
14.13. Outlaw Grave.   *233*
14.14. Photographers awaiting Ellsworth Kolb to boat Whirlpool Rapid in 1916.   *235*
14.15. Room of Doom, previously known by local residents as Big Whirlpool.   *236*
14.16. Second dam site proposed on Grand River below Westwater, Utah.   *237*
14.17. C. R. Sherrill memorial.   *238*
14.18. Cisco post office.   *239*

FOREWORD

Roy Webb

I was at a meeting of Colorado River guides recently—a confluence, one might say—and someone commented that they didn't know of many good sources for the history of Westwater Canyon. I was happy to point out that there happens to be a very good source for just that exact topic: *Westwater Lost and Found* by Mike Milligan. It falls into that happy category of "everything you ever needed to know" in one well-written book. I've known Mike Milligan for so long that I can't even remember where we met, and have always welcomed the chance to sit down and spend time with him. We've shared a long interest in the history of the Colorado River and have corresponded on email or run into each other at river guides meetings and history conferences. I was aware that Mike was working hard at researching and then writing a book, and when Mike's *Westwater Lost and Found* came out in 2004, I knew right away it was a tour de force, a deep and comprehensive study of one of the least-known stretches of the Colorado River. Although thousands of boaters go down it every year, no one had ever written its colorful, fascinating, and sometimes tragic history. With the publication of *Westwater Lost and Found*, Mike cured that problem without a doubt.

The first version of this book was encyclopedic; not only did Mike reveal many compelling, little-known human stories, but he wrote a reference work on the long history of this remote and often-ignored land. I enjoyed reading it and recommending it to others, and I found myself going back to it at times for a quick look at a story or to check a fact. And I was always glad to recommend it to anyone who asked. But I've found in my own work that as soon as something is published, you start to learn more and more and inevitably end up feeling like you need to write another book; I like to say something swirled in my head like a stick in an eddy. Mike felt that same compulsion to keep going, to look for one more obscure newspaper article or long-forgotten account of an early traveler. What about those new questions about Outlaw Cave? Was there really a crossing of the Old Spanish Trail, the longest and most difficult overland route in the country, near Westwater? The result is in your hands today.

Because of its incredibly detailed and in-depth, but never pedantic, coverage, to read *Westwater Lost and Found* is to be talking to Mike. Mike's a big guy with a quiet voice that makes you glad you're spending this time with him. Then there's a quick flash of humor and a smile, and it's off into another fascinating Westwater story. And this is a big book, full of quiet and meaningful undertones, just like its author. The pages turn like a novel; with each one wanting you to know more, to see how that story turned out. And there's always another story: Mike is an indefatigable researcher. Through his relentless digging, he's unearthed documents that were only known to former laborers in those archival halls we like to call the "dusty archives." (I spent forty years as an archivist at the University of Utah, so I get to say that.) Reading Mike's work, the phrase "contribution to the literature" comes to mind. That means that he's not only expanded the body of knowledge, but he's done it in a way meant to be read; he's added to the literature on the river. That's always a noteworthy achievement, one every historian should strive for.

Colorado and Green River runners can be positively tribal, loyal to their particular stretch of river; and river historians tend to specialize, some on the Grand Canyon, others on the upper rivers. I've done it myself for years. But to our delight, Mike's expanded edition ties Westwater to the larger history of travel down the great canyon rivers and the Colorado Plateau. I've studied nothing but the history of the Green and Colorado for decades, and I found myself learning new stories on almost every page. Besides the history of river travel, Mike's work has provided us with a comprehensive well-researched history of the entire region around Westwater, from the Book Cliffs to the north and the Four Corners to the south. Add to this the vast number of historic photographs that enliven the book, and Mike has produced a work that belongs not only in every river runner's library but on the shelves of anyone who loves the Colorado Plateau.

I have a good friend from the University of Utah's Marriott Library who is a veteran of the Vietnam War. During that conflict, he lived through dangerous, traumatic, life-threatening experiences. What I've always admired about this friend is that unlike so many who suffered those same traumas and, sadly, turned to drugs or drink, this friend turned his memories into the study of the history of Vietnam. He became a nationally known expert on the railroads of French Indochina, for instance, or the relationships between Vietnamese women and Chinese merchants. No detail of that country's long and often difficult past was too small for him to find and write or speak about. So it has been with Mike Milligan ever since he suffered a trauma that changed his life. That story is his to tell, and he does in a very powerful and moving way in the introduction. Mike turned his trauma into a lifelong fascination with Westwater Canyon, its landscapes and characters and stories, and *Westwater Lost and Found: Expanded Edition* is our silver lining to that awful event. As Mike says in the introduction, "I felt compelled to research further." And we're glad he did.

ACKNOWLEDGMENTS

It's always difficult to acknowledge who helps with a project of writing a book. It's easy to sincerely thank someone for their assistance; however, it is difficult to remember the names of everyone who has helped me along the way. Many people I acknowledged in my first book *Westwater Lost and Found* may be repeated here because their help continues to influence what I research and write about.

    I need to always revert to the beginning of the support and encouragement that I received from former Bureau of Land Management (BLM) Westwater ranger, and founding trustee and director of Canyonlands Field Institute (CFI), Karla VanderZanden, and the late Dee Holladay of Holiday River Expeditions. Also, my gratitude goes to the late William C. "Bill" Suran and his generous assistance with Ellsworth L. Kolb material located in the Cline Library at Northern Arizona University (NAU). Bill motivated me to want to share with the boating community what he had shared with me. Before NAU digitized Emery Kolb's collection of photographs, Bill made the effort to send me Xerox copies of many of them that were thought to be of Westwater and the Gunnison River. Recently, I've received great assistance from Peter John Runge, head of Special Collections and Archives for Cline Library at NAU, and Kim Besom, Grand Canyon National Park Museum Collection, for their help with the Emery Kolb Collection, photos, and research about Ellsworth Kolb.

My motivation for writing this second book, *Westwater Lost and Found: Expanded Edition*, came from recent interactions with BLM Westwater ranger Bob Brennan, and Moab BLM archaeologist Lori A. Hunsaker. I haven't actually met Lori but for several years have been interacting with her by email and through Bob. Having shared with Lori a few articles I wrote that were intended for smaller publications, she suggested that I instead submit them for a book. I did. All of the Westwater rangers through the years have been helpful with my research. Alvin Halliday preceded Bob Brennan and in 1998 put me in contact with John Weisheit, who invited me on my first interpretive Westwater trip. It was the 1998 trip that prompted me to write my first book, *Westwater Lost and Found*. Before Alvin retired, he took photos for me of the woman's shoes in Outlaw Cave to have them researched by specialists John Magill and Tom Mattimore.

Before continuing, I want to pay my respect to those who shared stories and photos of their early lives residing at Westwater. Many, perhaps all, of them have passed on, but their names and communications remain with me: Owen Malin, John L. (Jack) Malin, Ila Reay, Beryle Marah, Roberta Knutson, Myrtle Holyoak, Ruth M. Grennie, and Jessie Gruver. They were all excited to share what they remembered as a nostalgic childhood living at the former Westwater Railroad town. I have attempted to capture their spirit when writing both of the Westwater books. One might say that I've read enough about them that sometimes I feel as if I dwelt among them.

Learning of the North Branch of the Old Spanish Trail (OST) and its connection to Westwater was enlightening. I appreciate that the late William (Bill) Chenoweth was generous and shared his maps and writings with me. These materials became the foundation for me to begin my own research of the North Branch OST. I am grateful to Joe Fandrich for introducing me to Bill's research. The late Lloyd M. Pierson also contributed significantly through his research and writings and by introducing us to Colonel Edward R. S. Canby's contribution to the Old Salt Lake Wagon Road in 1860. After Bill died in 2018, I learned of Jon Horn, with Alpine Archaeological Consultants, who has shared some of his knowledge of the trail with me. I am grateful also for Lynn Brittner, the executive director of the Old Spanish Trail Association (OSTA), for her help getting "Westwater Camp: Water, Wood, and Grass" (chapter 1 in this volume) published in their triannual *Spanish Traces*.[1] Also, I appreciate their editor Willy Carleton, whom I worked with for *Spanish Traces*. Forrest Rodgers with the Moab Museum was also helpful.

Paul Zaenger, retired National Park Service (NPS) ranger of Black Canyon of the Gunnison National Park, assisted tremendously, helping to identify Ellsworth Kolb's photos of the Gunnison River. Paul was uniquely qualified because he had access to a copy of Ellsworth Kolb's manuscript, I was able to share with him photos from Kolb's collection, and with the assistance of other park rangers, he was able to identify the location of a number of the photos. He is succeeded by Forest Frost, who has assisted me with photos from the Fellows and Torrence Survey of 1901. I was further able to obtain assistance identifying photos from kayakers Milo Wynne aka Captain Black, Tom Michael Janney, and Tom Chamberlain. Milo has kayaked the Black Canyon of the Gunnison River fifty-two and a half times. Their experiences in the canyon were fascinating to learn about, and because of their need to inspect the technicality of the rapids and falls it made these features highly familiar to them. It was with their help that we are able to recognize that the rapid, or fall, known currently as Great Falls, is the rapid Ellsworth Kolb identified as Torrence Falls. Another kayaker, Kent Ford, also assisted me with information and leads regarding Walter Kirschbaum.

Ross Henshaw accompanied me numerous times traveling to Westwater and the Book Cliffs for my research along the back roads. Other friends who were former fellow river guides and who also accompanied me on the back roads are Roy Christenson and Doug Guest. A neighbor, Stacey Glad, helped decipher James E. Miller's letter to Frederick S. Dellenbaugh. Most of Miller's handwriting was legible; even so, I needed a more experienced set of eyes to help decipher a few words.

I appreciate the availability and knowledge of authors and river historians Roy Webb, Brad Dimock, John Weistheit, and more recently Tom Martin. Roy did not hesitate to accept my invitation to preview *Westwater Lost and Found: Expanded Edition* and write a foreword. Roy and I go back to when he worked as an archivist in Special Collections at the J. Willard Marriot Library at the University of Utah. In 2001, Roy worked with my grandmother Mary Gold Armstrong (Milligan), who donated her writings and slides to the J. Willard Marriott Library at the University of Utah, from when, as a passenger, she rafted the Colorado River through Glen Canyon, and the San Juan and Yampa Rivers in the late 1950s and early 1960s. As I age and am not as active on the rivers, it is always nice to speak with others about them.

And there are a host of individuals who assisted me with collections and information from the Beinecke Rare Book & Manuscript Library at Yale University, Cline Library at Northern Arizona University, Denver Public Library, Frontier Historical Society and Museum, Harold B. Lee Library at Brigham Young University, Huntington Library, J. Willard Marriott Library at the University of Utah, Moab BLM, Moab Museum, Montrose County Historical Museum, Museums of Western Colorado in Grand Junction, New York Public Library, Smithsonian Institute, and others. Included in this acknowledgment is the assistance I received from contributors to ancestry.com. I was able to learn more about James E. Miller, O. D. Babcock, and Richard "Rich" Adolphus McGruder from Martin Sperry, Denice Hellekson, and Glenda Lehman respectively. I found it rewarding to share with them a piece of history from their ancestor's life that they were only vaguely familiar with.

As my list of acknowledgments narrows down to the end, I wish to compliment the efforts and patience that my editors Rachael Levay, Allegra Martschenko, and Robert Ramaswamy made in getting *Westwater Lost and Found: Expanded Edition* published. I especially appreciate Robert's guidance getting this to the end. And whoever you are, thank you Reader 1—your contributions were invaluable.

Through the years my wife, Marla, always supported me in my research. Sometimes she even suggested that I need to get out of the house and take a trip. A few times those trips were for interviews or rafting and included my now-adult children Lindsi, Madison, and

Buck. Lindsi and Buck worked as river guides for Western River Expeditions, where I started. I love and appreciate all of them. Last, I thank my God for His help throughout this whole process. I sought out inspiration throughout writing both books in hopes of not only delivering the information but making it memorable. My desire writing both *Westwater Lost and Found* and *Westwater Lost and Found: Expanded Edition* was to leave readers with an emotion for Westwater and the individuals who made up its history, and for you, the reader, to perhaps experience a glimpse of discovery as I have. I believe also that God has placed in my path those individuals I have named in this acknowledgment, and I thank Him for that too.

LIFE'S DEPTHS

So this is why I am here! No concern for life, I wanted just to participate not knowing why I was back. I cannot foretell the future so expected there wasn't one. Instead I figure I was here to go full circle, back to where it all began. Back to when the nightmares and self-depredation began. Or was it?

Submerged I could not determine up or down, sideways or backward. There are absolutely no discernible directions. The water is dark—no there is light, it is translucent so I cannot see but it is definitely not dark. My eyes are swollen as sand or mud gathers in the lids when I open them to search for where I am. I can see yet I cannot see.

Shortly, I hear shouting, Pauline, Pauline, Pauline. I remember why I am here. Full circle, I am here to share my last day of earth life with her. Her, whose name I am hearing beneath whatever depths I am at. Two feet, forty feet, I don't know, I cannot see. But is she still there. Pauline, Pauline, Pauline.

Holding my breath is natural I suppose since it happened so suddenly. Now I wonder how long I must continue or should I stop. Push all of the remaining air out and take a big drink. No, I will wait a little longer. Long enough to meet Pauline, maybe? Let the river do with me as the river must, I am ready.

Suddenly I pop free, up to the top I see expectant comrades awaiting my arrival. None of them are Pauline I determine. I am back. Perhaps today is not the day to go full circle after all. I take a deep breath and lift my arms for my comrades to assist me back into the boat. Tough though it might be, I changed my mind. I am not ready yet.

MDM April 27, 2000

WESTWATER LOST AND FOUND

INTRODUCTION

It's been a wild ride digging up historical stories to share with my Westwater friends. I hope that my readers appreciate the experience of discovery as much as I have. This said, although *Westwater Lost and Found* (2004) provides a comprehensive history of the region, there were a few unanswered questions about Outlaw Cave; James Miller's missing letter to Frederick S. Dellenbaugh regarding an 1897 excursion down the Grand River, an earlier name given for the Colorado River above the confluence with the Green River; and the North Branch of the Old Spanish Trail (OST)—all of which I felt compelled to research further. Fortunately, with advanced digital technology and easier access to locating and communicating with individuals, historical societies, and libraries, I was able to track down additional information that expands on my first book. *Westwater Lost and Found: Expanded Edition* expounds on two stories about Outlaw Cave, the dentists Miller and Babcock's 1897 excursion down the Grand River, and a historic trail and road addressed briefly in the first book, and it provides important little-known historical documents related to Westwater and its relationship with the Upper Colorado River history. I'm especially grateful to be able to share Ellsworth Kolb's manuscript of his attempt to transit the Grand and Gunnison River tributaries in 1916 and 1917. As well, I have appreciated the opportunity to share the contents of James E. Miller's letter addressed to Frederick S. Dellenbaugh regarding his and O. D. Babcock's recreational boat excursion on the Grand River in 1897, and portions of Frederick Kreutzfeldt's (Creutzfeldt's) 1853 journal entries for Captain John Gunnison's central route survey of the thirty-eighth and thirty-ninth parallel for a Pacific Railroad. On my first river trip working as a swamper (river guide apprentice), I recall stopping at Rock Creek in Desolation Canyon to obtain water. We docked our rafts on a short beach upstream of the creek and while our passengers hiked to the ranch, and several of the guides went to refill the water coolers, I was left alone on shore with the boats. While there, I recall a feeling of being not far removed from stepping in the literal footsteps of early explorers such as Major John Wesley Powell's party, or members of the Wild Bunch. Although it was over 100 years earlier, because of the remoteness of the country, and far fewer rafting parties than there are currently, there was a slight chance that one of the historical figure's footprints might not have been trampled on, and I experienced some type of connection to them.

This experience initiated a passion to research the historical events of the Colorado and Green Rivers. I began purchasing and reading the classics by John Wesley Powell, Frederick S. Dellenbaugh, the Kolb brothers, George Flavell, Julius F. Stone, Clyde Eddy, and others to learn and compare their experiences with my own. Needless to say, although I had a number of dramatic experiences, none of them compared to the hard-fought voyages, portages, linings, uncertainties, hunger, and depravations of these historically hardened river men. Eventually, my studies led to Westwater Canyon, of which there were no books written. Initially, the only information I found came from Westwater Books' *Canyonlands River Guide*, where he inserted a couple of short blurbs below the photos of Ellsworth Kolb and Harold H. Leich that included the years that they boated through Westwater Canyon. Shortly afterward, whenever I ended a river trip, I spent much of my free time at

FIGURE 0.1. Three Spanish crosses located in the vicinity of Big Hole. Photo by Bob Brennan (2019).

the Moab library using their microfiche readers to search for articles from the *Grand Valley Times* (1896–1919) and the *Times Independent* (1919–current) on Kolb, Leich, and other subjects related to Westwater and the Grand River.

This was the beginning of over forty years of Westwater and Upper Colorado River research that resulted in *Westwater Lost and Found* (2004) and *Westwater Lost and Found: Expanded Edition*. There remains more history of Westwater and the Upper Colorado River to discover; however, finding it may be more difficult. Similar to the trappers who infiltrated the regions of the Green and Colorado Rivers at the turn of the nineteenth century, many of the earliest individuals who may have inadvertently boated or rafted through Westwater Canyon and the upper reaches of the Colorado River were likely illiterate trappers and miners who left no documentation of their activities. Preceding them is evidence of possibly the Spanish being in the Westwater region, where three inscribed Spanish crosses were recently discovered on a wall in one of the side drainages. Despite a lack of biographical historical documents, there is a continuing effort to digitize the remaining Colorado newspapers, which will likely reveal more early boaters on the Upper Colorado River.

An interesting observation throughout my research is that there are considerable overlapping or interacting historical figures involved in the Colorado, Grand, Green, and Gunnison River regions. The connection begins with the North Branch of the OST and continues with Captain John Williams Gunnison, whose impact on Colorado left a county, city, and river named after him. As documented in this book, he camped at Westwater Creek and members of his party led their famished mules and stock to feed and water at Westwater before leaving the Grand River in pursuit of the OST near the Green River crossing. The Denver & Rio Grande Railroad (D&RG RR) and Denver & Rio Grande Western Railroad (D&RGW RR) were present since the early 1880s, connecting several river towns along the Colorado, Green, and Gunnison Rivers at Glenwood Springs, Rifle, Montrose, Delta, Grand Junction, Westwater, Cisco, and Green River. Newspapers were present in most of these towns and at Moab.

Although it appears that no individual completed a transit of the entire free-flowing Grand and Colorado Rivers, we have biographical information from Ellsworth Kolb, who came closest because he transited the Grand Canyon prior to the Hoover Dam being constructed and completed his journey to the Gulf of California. All that he lacked for the credit was sixty-five miles of flat water on the Colorado (Grand) River between Moab and the Confluence. Including Kolb and Bert Loper, another historical river name found at Westwater is John Colton "Jack" Sumner, who reportedly sustained a "knife wound in the groin" there in 1902.[1] Sumner resided in Grand Junction since 1886 raising the question, did he do any trapping or mining by boat on the Grand River as far as the Confluence? Outlaw brothers Bob and Jack Smith reportedly traveled down the Grand River to Arizona a year prior to the D&RG RR train robbery in 1887. They must have felt comfortable on the river because during their escape from the law they hired a German immigrant at Green River to build them a boat on that river so that they could continue their escape downstream. In 1887, Harry McDonald ran a boat with Jess Fuller from Grand Junction to the Utah border. McDonald was a boatman for part of the Brown & Stanton's Denver, Colorado Cañon and Pacific Railroad (DCC&P RR) Survey in 1890, and again with the Best Expedition in 1891, which ended their mining expedition at Lee's Ferry after they lost a boat in Cataract Canyon. Elmer Kane was a boatman for both of the above expeditions and had testified during the Colorado Riverbed case, held between 1929 and 1931, that he had taken a raft down the Grand River from Grand Junction to Moab in 1888. Charles Brock, of Grand Junction, was also a boatman for the DCC&P RR, assisting surveyor Frank Clarence Kendrick down the Grand River to Green River, Utah, in 1889. Brock later settled on land near Westwater, where he was killed by Captain Wilson E. Davis on August 25, 1892. Nathaniel Galloway's son Parley, also a trapper, boated through Westwater Canyon in 1926 or 1927, and he guided Clyde Eddy through the Grand Canyon to Needles, California, in 1927. How much of the Grand River did he and his brother John trap for beaver? And how far did the mysterious Beppo Saeckler make it down the Colorado River in 1930?

Due to smaller populations, it appears that many individuals lived and worked within short proximity of each other throughout their lives in the vicinity of Green River, Utah, and Grand Junction, Colorado. Florence Creek, at the end of Desolation Canyon on the Green River, may have been named after Florence Harris Fuller (1866–1930), owner of the Pace-Fuller Ranch at Westwater.[2] Florence was a cattle woman who was well known in Green River, throughout Grand County, and in Grand Junction. On the east side of the Colorado River, upstream of the BLM Westwater Ranger headquarters, Florence's cattle ranch was one of the largest in Grand County. Longtime Westwater Ranch owner and sheep man Emmett Elizondo (1897–1992) resided in Grand Junction and Fruita, Colorado. And many other former residents came from, or had family, in Cisco, Grand Junction, Fruita, and Cedaredge. There is a little-known connection with Westwater involving the killing of Wild Bunch outlaw George "Flat Nose" Curry in Desolation Canyon on the Green River on April 17, 1900, and the murder of Moab sheriff Jesse Tyler in the Book Cliffs.[3]

As I conclude *Westwater Lost and Found: Expanded Edition* and search for biographical information and stories, it has become simpler to locate and reach out to the descendants of historical persons, through the use of genealogy programs. Using Ancestry.com I located descendants of both Drs. James E. Miller and O. D. Babcock with the hope that they might have more biographical information on their ancestors and that perhaps they might know the whereabouts of the photos that the dentists made of their 1897 trip down the Grand River. Fortunately, I did learn more about their lives; nevertheless, their descendants knew very little about the boating excursion and nothing about the photos. In retrospect, it was rewarding for me to share information with them about their ancestors' historical boating experience. Also, I have not been able to document when Dr. Miller met Major John Wesley Powell in Glenwood Springs. The two men haven't appeared together in any of the available Colorado digitized newspapers, and there isn't a complete registry for Colorado Hotel in order to document when Powell stayed there. From additional genealogy sources, I was able to learn more about Richard (Rich) Adolphus McGruder, who lost his left arm when he worked on the Gunnison Tunnel in the Black Canyon and it collapsed on him and trapped over thirty-five fellow workers in 1905. He is associated with Outlaw Cave history in Westwater Canyon, and possibly his new bride in 1919 is a candidate for the woman's shoes found in the cave.

Generally speaking, libraries, museums, and so on work independently of each other, and there are likely important historical documents that will eventually be digitized and thus made more widely available. This was the case that I experienced when I located James E. Miller's letter written to Frederick S. Dellenbaugh, housed in the Robert Brewster Stanton papers at the New York Public Library. It was an unexpected discovery. Another discovery is the Frederick Kreutzfeldt (Creutzfeldt) journal held at the Smithsonian Institution Archives. Kreutzfeldt was a German botanist who accompanied Captain John W. Gunnison's central route survey for a Pacific Railroad in 1853. The unpublished journal was written in German and translated into English.[4] I first learned of its existence on May 28, 2020, and immediately requested a copy from the Smithsonian Institute but because of the coronavirus (COVID-19) pandemic, it couldn't be accessed. As I was nearly ready in January 2022 to submit *Westwater Lost and Found:*

Expanded Edition to be reviewed for publication, I received an email from archivist Deborah Shapiro at the Smithsonian on December 22, 2021, with an attached typewritten transcript copy of Kreutzfeldt's journal. The new information caused me to revisit chapter 1, because Kreutzfeldt's journal notes did not support the premise that Captain Gunnison camped at Westwater. Bill Chenoweth's extensive research following Gunnison's path into Grand County relied solely on Lieutenant Edward G. Beckwith's narrative, which could lead to the conclusion that Gunnison's camp was subsequently moved to Westwater and the Grand River to nourish and rest their mules. Kreutzfeldt's journal did not appear in any of the primary sources that I researched on the OST and the North Branch.

Kreutzfeldt's journal is a much-lesser-known third biographical source of information that, along with Beckwith's report and Dr. James Schiel's account, helps to document Gunnison's central route survey of the thirty-eighth and thirty-ninth parallel for the Pacific Railroad Exploration and Surveys in 1853. As more original historical resources become available to the public, they can help support, or correct, what has been written and avoid a possible misinterpretation of historical events. This is an example of the usefulness of the internet and being able to locate sources that were not previously available to historians.

The unfortunate Kreutzfeldt was the botanist for Colonel John C. Frémont's ill-fated winter expedition along the thirty-eighth parallel, where ten men died from exposure and hypothermia in 1848, and Captain John W. Gunnison's central route survey for a Pacific Railroad in 1853, where Kreutzfeldt was killed along with Captain Gunnison and six other members of the party by Pahvant Utes on October 26, 1853.

Additional questions continue to build, and as more sources from libraries, museums, historical societies, and newspapers are digitized and made available on the internet to the public, our ability to further research Westwater and the Upper Colorado River and other topics is likely to increase.

In order to have the Westwater and regional histories that I researched readily available on investigative trips, I typed up major parts of stories and articles and kept them in a large binder that fit snugly into a 40MM Ammo can. As a resource during my travels, the binder was something I brought with me on river trips and when I drove on the back roads of Westwater, Cisco, and the Book Cliffs. The binder was shared liberally with anyone in my company, and it was those who thumbed through its pages who convinced me to write my first book. Separately, I collected poetry, song lyrics, and quotes about rivers and the wilderness that helped me to internalize my feelings for these natural places. The quotes are also kept in the large binder with the Westwater material. Words portraying images are important to me. Personally, I feel inadequate at formulating my own written images through words and sometimes resort to borrowing the words from those who are more gifted. From the stories about Huckleberry Finn, Mark Twain writes, "We said there warn't no home like a raft, after all. Other places do seem so cramped up and smotherly, but a raft don't. You feel mighty free and easy and comfortable on a raft."[5] Just like that, Huck Finn describes how I feel about boating.

Toward the end of my five-year career as a professional river guide, I recall floating along Peter's Point on the Green River in the early morning shade when I was struck with these very feelings. I remember my passengers were relaxed as they quietly observed the magnificent sculpted canyons in that region, and it was so quiet and serene that I could hear droplets of water fall from beneath my elevated oars as they returned to the river. It was an intimate moment for contemplation and inspiration enhanced by my knowledge that I might not be back. Although I grew up in a suburb of Salt Lake City, I was never comfortable living there or any large city. It wasn't until I began boating that I could feel a distinct positive difference in my personality and confidence. From my youth I had plenty of experiences in the outdoors and from hunting; having said that, the river experience was different. It unknowingly released many inhibitions and allowed me to be freer with myself and others. Had I believed I could make a responsible career out of river rafting, I likely would have done it.

Because I didn't believe I could make it a livelihood, I returned to the city, finished my degree, got a job, got married, and had children. I returned to the river periodically with friends, or as a guide for private groups, and over the past twenty years primarily as a Westwater historian. Yet, when I couldn't be on the river and had free time, I researched

Westwater and read the latest historical river books. This activity did not preoccupy my time to the extent that it affected my work and raising a family, but when I needed a break I had somewhere to escape to: the river. In addition to sharing the historical discoveries found in *Westwater Lost and Found* (2004), the book is also intended to provide a personal experience of boating down the Colorado River through Westwater Canyon, whether on or off of the river.

On April 18, 2018, I was invited with Grand Canyon geologist Dr. Peter Huntoon as one of the specialists for a single-day Westwater Canyon interpretive river trip sponsored by Colorado Plateau River Guides (CPRG). The interpretive trips are organized to educate professional river guides representing companies located at Grand Junction, Green River, and Moab about the various canyons that they traverse.

The Colorado River through Westwater Canyon was running lower than I had ever rafted it, at 2,100 cfs (cubic feet per second). Both Skull and Razor Rocks were well out of the water. I'd seen the rapid at nearly this level in 2003 from the cliffs above, and from that height there appeared to be plenty of space to split the two major rocks in Skull Rapid. Looking at the rapid from river level is a different matter and requires precise timing to get through it cleanly. I think of a quote by historic Grand Canyon boatman and photographer Ellsworth Kolb, who described a plan getting through Skull "Whirlpool" Rapid in 1916 by "making a corkscrew curve with a back action kick and a swipe at the scenery."[6] Well, when Westwater ranger Bob Brennan swiped at the scenery, our boat landed between Razor Rock and the rocky shore, temporarily stuck. The other boats in our party were too far right and squeezed between Skull Rock and the cliff, where they were pooped out through the "birth canal" into the eddy behind the rock. None of the runs were particularly pretty; even so, they were pretty entertaining. Incidentally, Kolb also had his troubles in the rapid, when his boat turned over briefly. Fortunately, he was able to right the boat midway through the rapid and finish the run.

Ellsworth Kolb said of Westwater Canyon that "it is the Grand Canyon in miniature."[7] Dr. Peter Huntoon helped the guides appreciate the uniqueness of Westwater Canyon when he compared its geography to the Grand Canyon. The missing strata that make up an unconformity that exists in both canyons represent a far greater length of time between sequences in Westwater Canyon than in the Grand Canyon. It is a beautiful canyon with breathtaking views where the Colorado River follows a narrow slit in the earth exposing 1.7-billion-year-old Precambrian rocks. There are petroglyphs, a small waterfall, old dugouts, and the Outlaw Cave of mystery within the short canyon's walls. What else could a person want on a one, or two-day river trip?

It was a great experience to return to Westwater Canyon. I'm not sure whether it was my last time through the canyon, or whether I will return. One thing is certain: if I do, the river is never the same. I'm reminded of a quote from the 1996 movie *Same River Twice*, where an old river guide says, "Part of the reason we keep coming back here is we don't exactly know what's going to happen, that's part of the thrill, it's never the same river twice."[8] That's the uniqueness of Westwater Canyon; it's never the same river twice. And whether I am able to return to the river physically, or through continued research, it is never the same. Knowing the region's history, I look at the entire experience differently and can imagine Utes on horseback crossing the Colorado River upstream of the Westwater Ranger Station, or picture surveyors and military expeditions watering and fattening up their livestock for the dreaded trek across the Cisco Desert, an old railroad town, scattered sheep, and unsuspecting trappers and miners in heavy wooden boats attempting Westwater Canyon. Just as flora, fauna, and geology contribute to our appreciation of the river's waterways, so can the footprints of historic humankind leave an impression when these people's presence is known and they have hopefully taken care of the land.

As I indicated in my first book, for personal reasons I avoided boating Westwater Canyon and instead pursued my research of the area by land from 1984 until 1998. I began to research Westwater Canyon in 1981, and, although at times it was difficult, I continued to do it after I lost my mother in Skull Rapid on August 31, 1983. Fortunately, I was encouraged to continue with the research by my friend's, former Westwater Ranger and cofounding director of Colorado Field Institute (CFI), Karla VanderZanden, and the late Dee Holladay of Holiday River Expeditions. Ultimately, researching Westwater became somewhat of a release for me and helped me to remain in contact with the river.

Shortly after my mother died, my stepfather approached me to ask if I would participate in a lawsuit against river companies that was brought on as a result of a number of boating accidents that occurred during the record high-water season of 1983. I don't remember the particulars of the lawsuit; however, I believe it involved companies not having sufficient means of handling emergency situations on river trips. Unlike today, in 1983 about the only way to communicate while on the river in the middle of a canyon was use of long-range walkie-talkies. I understand why my stepfather was approached about the lawsuit—he was devastated, distraught, angry, and confused, and although he didn't outright blame me for the accident he did want to find some kind of resolution. I too was devastated and guilt ridden, and I reflected in my mind numerous times about what had happened; nonetheless, I refused his invitation to cooperate in the lawsuit. Although I had lost my mother, I had over the previous five seasons of river running seen the rivers' many more positive influences than negative ones on people's lives, even my own.

Returning to the river, both literally, and through river books and research, helped me to recall the positive experiences I had and to heal. I perceived from the experiences that I had with fellow river guides, private boaters, and passengers that rivers had a similar influence on them too; that they had found an escape from the working world, politics, and busy cities and found a love and liberty within this adventurous outdoor wilderness experience. A recent documentary that appeared on Netflix titled *The River Runner* (2021) expressed to a far greater scale some of my feelings regarding rivers and their influence on us. The film follows world-renowned expedition kayaker, cinematographer, and producer Scott Lindgren and depicts how river running probably saved him and his brother from a life of crime, or worse. River running did become his livelihood! He also had a devastating loss of his best friend, Chuck Kern, who died while kayaking the Black Canyon of the Gunnison River on August 14, 1997, and he too returned to the river. Lindgren said,

> The river sang to my heart. I'd been fighting my whole life—kids, teachers, cops, parents—and here was a force so powerful that my

only choice was surrender. I recognized the river as a teacher, offering me a gateway to the world. It channeled all the energy that was going to get me locked up or killed into something productive. I couldn't get enough.[9]

I observed a seventy-something-year-old stockbroker loosen up and take his first-ever vacation with a grandson down the Green River. A woman passenger trying to overcome alcoholism was warned she'd relapse by going on a river trip, and instead she was strengthened in her resolve to quit while on a five-day river trip through Desolation Canyon. I saw youth and adults enthusiastically catch their first (cat)fish, and it was easy for me to allow nature to discipline a couple of fighting young siblings on my boat by taking them through Westwater Canyon and scare the hell out of them. And many other families and friends bonded together from the whitewater, the solitude and beauty of the canyons, and the experience of camping in tents, or outside beneath a canopy of stars. Needless to say, nearly everyone enjoyed the various locations where we set up a room with a view (latrine). It's not easy to leave the river, and who would want to?

The following chapters are a continuation and expansion of Westwater history and the discovery of its centrality to the histories of other regions of the Upper Colorado River. Without Westwater Canyon obstructing early river travel, we would have far less knowledge of the historical boaters on the Grand River, and at the head of Westwater Canyon the discovery that the valley was historically important because of its abundance of wood, grass, and water for Native Americans, trappers, surveyors, and settlers traveling between the Green and Grand Rivers along the North Branch of the OST. In addition to new information about the North Branch of the OST, with this book I have added further insight into two stories related to Westwater's Outlaw Cave and added historical documents and insight into the character and boating experiences of the earliest-known parties who tackled Westwater Canyon's troublesome rapids.

1

WESTWATER CAMP

Water, Wood, and Grass

After Westwater Lost and Found *(2004) was published, I was made aware of an important historical event: Westwater may have been a significant camp along the North Branch of the Old Spanish Trail (OST) between Taos, New Mexico, and California. My editor John Alley was able to include a note in the original book with a succinct description of Westwater camp at the bottom of page 28. If you purchased a copy of* Westwater Lost and Found *(2004) and it doesn't have the note, then you have an original edition.*

In 1998, I was introduced to John Weisheit, who was the editor of the Confluence magazine *for members of the Colorado Plateau River Guides (CPRG). After I met John, he invited me on a number of CPRG-sponsored interpretive Westwater trips as a historian to share my information with professional river guides from various companies mostly based in Grand Junction, Green River, and Moab. During these trips I toted a large binder that contained hundreds of articles and notes from research I had gathered on Westwater and shared it with the guides at camp and during lunch stops. It was at the prompting of these new river friends that I was encouraged to write* Westwater Lost and Found *(2004).*

https://doi.org/10.7330/9781646425457.c001

FIGURE 1.1. Westwater launch site looking upstream in the direction of Ruby Canyon. Upstream view includes where early Westwater residents crossed the Colorado River when it was low, and possibly may have been where Colonel William Wing Loring in 1858 observed "numerous Indian trails, leading to Salt (La Sal) mountain and the San Miguel and Dolores rivers" (LeRoy R. Hafen, intro. and notes., "Colonel Loring's Expedition across Colorado in 1858," *Colorado Magazine* 23, no. 2 [March 1946]: 61). Traveling westerly along the North Branch of the OST, Westwater is the first access to the Colorado River after leaving Salt Creek. Photo by author (2009).

During one of the interpretive trips, I was introduced to geologist Joe Fandrich, who at the time owned, or leased, Westwater Ranch. I don't recall whether it was a working farm at the time that he was there, because his main interest was to research microspherules and a Quaternary Ice-Dam Lake at Westwater; both subjects are beyond me to explain. Shortly after Westwater Lost and Found *(2004) was published, Joe shared with me a copy of an article about Westwater being a prominent campsite along the North Branch of the OST that was written by another geologist, his friend, William Lyman "Bill" Chenoweth of Grand Junction. Except for the river crossings at Moab and Green River, the OST wasn't something I was very familiar with, and this was new and exciting information for me to read. Bill was a retired highly recognized uranium geologist who spent considerable time documenting the OST. He and others living at Grand Junction were instrumental, along with the Old Spanish Trail Association (OSTA), getting the OST and its North Branch designated as the fifteenth nationally recognized historical trail in the United States.*

Chenoweth's research motivated me to delve further into researching the North Branch of the OST and various trapper trails and the men who traveled them, which led me to other important writings and research performed by Lloyd Pierson of Moab and Jack Nelson of Grand Junction. Between these three men and their associates, they did a lot of legwork documenting the early trails and roads in Grand County and western Colorado. My interest renewed, I felt that if Westwater was a camp along the North Branch of the OST, then it, like other historical sites, should be recognized with a historical marker and have its history shared.

In *Utah Place Names*, John W. Van Cott states that the name of Westwater derived from "where the railroad exits into the valley at the west end of Ruby Canyon."[1] Another source for the name Westwater described it as "where the tracks left the river, and gave warning that you had better see that the water kegs were filled for a long dry march ahead."[2] The railroad tracks, however, didn't always follow along the Colorado River and exit from Ruby Canyon. Furthermore, when the Denver & Rio Grande Western Railroad (D&RGW RR) was incorporated in Utah in 1881, it chose the more economical narrow-gauge tracks that were spiked down farther inland in 1883. Perhaps, instead, the name that was assigned to the original railroad station derived from an earlier era, when the area was a common camp used by explorers, surveyors, trappers, merchants, settlers, likely Native Americans, and others as they prepared themselves and their mules, horses, and other stock with water, grass for grazing, and wood that could be used for fire, roads, and wagon repairs before heading west over the Cisco Desert to converge with the main OST near Green River.

In 1883, the Denver & Rio Grande (D&RG) Railroad of Colorado spiked down narrow-gauge tracks through northern Grand County that connected Salt Lake City with the recently settled town at Grand Junction (1881). To keep up the tracks and provide fuel for the steam locomotive

FIGURE 1.2. A small Westwater railroad town existed in the vicinity of where the parked van is. Beyond the van is Westwater Ranch, which historically has been some of the most valued real estate in Grand County, Utah. Photo by author (1987).

engines, the railroad set up a number of stations or sidings throughout the train route over the Cisco Desert and Grand Valley. West Water, along with Cisco and Thompson, was one of the original stations. According to D&RG RR historian Jackson Thode, the name Westwater first appeared in 1883 as two words, West Water.[3] The original location was approximately twelve miles inland from the Colorado River, near Exit 220 off of I-70, where a dirt road veers to the northeast and some remnants of the station can be found next to Westwater Creek. The 1883 narrow-gauge tracks completely bypassed Ruby Canyon.[4]

By avoiding Ruby Canyon and the Colorado River, the financially struggling yet newly incorporated D&RGW RR chose to build around the canyon atop the Mancos shale using the most economical and easiest constructed narrow-gauge track. One source described the result over the Cisco Desert as a "frightful combination of curves and roller coaster grades."[5] A major drawback using narrow-gauge tracks was that the engines were smaller, which meant they ran slower than the wider standard-gauge tracks and hauled less freight. There were also considerable maintenance issues. Along with these drawbacks, the D&RG RR, which was based in Colorado, primarily used a standard-gauge track, which ultimately influenced the D&RGW to upgrade their tracks to standard gauge by 1890. It was during this change to a standard-gauge track that the train route was moved nearer the Colorado River and emerged from Ruby Canyon at Westwater (by this time, one word). The new Westwater train station and water stop were located approximately one mile northeast of the Westwater Ranger Station, where there is a pullover with sidings along the main dirt road.

On April 10, 1889, Frank Clarence Kendrick was conducting a railroad survey for the DCC&P RR; upon surveying Westwater he wrote in his journal, "This is a very fine valley."[6] The area was also described as "a wooded country filled with game."[7] The Westwater valley may have been settled as early as 1880.[8] In 1884, a small community sprung up from what was considered some of the most fertile land in what would later be Grand County. And by 1887, Westwater Ranch was already established in the valley under the name Bar X Ranch. More settlers and squatters followed after the railroad converted to the standard gauge.[9] The community had access not only to the railroad but also to an already-established road that was used for travel between Salt Lake City and Colorado. Most of the "Old Salt Lake Wagon road" follows a much older, forgotten Northern Branch of the OST.

In early July 1860, 100 prospectors left Denver for two months to explore western Colorado and portions of eastern Utah "over a region of country that has hardly ever been penetrated . . . and never fully described by any one."[10] D. C. Collier Esq. was designated as a guide, historian, and secretary for the party, and he provided details of their explorations in Denver's *Rocky Mountain News*. The prospectors went as far north as the confluence of the White and Green Rivers in Utah. There, the party split up, with some choosing to prospect further northeast, others to return to Denver, and the remainder to follow the original plan and head southeast to the Grand (Colorado) River; once the Grand was reached, a few more men headed back to Denver. The remaining sixteen prospectors continued exploring south and southeast until they reached the Rio Grande River. Based on Collier's comments, it appears that the party avoided contact with Utes and other

FIGURE 1.3. A 1916 photo by Westwater resident Beatrix Simpson of a farm and Westwater Ranch in the distance. The road in the lower right corner running from left to right is part of the Salt Lake Wagon Road. A section of the road is still in existence running parallel to the railroad tracks. The photo appeared in a 1917 Railroad Red Book and in Moab's *Grand Valley Times* on February 9, 1917. Image scan by Colorado Railroad Museum Collection, Golden, Colorado.

prospectors until it was necessary toward the end of the expedition, when, with their supplies diminished, they sought help at Fort Garland, formerly in New Mexico territory. In Collier's notes to the newspaper, he wrote that several times during his group's travels the trails they followed intersected with the "Fort Garland and Salt Lake wagon road." Notably, because the Fort's supplies were also low it was required that party members apply for assistance from the quartermaster. When they approached the quartermaster for assistance, he was with Colonel Canby, who had just recently arrived at Fort Garland on the Salt Lake Wagon Road. Colonel Canby with his troops were asked to try and locate a shorter route to New Mexico and to improve the existing road along the way from Camp Floyd, near Salt Lake City, to Fort Garland.[11]

Historically, the Fort Garland and Salt Lake Wagon Road went by several other names, including the Great Fort Garland and Salt Lake City Wagon Road, Salt Lake Wagon Road, Old Salt Lake Wagon Road, Road to Colorado, Road to Salt Lake, and Loren's (Loring's) Trail. It was the "first named road which carried wheeled vehicles" through what eventually would be Grand County.[12]

FIGURE 1.4. General Edward R. S. Canby. Photo from Timothy Hughes Rare & Early Newspapers website (http://www.sonofthesouth.net/leefoundation/civil-war/1865/general-r-s-canby.htm) for April 15, 1865.

Until 1990 the Salt Lake Wagon Road appeared to be historically ignored or forgotten, when retired uranium geologist and western Colorado historian Bill Chenoweth and former Colorado state legislator and member of Colorado State Parks Board Judge James M. Robb questioned the road's existence when it appeared on an 1875 map by Henry Gannett of the Ferdinand V. Hayden Surveys of Colorado and eastern Utah Territories. A few years earlier, in 1987 or 1988, Chenoweth wrote and delivered a three-page memo titled "Historic Crossing of the Colorado River in the Grand Valley" to the Grand Junction / Mesa County Riverfront Commission. In 1990, Chenoweth's paper about the Salt Lake Wagon Road paralleling the Colorado River and a historic crossing at Grand Junction fortuitously coincided with a project Robb, as a founding co-chair of the commission, was involved with developing—a trail and park system to help clean up a twenty-six-mile corridor area along the Colorado River in Mesa County. It was the discovery of the

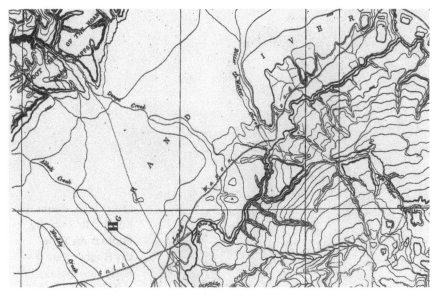

FIGURE 1.5. Map of Westwater area by Hayden Survey, 1875–1876. Bitter Water Creek refers to what today is Westwater Creek. F. V. Hayden, *Geological and Geographical Atlas of Colorado and Portions of Adjacent Territory* (New York: Julius Bien, lith., 1877).

Salt Lake Wagon Road and its history that helped Chenoweth and Robb to establish many historical coordinates of the road through northern Grand County, Grand Junction, and western Colorado. More important, they discovered that the Salt Lake Wagon Road followed a much older, sparsely documented North Branch of the OST.[13]

Independent of each other, Chenoweth and Robb became interested in the OST in 1987. Learning that the Northern Branch of the OST traversed their city made the investigation more personal. Not only would their research benefit the Colorado River corridor through the town of Grand Junction; it was also important for them to bring to light the colorful history of the OST and its North Branch and have it recognized as a historical trail under the National Trails System Act of 1968 (https://www.nps.gov/articles/000/national-historic-trails.htm). By 1992, a committee was formed in Grand Junction to work on having the trail nationally recognized, and, in 1994, they merged with the newly founded OSTA. Their combined efforts came to fruition when President George W. Bush signed into law Senate Bill 1946 on December 4,

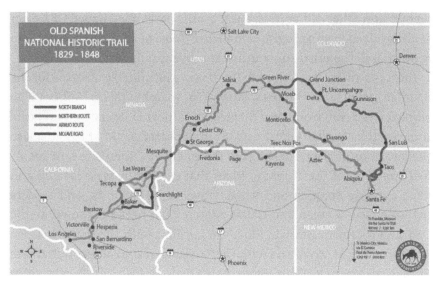

FIGURE 1.6. Map of three primary branches of the Old Spanish Trail. Map courtesy of the Old Spanish Trail Association.

2002, resulting in the OST and its North Branch being federally recognized, as mentioned earlier, as the fifteenth historic trail in the United States. Along with the thorough research found in Leroy R. and Ann W. Hafen's *Old Spanish Trail* (1954), Chenoweth, Robb, Jack Nelson (also of Grand Junction) and Lloyd Pierson (of Moab) documented the paths of the *Forgotten Pathfinders* and the ruts of the Salt Lake Wagon Road, making a huge contribution to our understanding of the North Branch of the OST through Colorado and Utah.[14]

The Hafens described the OST as the "longest, crookedest, most arduous pack mule route in the history of America."[15] For a short time in history, the trail played a vital role in developing the Southwest. New Spanish territories of California and New Mexico were separated by the Grand Canyon and other obstacles that prevented commerce between them by land. It wasn't until late in the eighteenth century that Spain sanctioned expeditions to explore a route linking the two settlements. Los Angeles sits at a slightly lower latitude than Santa Fe, and currently there are approximately 850 road miles between them. Because of the terrain and other difficulties, a 1,200-mile parabolic-shaped OST eventually evolved, beginning at Santa Fe, or Taos, heading northwest into central Utah then turning southwest to eventually reach Los Angeles.

The 1,450-mile-long Colorado River was a formidable obstacle for the Spanish, Mexicans, trappers, surveyors, merchants, and others who worked their way from New Mexico to California. Some early reports indicate that Native Americans often appeared reluctant to disclose the locations of river crossings to the intruders. There are four identified crossings of the Colorado River that eventually were located and used by early Spanish and Anglo travelers, merchants, and traders between New Mexico and California on what became known as the OST and its North Branch. Most are familiar with the main Spanish Trail crossing at Moab and with the Crossing of the Fathers by Fathers Francisco Atanasio Domínguez and Silvestre Vélez de Escalante in 1776, a site now buried beneath the waters of Lake Powell in Glen Canyon. There was a lesser-used crossing near the Dolores River's confluence with the Colorado River. However, the primary crossing for the North Branch of the OST on the Grand/Colorado River was at Grand Junction and identified as the "Crossing of the Grand." Prior to 1921, the Colorado River between Grand Junction and the confluence with the Green River was previously known as the Grand River.[16]

Sections of the North Branch of the OST may possibly predate the main branch. As early as 1686, Spanish friar Alonso de Posada was aware of Utes coming from as far north as Utah Lake to New Mexico. The routes they traveled likely were preexisting game trails that were developed and enlarged by Utes, Navajos, and other Native Americans as they hunted, sought out water sources, migrated, and developed trade among other tribes and eventually the Spanish. Subsequently, sections of Native American trails were used by the first explorers and trappers out of New Mexico as they headed north into Colorado and Utah. It wasn't until 1826 that an overland route from the Salt Lake area to California was pieced together by Jedediah Smith. He returned again to California in 1827, which opened up a route that would lead to finally piecing together the OST and linking New Mexico with California. The commonly used main OST route coming through Spanish Valley was first transited in 1830–1831 by William Wolfskill, George C. Young, and a number of other trappers.[17] Two years earlier, in 1828–1829, merchant Antonio Armijo with sixty men and 100 mules followed a more southerly, less-used route starting at Abiquiu, New Mexico, to become the first party to travel between the two settlements.

Except for the expeditions led by Juan María Antonio de Rivera in 1765 and by Fathers Domínguez and Escalante in 1776, little is known about other Spanish explorers or traders because without proper authorization it was illegal to enter Ute lands and trade with them. Beginning at Abiquiu and Santa Fe, respectively, the three known expeditions traveled northward following the Dolores River then east of it nearer to the North Branch OST, and in some instances touched upon it while in Colorado along the Uncompahgre and Gunnison Rivers. After the Domínguez and Escalante Expedition reached the confluence of the Uncompahgre and Gunnison Rivers, it took an easterly direction along the northern branch of the Gunnison River; expedition members then headed north, which placed them east of the North Branch OST, as they took a longer route to reach Utah Lake. They returned on trails that were closer in proximity to the main OST and crossed the Colorado River at the Crossing of the Fathers.

In 1821, when Mexico gained its independence, restrictions from Spanish rule against entering Ute lands were eased slightly, and by 1824 an influx of French and Anglo-American trappers had entered their country. After the Louisiana Purchase in 1803, American and French trappers moved north and west, at first trapping the rivers connected with the Missouri and Mississippi Rivers. Mexican territory was off limits without obtaining a license and paying fees for beaver and other hides. Eventually, a number of French and American trappers entered New Mexico and settled or established headquarters at Taos, including Kit Carson, the Robidoux brothers (Antoine, Michel [Miguel], Francois, and Louis), Antoine Leroux, Jean Baptiste Chalifoux, "Old Bill" Williams, "Peg Leg" Smith, James Ohio Pattie, William Wolfskill, Etienne Provost, and others. It is possible that the mysterious Denis Julien may have briefly resided at Taos in 1827.[18]

Before the OST to California was fully established in 1830–1831, other trails made their way into the Rocky Mountains blazed by trappers headed out of Taos to the Colorado and Green Rivers. Those traveling

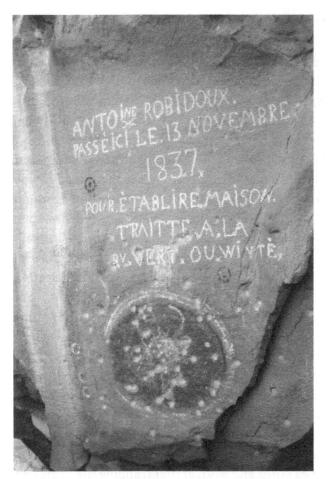

FIGURE 1.7. Antoine Robidoux inscription found along an early trapper trail entering into the Book Cliffs that led to the Salt Lake, Green River, and Rendezvous areas. Since this photo was taken, a section of the lower left side of the panel has broken off. Photo by Vicki Lynne Amis (2001).

from Santa Fe followed the OST to San Juan Pueblo (Ohkay Owingeh Pueblo), where the trail split. The main trail continued northwest, and the other headed east toward Taos or the western fork of the North Branch OST. Antoine Leroux explained that this route generally was used "when there was much snow in the mountains on the Abiquiu (main) route."[19]

There was a west and east fork of the North Branch through the seventy-four-mile-wide San Luis Valley.[20] The two forks converged at Saguache, Colorado; then the trail continued a northwesterly route over the Cochetopa Pass. Variant trails spread out after passing over the Continental Divide at the Pass due to the difficult terrain; however, they eventually converged again near the confluence of the Uncompahgre and Gunnison Rivers. It was near the confluence that the Fort Uncompahgre trading post was established by Antoine Robidoux possibly as early as 1827.

After crossing the Gunnison River shortly below its confluence with the Uncompahgre, the trail continued through nearly forty miles of desert, bypassing steep and difficult terrain where the Gunnison River flowed nearby but was not accessible. Shortly after the Gunnison River emerges from the canyons, it converges with the Colorado River at Grand Junction, Colorado. It was shortly before the rivers merge that the "Grand River Crossing" was used by parties to continue north into the Book Cliffs to the Winty region of the Uinta Basin and Salt Lake area, or northwest to merge with the main OST. The older trapper trail left the River at Salt Creek and went northwest to one of the only entries into the Book Cliffs / Roan Mountains at Westwater Creek, where the Antoine Robidoux inscription is located.[21] During the fur trade from about 1824 to 1840, this variant of the trail was traveled extensively by numerous brigades of trappers as they made their way north to trap the Green River and Uinta Basin regions. The primary trail through the Book Cliffs likely entered Hay Canyon and exited Willow Creek Canyon to the Winty or Uintah area, where another Robidoux trading post was located.[22] The trail was also used by trappers and traders going to the annual Mountain Man rendezvous, which lasted from 1825 to 1840, and the Salt Lake area. Along the Hay Canyon and Willow Creek route, there are inscriptions from Denis Julien (183?), Louis Robidoux (1841), Antoine Leroux (1835), and B. Chalifou (probably Juan Baptiste Chalifoux—1835).[23]

The westerly North Branch trail from Salt Creek followed closer to the Colorado River, where Westwater, and sometimes Cisco and McGraw Bottom, were recognized as primary water sources along the route to the main trail. The most promising camps included water, grass for grazing, and wood. These resources were available at Westwater for travelers of the North Branch OST through northern Grand County as the trail headed west to merge with the main OST near Green River. Of the three known water stops along the Colorado River, Westwater was identified by Bill Chenoweth and Lloyd Pierson as the only location visited by all of the early documented parties.

A central figure in our understanding of the Westwater campsite and a number of other locations identified as part of the North Branch of the OST was the renowned trapper and guide Antoine Leroux. Mostly unknown today, Leroux was renowned in his day, especially as a guide. Because he lacked the credentials of surviving a grizzly bear mauling or guiding any of five highly publicized expeditions led by Frémont, there is little biographical information written about Leroux.[24] A Kit Carson biographer, DeWitt C. Peters, wrote that "Leroux was an old and famous trapper and mountaineer whose reputation and skill as a guide in the Far West, was second only to Kit Carson's. A few of his warm partisans, ... at one time considered him superior even to Kit Carson."[25]

Perhaps destined to be a mountain man and trapper in the Southwest, Joaquin Antoine Leroux, aka Watkins Leroux, was born in St. Louis in 1801, two years prior to the Louisiana Purchase. Founded as a trading post in 1764, St. Louis was the home of many mountain men and trappers, including the Robidoux brothers, who would find their way to New Mexico about the same time as Leroux, around 1824. Leroux's roots in the Southwest were established long before his birth. In 1748 his maternal grandmother, Maria Roselia Jacques, while residing in Taos, New Mexico, survived the slaughter of most of her household and neighboring citizens by Comanches.

> Surviving the Taos massacre, she was captured by the Comanches who held her for ransom. She was later sold to Pawnees where she was eventually ransomed by a French merchant, who married her and brought her to St. Louis. Leroux would eventually return to Taos where his grandmother was raised and make it his home.[26]

As Leroux lived among his friends and trappers who traded at the trading posts in St. Louis, tales of rivers, mountains, beaver, and Native Americans must have had a huge influence on him. At the age of twenty-one, Leroux answered an employment ad for "enterprising young men" to join the Rocky Mountain Fur Company (RMFC), led by William Henry Ashley and Andrew Henry, in 1822. Listed as one of the original RMFC employees known as "Ashley's Hundred," Leroux spent nearly two years learning to trap, hunt, and survive with the likes of Jedediah Smith, Tom Fitzpatrick, Hugh Glass, Jim Bridger, and William Sublette in the wilderness along the upper Missouri River. By 1824, three years after Mexico gained its independence from Spain and lightened trapping requirements in their country, Leroux, the Robidoux brothers, and a number of other Anglo and French Canadian trappers made their way to New Mexico, where most of them either settled or began trapping enterprises based in Taos where it was easier to avoid paying fees for their pelts.

Antoine Leroux worked as a free trapper for thirty years among many of the legendary trappers. He was neighbor and close friend of Kit Carson. Until he was named lead guide for the Mormon Battalion in 1847, his activities were obscure and mostly unwritten. Many of the mountain men and trappers were illiterate, and their stories died with them. Jim Bridger was unable to sign his name but benefited from other's writings. Antoine Leroux was educated and spoke English, French, Spanish, and a number of Native American dialects and sign languages. There is no evidence that Leroux kept a journal; even so, we have some written material on his activities, from letters he wrote describing the Southwest that were printed in major newspapers throughout the country to military reports from expeditions that he guided.

By 1840, the beaver market had declined and, as silk hats replaced the need of pelts for top hats, mountain men pursued other interests or settled down. Because of their vast knowledge of the West, some old trappers became military guides. Three of the prominent guides were Leroux, Kit Carson and Tom Fitzpatrick. Leroux was a guide in demand because of his vast knowledge of the Southwest and was sought out by a number of early military expeditions, surveyors, and caravans throughout the 1840s and 1850s. He was also a successful rancher and likely didn't need to work as a guide. Baldwin Möllhausen, topographical draftsman and naturalist for Lieutenant Amiel Weeks Whipple's 1853 southern route survey along the thirty-fifth parallel for a Pacific Coast Railroad, wrote in his journal about securing Leroux as their guide that "the confidence which he inspired,—a confidence that had been earned by thirty years' toil in primeval wildernesses—made us all rejoice not a little at having secured his services." Möllhausen was also impressed with Leroux's "very minute detail" when one night, as they slept alongside each other, he told the graphic story of Colonel John C. Frémont's 1848 failed attempt at surveying the thirty-eight parallel during a severe winter.[27]

Leading into 1853, there was considerable interest in building a transcontinental railroad across the country to the Pacific Ocean. Several routes were proposed, and to resolve the issue money was appropriated for the Army Corps of Topographical Engineers to determine the most practical and economic route for a railroad from the Mississippi to the Pacific Ocean. Beginning in 1853, several surveys took place along the proposed routes, including one that followed closely along the North Branch of the OST. The route was strongly advocated by Frémont's father-in-law, Senator Thomas Hart Benton of Missouri. Late in 1848, Frémont attempted a survey for a year-round railroad route along the same general route of the thirty-eighth and thirty-ninth parallels being proposed by Senator Benton. Unfortunately, Frémont was not successful, as he started too late in the year and was hampered by winter snows that cost ten men in his company their lives and the maiming of others for life from frostbite. It was not one of Frémont's proudest moments.

In the early spring of 1853, Senator Benton invited the legendary trapper and guide Antoine Leroux to Washington, DC, to appear before Congress regarding the proposed route of the thirty-eighth and thirty-ninth parallels. Leroux also wrote an extensive letter that appeared in a number of newspapers throughout the East expounding on four routes from New Mexico to California that he had personally traveled and the country between them. He wrote, "I have trapped on nearly every stream between Cooke's route (Mormon Battalion, Northern New Mexico, followed the Gila and Colorado Rivers to San Diego) and the Great Salt Lake, and am well acquainted with the region of country between them."[28]

Moreover, Lieutenant Thomas W. Sweeny wrote, "Antoine Leroux was perhaps as well informed about the little known spaces of the unexplored West as any man of his time."[29]

Westwater Camp | 31

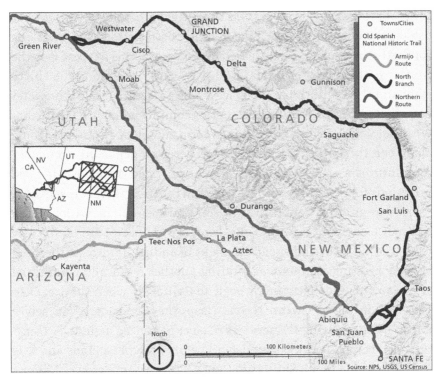

FIGURE 1.8. North Branch of the Old Spanish Trail. Because of insufficient evidence that the West Fork of the trail through San Luis Valley was used for commercial activities between New Mexico and California during the trail's significant period (1829–1848), the West Fork of the North Branch is no longer shown as part of the Old Spanish Historical Trail. Map courtesy of the National Park Service.

In 1847–1848, during the Mexican-American War, Leroux was lead guide for Colonel P. St. George Cooke and the Mormon Battalion, and they built a road from New Mexico to California. He was also guide to Captain Lorenzo Sitgreaves, who in 1851 led a small crew of topographers, naturalists, artists, and support personnel and thirty infantrymen along the Zuni, Little Colorado, and Colorado Rivers to map and explore a shorter route to California. Their party was also instructed to evaluate the navigability of the three rivers. Leroux was already familiar with the navigability of the Colorado River from the Virgin River to the Gulf of California, having trapped it by boat in 1837.[30] He concurred with Senator Benton that when one was coming from the East, the route over Cochetopa Pass was the better path. In 1853, Antoine Leroux wound up guiding two of the four proposed railroad surveys along southerly routes from New Mexico to California. One of these was the central route survey of Captain John W. Gunnison along the thirty-eight and thirty-ninth parallels, which he guided as far as Westwater before returning to Taos to meet a prior commitment with Lieutenant Whipple, whose regiment he guided for a survey of a southerly route along the thirty-fifth parallel. Before Leroux's departure from Captain Gunnison's survey at Westwater, he provided them with detailed directions for reaching the main OST and the Green River crossing.[31]

Prior to guiding Captain Gunnison and Lieutenant Whipple, Leroux met Lieutenant Edward F. Beale on the Santa Fe Trail on his way to California to be the superintendent of Indian affairs. At the time of their meeting, Leroux was guiding another outfit and committed afterward to guide Lieutenant Beale to California when they reached Taos. According to Gwinn Harris Heap, they "considered ourselves fortunate in securing the services of so experienced a guide."[32] Unfortunately, Leroux became seriously ill before arriving at Taos and was unable to guide them. Similar to Captain Gunnison, Leroux, it seems likely, would have provided Beal with directions and landmarks to follow the North Branch OST as far as the main OST. Heap's journal was the first to describe the entire trail along with recording the mileage between camps.

In addition, Leroux guided Captain Randolph B. Marcy's northerly return trip in 1857 from Fort Union, New Mexico, to Camp Scott, Wyoming, with supplies for Colonel Albert Sydney Johnston's army during the short-lived Utah War. Captain Marcy had started out with his soldiers when he was ordered to wait for Colonel William Wing Loring and his troops. Colonel Loring hired Leroux in Taos, and together they traveled eastern Colorado, where they combined their troops and completed the journey to Camp Scott. After the Utah War ended in 1858, Colonel William Wing Loring was ordered to return with his troops to New Mexico and take a more southerly route than the one he had traveled with Marcy the previous year. It was a large contingent of military that included fifty wagons and 300 men who were assigned to repair existing roads and build their own when needed. Leaving Camp

Floyd on July 19, 1858, Loring kept a journal that included descriptions of their camps, landmarks, existing roads, and, most important, the daily mileage. Colonel Loring provided the most thorough record in existence of the trail, which helped Chenoweth, Robb, and Lloyd to reconstruct their route through Grand County and western Colorado. Unbeknown to them, the Second Lieutenant John Van Deusen Du Bois also kept a journal, which helped identify their camp at Westwater.[33] Colonel Loring's guide was Antoine aka Watkins Leroux.

Along the route, Colonel Loring at one point wrote that they were "marching slowly to make a good road for the train (wagons)."[34] Throughout his journal he reported attributes of grass, wood, and water at stops and camps. Both Loring and Du Bois indicate that there was an existing road (North Branch of the OST) between the Green River and Grand River that they generally followed or made improvements on to avoid sandy areas or difficult terrain for their wagons. After exiting the main OST to avoid long distances of a dearth of water, the party followed the existing trail south of Captain Gunnison's that reached the Grand River sooner. Loring's party reached the Grand River at McGraw Bottom, then traveled to Cisco, and on August 12 their party camped for several days at Westwater, where there were water, grass, and wood (and trout), while they worked on a road near the Utah-Colorado border. Colonel Loring described the Westwater camp, where "the valley we are in is some six miles in length and two or three in width, surrounded on all sides by high mural precipices. Soil good and covered with large cottonwood trees and sage bush, grass abundant and numerous fish in the river."[35] Lieutenant Du Bois added, "this camp is a pretty good one."[36]

Interestingly, Loring reported at this location "numerous Indian trails, leading to Salt (La Sal) mountain and the San Miguel and Dolores rivers."[37] Upriver of the Westwater Ranger Station, there reportedly was a Colorado River crossing used by early resident ranchers during low water. The Westwater area, as described by Lieutenant Edward G. Beckwith in his 1853 report, had a

> narrow bottom of fine grass two or three miles in length, with shady groves of cotton-wood on the banks of the stream. The red sandstone cañon walls are nearly vertical and two hundred feet high; beyond

FIGURE 1.9. Undated stereo image of Westwater where Westwater Creek drains into the Colorado River. The name on the image is Nottingham Point. A Dr. D. M. Nottingham's name appears in newspapers reporting Westwater news in 1906. The river bottoms in the photo are flooded by the Colorado River. This is the area where Colonel William Wing Loring is believed to have camped in 1858. Below Nottingham Point, the Colorado River narrows as it enters Westwater Canyon.

which smaller ledges rise above each other, terrace-like, for some miles towards Salt Mountain (La Sal), which bears south from our camps, some twenty miles beyond the river. The cañon narrows to the width of the river below the groves of cotton-wood.[38]

"They remained at their camp for three days ... keeping our animals at the river to graze."[39]

It seems evident that Antoine Leroux knew his way throughout the Southwest. Regarding the area between Taos and the Green and Colorado Rivers, he claimed to have made semiannual trips to Salt Lake before it was settled. According to two sources there existed a Mount Leroux in the vicinity of Green River that was named for him.[40]

Prior to 1853 there are little to no detailed descriptions given of the Northern Branch of the OST. During the period from 1853 to 1858, the only known detailed accounts of the North Branch of the OST that later became the Salt Lake Wagon Road come from the Beale, Gunnison, and Loring parties that were either guided or consulted by Antoine Leroux. Later in 1875, Henry Gannett further documented the route by identifying the Salt Lake Wagon Road on his map for the F. V. Hayden Survey. Of the known parties, only Captain Gunnison took a different northerly route after leaving Westwater. It was a comparison of the more detailed notes from Loring and Gannett that helped Chenoweth and Robb locate the Grand River Crossing at Grand Junction, Westwater camp, and other historical sites along the road/trail through Utah and Colorado. Leroux was familiar with the camps and where water, grass, and wood could be found.

It's unclear when Westwater was first used as a camp. Between 1822 and 1840, there was significant activity by trappers who shared little to no descriptions of their travels along the Colorado and Green Rivers. The OST was interchangeably used when describing both the main and North Branch. The well-traveled northern route heading west at Salt Creek to converge with the main OST may have been established around 1830, when the trail opened up to California. Sometime in October 1837, Leroux reported that trappers Isaac Slover and William Pope, with their families and two Mexicans, traveled by wagon along the North Branch OST from Taos. Because of the difficult terrain crossing the area below Cochetopa Pass, it is surmised that they used a two-wheeled cart. The same month, John Wolfskill, brother of William Wolfskill, followed the same route with thirty-three Mexicans leaving Taos on October 17, 1837, and arrived in California in February 1838. Perhaps the two parties traveled together?

On June 24, 1852, former trapper "Uncle Dick" Wootton departed Taos with 9,000 head of sheep to sell in California for a profit. Most recorded merchants traveled the main OST; however, Wootton chose to travel the North Branch to California. In a news article, he provided a list of water sources along the route and the approximate mileage between them. There were three water sources listed between the Blue or Benikera (Colorado) and Green Rivers. Of these he named the first two water sources "Big Salt Creek" and "Little Salt Creek" respectively. The latter was fifteen miles further west and is likely Westwater Creek (then called Bitter Water Creek), where there were good camps and "plenty of wood, water and grass every night during the whole trip." Both creeks are laden with alkali, which suggests the campsites near the Grand River were the sources for water. Wootton also reported that the following year, an emigrant party with "two thousand sheep, and from three to four hundred head of cattle" followed behind Captain Gunnison and that Leroux ran into them on his return to Taos.[41] With so much traffic in 1853, there appeared clearly a bias to promote the North Branch trail for the building of a Pacific railway. Chenoweth and Pierson identified a number of parties who camped or stopped at Westwater. See appendix B for a chronology.

Today, a small part of the Salt Lake Wagon Road survives at Westwater. It followed closely an older North Branch of the OST. Travel in the Southwest was harsh, and water, wood, and grass were critical for survival. Henry Gannett wrote of the Cisco Desert region: "Between the Grand and Green Rivers there is no permanent water along the route. Still rain-water is found at several points in holes, where it remains for several days. Grass, also, is very scarce along this portion of the route."[42]

When traveling beyond the Union Pacific Bridge to the Westwater boat launch, you are making your way on one of the few remaining exposed sections of the Old Salt Lake Wagon Road and the North Branch of the OST. Initially a narrow trail worn by foot, pack animal, or horse, the trail was later enlarged into a path and developed for wagons by Colonel Loring and Colonel Canby's military troops, becoming an important well-traveled wagon road between Utah and Colorado. The road was established when Colorado was sparsely settled. It was used for the military, stagecoaches, and freight wagons hauling supplies

FIGURE 1.10. Cisco Desert images near Green River, Utah. Photos by author (2019).

coming out of Salina to Utes near Montrose, and for mining activity in the San Juan Mountains. Before the railroad, it was a common route for members and missionaries of the Church of Jesus Christ of Latter-day Saints (Mormons) traveling from Utah to settlements in the San Luis Valley, where many converted Saints coming from the southeast settled.[43] There are insufficient records to know how many other parties may have stopped or camped at Westwater. It seems likely that many would stop there for grass, wood, and water.

In 2010 and 2011, the National Historic Trails Project was conducted for a number of trails in southern Utah. Part of the report involved the archaeology of Colonel William Wing Loring's Salt Lake Wagon Road. Of Westwater being a camp, the report strongly suggests that Loring's description and other supporting evidence appear to validate what Chenoweth and Pierson concluded from their independent research. The report surmises that Loring's party camped near the confluence of Westwater Creek and the Colorado River (note: this location is now private property).[44] When one reads the descriptions from Beale's (Heap), Beckwith's, Loring's, and Gannett's reports, they are similar.

Bill Chenoweth and James M. Robb's research of the Salt Lake Wagon Road was instrumental in identifying the "Crossing of the Grand" by early travelers along the North Branch of the OST. In 2001, an attractive historical marker designating the Crossing was attached to a boulder that sits off the side of the road along 28 ¼ Road and Unaweep Avenue in Grand Junction. It is one of several markers throughout Colorado that designate historical locations along the North Branch OST. Their work—along with that of Jack and Katherine Nelson, Lloyd Pierson, and

FIGURE 1.11. Whitewater enthusiasts at Westwater Canyon launch site. The one- and two-day whitewater trip is very popular, and more than 10,000 commercial and private visitors each year come to raft and kayak the canyon. Photo by author (2009).

others from OSTA—contributed tremendously to having the Main and North Branches of the OST designated as the fifteenth nationally recognized Historic Trail in the United States. Before Bill Chenoweth passed away on July 23, 2018, he generously shared his research with interested parties in Utah, including the BLM at Moab. He wanted to recognize as much of the North Branch of the OST as possible and was certain about Westwater being a primary camp on the trail. There are currently no historical markers of the North Branch of the OST in Utah. It would be appropriate if posthumously a marker could be placed at Westwater identifying the camp and history of the North Branch of the OST on behalf of Chenoweth, Robb, and Pierson for their efforts identifying it.

Perhaps the name Westwater was derived from the D&RGW RR as it headed west across the Cisco Desert. However, the tracks heading west did not initially emerge from Ruby Canyon as described by the source. The naming of the railroad station was made seven years earlier. Or possibly, the name is derived from an earlier historic source. Perhaps, just maybe, the name was derived from the last good camp with water, wood, and grass before heading west across a desert that is destitute of these critical resources until travelers reach the next permanent source of water at the Green River. A directive to go west from this camp to the next source of water may have morphed into its being named Westwater.

2

THE OUTLAW BROTHERS

While writing Westwater Lost and Found *(2004), I encountered frustrating details missing from a few stories that I couldn't resolve because of limitations working with archaic methods of research prior to the internet. In particular, many boaters who stop at Outlaw Cave question the woman's shoes that are found with other debris on top of an old iron stove, and my desire persisted to locate supporting evidence related to the original story of the outlaw brothers residing at Outlaw Cave that Dee Holladay of Holiday River Expeditions shared with the river community—a story that continues to be told.*

The advancement of the internet over the past twenty years contributed heavily to my ability to locate formerly missing or incomplete information not found in Westwater Lost and Found *(2004). With the advent of digitized newspapers, documents, photographs, genealogy websites, and direct contact using email and messaging with individuals, museums, historical societies, and libraries, the internet has introduced us to a significant amount of research that can be performed in our own homes. Considerable information can now be easily found using search tools that are available on most websites. It was*

https://doi.org/10.7330/9781646425457.c002

FIGURE 2.1. Outlaw Cave, in the middle of Westwater Canyon along the Colorado River. Photo by author (2005).

the internet and a search tool at Utah Digital Newspapers that brought me to a wealth of new and supporting information that form the basis of this book.

By sharing Westwater's history in Westwater Lost and Found (2004), I removed what likely was a self-imposed burden from my shoulders. Initially, I began to research the previously undocumented popular Westwater Canyon for personal reasons, and as I accumulated considerable histories on both the canyon and region at some point, I realized it should be shared with the boating community and historians.

Except for my interest in researching and writing more about Westwater camp along the North Branch of the Old Spanish Trail (OST), I relaxed from any additional research until a few years later, when out of curiosity I typed Westwater in the search tool for Utah Digital Newspapers and it came up with more than 3,000 hits. I stayed up nearly all night inspecting each of the sources in the hopes of locating new and additional information on the subject. Toward the end of my search, I located an article that appeared in only one of the early Utah newspapers about a woman drowning near Cisco in 1887.[1] Finding this article prompted me to continue researching Westwater and the Upper Colorado River using tools made available through the internet.

Without these tools, I highly doubt that the story regarding the outlaw brothers in Westwater Canyon could be pieced together. Other than who built Outlaw Cave, and when it was done, the story of the outlaw brothers is perhaps the biggest mystery to solve about Westwater Canyon. The late Dee Holladay of Holiday River Expeditions learned the story of the outlaw brothers from former residents Ray and Mary Rose of the Rose Ranch near Cisco takeout. In Westwater Lost and Found (2004) I provided a plethora of information *surrounding the cave; even so, no written record revealed a source for the outlaw brother story. As remote as Westwater Canyon was in the 1800s and early 1900s, even until the 1950s, I doubted any evidence of the brothers existed. Although unsubstantiated, the story continues to be told of two outlaw brothers who robbed a bank in Vernal, Utah, and proceeded to then find refuge in Outlaw Cave during a severe winter. One brother was wounded and eventually died and is buried not far downstream from the cave. The closest potential lead may have come from my original book, where I introduce Bob and Ira Smith; however, I left the Smith brothers on the Grand River heading to the Utah border in a boat with no further details.[2] Digital newspapers helped me locate more information about the brothers, and the writings of Gunnison sheriff Cyrus Wells "Doc" Shores provided details that may perhaps solve the mystery.*

Outlaw Cave in Westwater Canyon is riddled with many unanswered questions. In 1933, when Harold H. Leich completed his solo boating traverse of Westwater Canyon, he camped near the Denver & Rio Grande Western Railroad (D&RGW RR) Pumphouse near Cisco, where he met the pump station engineer Roscoe C. Hallett (1890–1971). Hallett had lived nearly his entire life at Westwater and later at Cisco, and as a moundsman he dug pits and erected mounds as reference markers for a 1910 government survey of the canyon and region and was very familiar with Westwater Canyon and the cave.

In Leich's handwritten journal he wrote in his entry for August 17, 1933,

> I asked Hallett about an old mine tunnel I had seen in the middle course of the gorge on the left bank. He said the hole had been dug back in the 60's or 70's & was used in the 80's by a gang of Spanish counterfeiters, secure in their mountain stronghold from the law. Spurious coins have been found there in recent years.[3]

Although not specifying the ethnicity of the gang, longtime Westwater resident Elwood Clark Malin (1885–1960) wrote to the *Times Independent* about the cave and said that when he came to Westwater in 1904, "he was down at the cave and was told a band had been using the place for making bogus money."[4] Both men referred to its name as Counterfeit Cave.

One can only speculate where Roscoe Hallett learned of the cave's origin to have been in the 1860s or 1870s. The region was mostly uninhabited by settlers during that period. It wasn't until the 1880s that small communities developed along the newly laid tracks of the D&RGW RR at Cisco and a former inland site at West Water.[5] Neither of the settlements was near the Grand (Colorado) River. Uncompahgre (Tabeguache) Utes occupied Grand Junction area until 1881, when they were forced to leave for reservations in Utah. In addition to the counterfeiters previously mentioned, there were some placer mining booms reported in the early 1880s at Westwater.

The region began to be settled mostly along railroad tracks and major crossings of the Colorado and Green Rivers. Outside of the settlements, much of the area was desolate harsh country that was ideal for outlaws in hiding. Between 1880 and 1900, there were numerous news reports of horse thieves in Colorado and Utah escaping the law by herding the stolen horses into the Dolores Triangle; Westwater was located along the Colorado River on the northwestern border of the triangle.[6] Lawmen were reluctant to pursue outlaws after they entered the triangle, because of the terrain and incalculable locations for bandits to hide or ambush them. An unsubstantiated story related to Outlaw Cave is that horse thieves left their stolen horses to pasture near the River between the Little Dolores River and Marble Canyon while they holed up in the cave. This could explain wild horses that were found in the area.[7]

Outlaw Cave's name is of recent origin and is derived from a story that was handed down to Dee Holladay of Holiday River Expeditions. Previously, because of the story of a Spanish gang of counterfeiters residing in it during the 1880s, former residents of both Westwater and Cisco, as indicated earlier, called it Counterfeit Cave.[8] Dee began commercially boating the Colorado River through Westwater Canyon in 1966. Fortunately, his interests extended beyond the whitewater, and he gathered histories and stories from residents living in the area. The outlaw brother story was derived from Dee's friendship with Ray and Mary Rose, who leased the Rose Ranch upriver of the Cisco boat landing from J. Perry Olsen of Grand Junction. Ray told him that the previous owners of the ranch claimed that two brothers robbed a bank in Vernal at the turn of the twentieth century. They hid out in the cave during a harsh winter, until one of the brothers died from wounds that

FIGURE 2.2. Dee Holladay at Outlaw Cave. Photo by John Clark, of Holiday River Expeditions, courtesy of Dee Holladay (early to mid-1970s).

he received during their escape. Reportedly, the deceased brother's grave is located approximately a half-mile downstream from the cave. Evidence validating the outlaw brother story as it was told to Dee Holladay has not been found.

Chloe A. Hallett and her two sons Charles V. and Roscoe C. are the original owners of the Rose Ranch, located at mile 111 on Westwater Books' Canyonlands River Guide.[9] Chloe and her husband, Charles H. Hallett, initially homesteaded land along Westwater Creek near the head of Westwater Canyon in 1892, and it was officially deeded to him with a US patent on November 1, 1897. He may have died shortly afterward, because his wife, Chloe, sold the land five months later on March 22, 1898. Charles doesn't appear to have made it to Cisco, where Chloe is shown as widowed on the 1910 Census. Charles H. Hallett was portrayed as a good family man; however, there were circumstances since he arrived at Westwater that put him in Utah and California

FIGURE 2.3. Outlaw Grave. Photo by Bob Brennan (2021).

newspapers numerous times for both good and bad: He was a witness during the murder trial of Captain Wilson E. Davis in 1892, and then he himself was on trial with James H. Smith for killing Royal Grant in a land dispute in 1894. Juxtaposed between these incidents, he was involved with a false claim of knowing the whereabouts of a missing millionaire Dr. Thomas E. Tynan of San Francisco.[10] It appears that he would have had some stories to tell. However, by 1910, a widowed Chloe and her two sons moved downstream and homesteaded the property near Cisco landing.[11] The outlaw brothers story as reported to Dee was that the Vernal bank robbers hid in the cave during a severe winter and that the Halletts (or perhaps an earlier resident at the Cisco Pumphouse) helped take food and supplies to them by ice skating, where possible, up a mostly frozen Colorado River.

We are more aware of the Outlaw Cave's history at the onset of the twentieth century, and it doesn't appear that any outlaw brothers resided in it. However, both Charles V. and Roscoe Hallett had been through Westwater Canyon, and either one of them may have relayed the story of the outlaw brothers from other sources. Roscoe claimed to have assisted with a government survey of the canyon and shared some of the cave's history with Harold H. Leich in 1933. If we can't locate any evidence that it was Vernal bank robbers who hid in the cave, then possibly some of the facts were distorted through the years? The story as given to Dee Holladay would have taken place sometime near the turn of the twentieth century.

Perhaps the story evolved from two brothers who instead of robbing a bank robbed a train. The story could relate to the first robbery of a Denver and Rio Grande Railroad train on November 3, 1887.

We first learn of brothers Bob, alias Ira, and Jack Smith two years earlier in 1885, when they may have been involved with the murder of rancher Sam Jones of Unaweep Canyon, Colorado. On May 19, 1885, Sam Jones saddled his horse and left his ranch in Unaweep Canyon, heading for Silverton, Colorado, where he anticipated receiving several thousand dollars from a lawsuit. He never made it back home. His decomposed body with bullet holes in it was found in the West Creek area of Unaweep Canyon, where it had been dumped over a precipice. Bob Smith discovered the victim's bullet-riddled vest and where the body was dragged and sent over a cliff. Bob was also quick to implicate Jones's partner, John L. Campbell, in the murder, of which he was consequently convicted. It wasn't until 1891, during a retrial of Campbell's murder conviction, that additional evidence surfaced that instead implicated Bob and his brother as the murderers. An unrelated story was revealed in the synopsis of the retrial that appeared in the *Grand Valley Sentinel* on July 18, 1891, describing a train robbery in 1887, that involved Bob and Jack Smith, who escaped capture by "sailing down the Gunnison River into the Grand (Colorado) River and on to the Utah Line."[12]

On the morning of November 3, 1887, Bob, his brother Jack Smith, Ed Rhoades, and Bob W. Wallace (real surname Boyle) robbed a D&RG train near the Unaweep Switch, three miles east of Grand Junction, Colorado. It was the first robbery of a D&RG passenger train after the railroad had been established seven years earlier. The robbers had an ingenious getaway plan involving a boat. However, the plan was frustrated because of bad luck and by a relentless sheriff that resulted in them being pursued for more than two months under extreme winter weather conditions for a measly $150.[13]

FIGURE 2.4. Train Robbery wood engraving. *Harper's Weekly*, January 16, 1892. iStock-977715972.

The Salt Lake express train coming out of Salt Lake City was headed eastbound toward Delta, Colorado, when shortly after 1:30 a.m. the engineer Ed Malloy observed rocks and railroad ties blocking their path, prompting him to slow the trains speed as they neared Unaweep Switch. Bringing the train to a stop, Malloy and the train's fireman Fred Sellinger were immediately accosted by four masked men and told to get down from the train and raise their arms high. While one of the outlaws held a gun on the engineer and fireman, the other three robbers approached the mail car to wake the mail clerk H. W. Grubb. Grubb was unaware of what happened until he opened the mail car's door and had a pistol pointed at him. The outlaws then ransacked the mail, looking for cash and valuables. Finding little to nothing of real value, they proceeded to the express and baggage car. Dick Williams was responsible for the express car and recognized that the train was being robbed. He initially resisted opening the car door until the robbers threatened to dynamite it. Inside, there was a messenger safe holding approximately $150; a second larger and more secure safe held more than $3,000. It wasn't until the robbers threatened Williams's life that he reluctantly opened the smaller safe. However, he did not have the combination to open the larger "through safe" that belonged to the express company. For security against such acts, the D&RG RR prohibited giving the combination to anyone on board the train; it could only be accessed by agents located at specified stopping points along the route. After thirty-five minutes of threatening Williams to open the larger safe, the discouraged robbers finally believed him, conceded defeat, and let him live. They had bluffed Williams earlier about having dynamite that they didn't have, and without any dynamite, or a combination for the larger safe, the outlaws disappeared into the night with a much smaller haul than they had anticipated.

It did not take long before the robbery was reported to Grand Junction, and a posse was swiftly assembled. The posse arrived at Unaweep Switch shortly after the robbery took place; it was still early in the morning. Spreading out, the posse unsuccessfully searched the entire area for the outlaws' tracks or signs of their departure. Finding nothing, they disbanded after a couple of fruitless days of searching. Where they left off, Gunnison sheriff Cyrus Wells "Doc" Shores began his own tracking. On the morning of the robbery, Sheriff Doc Shores was telegraphed by the D&RG RR and asked to participate in the hunt. Doc Shores doubled as a deputy US marshal that allowed him jurisdiction to investigate crimes in other counties. The D&RG RR desperately wanted to make an example of the robbers and turned to Doc Shores for his renowned tracking abilities.

FIGURE 2.5. Gunnison Sheriff Cyrus W. (Doc) Shores (1834–1944). The photo was taken by his friend Grand Junction and Gunnison, Colorado, photographer Frank E. Dean. Courtesy of the Museums of Western Colorado, Grand Junction, Colorado. As a side note, Dean was the photographer who assisted Ellsworth Kolb and Bert Loper when they boated through Westwater Canyon in 1916.

Arriving at the scene, Sheriff Shores was perplexed. He and his brother-in-law M. L. Allison of Grand Junction spent two days circling the area along the railroad tracks that followed alongside the Gunnison River to Delta. The switch was located at a point where the Gunnison River is generally too deep to ford with horses, yet without the outlaws having left any tracks Shores began to suspect that they must have come from the other side of the river. Allison surmised that the "train robbers had wings."[14]

The next day Shores and Allison ferried their horses across the Colorado River below its confluence with the Gunnison River at Grand Junction in order to begin a search across the river from where the train robbery occurred. Having no success, the men returned to Grand

Junction for the night. After crossing the river the next morning, the two men rode their horses directly to the location where they had stopped searching the previous day and continued searching upstream for tracks. Across the Gunnison River and a short distance upstream of where the robbery occurred, the search party discovered two distinct sets of footprints separated by approximately a half mile apart along the riverbank. To confuse the trackers the robbers had separated into two parties and as they emerged from crossing the river at the mouth of Bangs Canyon, each pair in the group followed the lead person's footsteps onto dry land for a distance, hoping that anyone tracking them would be dissuaded from believing they were the four train robbers. Further complicating the mystery, the two parties continued on foot for approximately fourteen miles into Bangs Canyon before they converged. A patient and thorough tracker, Sheriff Shores did not fall for their trickery. However, he found it unusual that they were on foot and didn't have horses or another means of transportation once they reached the other side of the river. The lawmen continued to track the four outlaws over difficult and rocky terrain for twenty miles before Sheriff Shores was convinced that the outlaws were headed to the Dolores River area, "where it would be good country to hide out in."[15] They needed to get there first.

Returning to his home in the town of Gunnison, Shores arranged for better horses and had them shipped to Whitewater, where he and Allison were joined by a special agent for the D&RG Express Company, James Duckworth. Riding through Unaweep Canyon, their party made better time and reached the Dolores River near Gateway that evening hoping to intercept the outlaws. Instead, they were told by a miner returning from Sinbad Valley near the Utah border that he had seen footprints heading in that direction, leaving the posse to believe that they were a couple of days behind the outlaws, who were headed to Sinbad Valley. Near Gateway they met a cow camp owner Tom Denning, whom they persuaded to join them because of his familiarity with the region.

The four men, led by Sheriff Shores, continued their ride to Sinbad Valley and arrived at a summit overlooking the valley just before dark. They then followed a steep Ute trail down into the valley that caused their horses to slip several times. Once they reached the bottom, inclement weather struck and a hard rain came down. They shot their guns into the air a few times in hopes that someone living in the valley might offer them shelter, but there was no response. They stopped to get out from under the rain. There was no dry wood to make a fire, so they kept warm by huddling together and draped their saddle blankets over them.

The next day the rain turned to snow. In the valley they located a cabin that was being used to make bootleg whiskey. Someone evidently resided in the cabin; however, they didn't appear during the several days that Doc Shores and his posse waited for the snow to subside. The severe weather gravely affected James Duckworth, who wound up getting pneumonia and would later die from it. Unknown to the posse, the outlaws, who were on foot, fared worse in the inclement weather and returned down Bangs Canyon to lower elevations and the Gunnison River.

After several days the lawmen traveled south toward the Dolores River, where they suspected the outlaws were headed. Reaching Paradox, the lawmen inquired about the four outlaws they were tracking, but there was no sign that the men had made it that far. With Duckworth ill and no sign of the outlaws, the group decided to return to Grand Junction. Unfortunately, the route back to Unaweep Canyon was blocked by ten to twelve feet of snow that had fallen during the storms. Forced to continue south they rode to the Dolores River, then followed it to its confluence with the San Miguel River. Snow continued to fall, and they stopped for a few days at a ranch near the placer mining town of Uravan. At Placerville, they split up to get help for Duckworth. Shores and Duckworth took a stage to a former railroad town of Dallas; Duckworth then took a train to Denver, where he died. Shortly afterward, Doc Shores reunited with Allison and Denning at Montrose; they then continued toward Grand Junction. Along the way the train stopped at Delta, where Shores and his men learned from residents the identities of the robbers and that a boat was involved. Up to this point Doc Shores questioned why the outlaws were on foot. Now he knew.[16]

The Smith brothers, Rhoades, and Wallace met shortly before the train robbery while working on the Midland Railroad in Carbondale, Colorado. The Smiths would have been familiar with much of the area, having worked in the state for a couple of years primarily in Mesa

County and along the western Colorado and eastern Utah border on ranches and herding cattle. Rhodes did some mining at several locations throughout Colorado and spent time in Grand Junction. Wallace was a bit more reserved about his whereabouts, and unbeknownst to his comrades they only knew him by an alias name, Robert Wallace.

While working together in Carbondale, they developed an ingenious plan to rob a D&RG Railroad train and escape by boat on the Gunnison and Grand (Colorado) Rivers. The plan may have been conceived by the Smith brothers, who, newspapers reported, had boated down the Colorado River to Arizona the previous year. Quitting their employment, they traveled to Delta and built a boat.[17]

Describing the strangers, Delta residents said that the four men came to their town shortly before the train robbery. They were on foot leading a black pack horse carrying supplies. The men set up a camp outside of town along the Gunnison River, where they proceeded to build a boat. The project attracted attention of the townspeople, who stopped to observe the boat's progress. For several days while the boat was being built, the strangers shared limited information about themselves during their casual conversations with the onlookers. However, additional enlightenment was revealed by Delta residents, who overheard the stranger's conversations among themselves, including their names. A day or two before the robbery, Jack Smith sold the pack horse to a resident, and the four men loaded the boat with guns and supplies then launched it onto the river and headed toward Unaweep Switch, where the robbery occurred.

After hearing the evidence presented by the Delta residents, Doc Shores now knew the suspects' names and the means for an escape. Because there wasn't previously any indication that a boat was involved, Shores surmised that something must have happened to it. When Shores and Allison first started tracking the outlaws, they searched numerous times along the banks of the Gunnison River near Unaweep Switch and didn't find any evidence of a boat. Later, after the outlaws were captured, they related to Doc Shores that "the boat was caught in an eddy near Whitewater and capsized. Although the occupants managed to right the boat and salvage their roll of blankets as it floated downstream, they lost all of their Winchesters and shotguns

FIGURE 2.6. Outlaw Cave. Photo by author (2018).

which sank to the bottom of the river."[18] They retained their pistols; however, they felt that they needed shotguns to pull off the heist. Their plans disrupted; the men then rowed the boat down to Grand Junction, where they hid it along the banks of the Grand River. To avoid suspicion, they shaved and cleaned themselves up, then went into town to purchase the necessary weapons. Afterward, the men left their boat hidden along the bank of the Grand River and walked up the road three miles to Unaweep Switch, where they piled rocks onto the railroad tracks to stop the train. When Doc Shores, Allison, and Denning arrived at Grand Junction, they searched the banks of the Grand River and located the boat. The outlaws were still in the area.

Returning to his hotel in Grand Junction, Doc Shores received a message from an agent with the Denver & Rio Grande to investigate a report that the outlaws were seen at Raven's Beak, which was north of Palisade along the Grand River. Inclement weather continued to affect the men as they left immediately during the night for Raven's Beak. Partway, they found a cabin to stay in, supposing it was warmer than the frigid weather they were caught in. Unfortunately, the cabin was like an icebox, and all of the men caught colds. Raven's Beak was a false alarm. The men returned to Grand Junction, where Tom Denning was hospitalized with pneumonia, Allison returned to his work, and Doc Shores took time to recuperate from his illness. Having gone through extreme harsh weather conditions, Shores could not help but believe that the outlaws had suffered more and had likely turned back, having been on foot. After Shores sufficiently recovered, he returned to where the boat was hidden, and it was gone.

Working alone, Doc Shores tracked the outlaws down the Grand River.

> It did not take me long to find where the boat had been dragged over the ice and snow in the unnavigable portion of the stream. The tracks of the men who pulled the craft were about a week old.
>
> I rode down the Grand as far as Cisco, Utah, where I was told that four men had been seen coming down the river in a boat. Later they came into town and caught a freight train going west. The next day I rode westward into the town of Green River where I again inquired about any strangers.[19]

There are no specific details about what conditions the robbers experienced as they worked the boat down the Grand River, and where they eventually left the river for Cisco. Later, after three of the outlaws were captured, they told Sheriff Shores that "they had been living out doors like wild animals and suffered a good deal of hardship and privation long enough to be glad to be taken in and kept where it was warm and given something to eat."[20]

As described before, at points on the Grand River, they had to drag their boat across ice; otherwise, they traveled in it. There were two locations within the Utah border in which the robbers could have boarded a train. One was at the head of Westwater Canyon, where a small railroad stop was inland about twelve miles from the river, and the other was at the mouth of the canyon at Cisco. It appeared that they wanted to continue by boat, but there were news reports that indicated the boat may have sunk. At Green River/Blake, one of the robbers hired a German immigrant to steal lumber and take it downstream to a designated location on the Green River for them to build another boat. Unfortunately, the German was captured and put into jail by Constable Farr, of Green River, after his makeshift raft hauling the lumber was caught on a sandbar. After the German did not arrive with the lumber, the robbers departed.[21]

The Smith brothers and Ed Rhodes stayed together and were soon captured around January 10, 1888, at Woodside, Utah, by Sheriff Shores's

FIGURE 2.7. Decommissioned Post Office at Cisco, Utah. Photo by author (1997).

brother-in-law M. L. Allison, Tom Denny, his undersheriff Sam W. Harper of Gunnison, and Sheriff Cramer of Mesa County. Sheriff Shores met them in Thompson on their return with the prisoners. The *Gunnison Review Press* reported:

> Very little property of value was found upon them or in the dugout. They had no guns but four revolvers, $6.50 in cash, only a pair and a half of blankets between them and were about out of grub, their boots were about worn out and their feet were protected by rawhide sewed or laced over their feet. They had evidently had a hard time.[22]

Later that month, on January 26, 1888, Sheriff Shores and the "Lone Fisherman" captured the fourth train robber, Bob W. Boyle, who was working near Price, Utah.[23]

The similarities of the story told of Vernal bank robbers escaping to Westwater's Outlaw Cave and the D&RG Railroad train robbery are intriguing. The Hallett family would not have been around to help them if they had briefly stayed in the cave. The Halletts did not arrive in the region until 1892, when both Charles and Roscoe were children. However, there may have been a previous rancher who resided near the Cisco Pumphouse and possibly helped the outlaws in some manner. Of course, they would share their exciting story of the two outlaw brothers, and for nearly eighty years it continued to be told until it reached Dee Holladay, where he shared it with the early Westwater boating community.

Regarding the story about one of the brothers being injured, Jack Smith was wounded in his cheek from an accidental shotgun blast from Ed Rhodes while they were hiding in Bangs Canyon. When it happened, the wound looked like it could be life threatening, and, concerned for his brother, Bob Smith left to go to Grand Junction for help. When he arrived at the Gunnison River and saw a posse that was searching for them, he changed his mind. When Bob was gone, Ed cleaned up Jack's wound and bandaged it as well as he could. Jack was sitting up smoking a cigarette when Bob returned. The weather conditions described by Sheriff Doc Shores match those given by Ray Rose to Dee Holladay. Part of the river was sufficiently frozen for a boat to be dragged over it, or for somebody wearing ice skates to deliver supplies to the wanton robbers.

During most of the time that Doc Shores was pursuing four unknown train robbers, there were reports that six men were involved with the robbery. On December 27, 1887, the *Denver Republican* reported, "Two of the gang who stopped the passenger train on the Denver & Rio Grande Railroad in October last near Grand Junction, Colorado, were captured yesterday at Vernal, Uintah County, Utah."[24] The two men who were arrested were later released after the truth about the robbery was learned. Could this be our Vernal connection?

3

THOSE DARN WOMAN'S SHOES FOUND IN WESTWATER'S CAVE

A question that crosses many boaters' minds when visiting Outlaw Cave in Westwater Canyon involves a pair of a woman's shoes. Found in the man-made cave midway through the canyon are two curious wooden beds, a Duffy Trowbridge Range and a small table cluttered with old cans, bottles, and other artifacts dated eighty years and older. Of the artifacts, a woman's pair of shoes stands out. Because of their age and the remoteness of the cave, one has to wonder what a woman was doing there, who she was, and when was she there.

Westwater Canyon is a popular seventeen-mile stretch of whitewater on the Colorado River above Moab, Utah. Until the mid-1960s the canyon was fairly remote and rarely visited except by infrequent cattle ranchers, bootleggers, horse thieves, outlaws, surveyors, trappers, and miners. A few individuals unknowingly entered the canyon by boat. Others were turned away because of Westwater Canyon's sinister reputation. An early name given to the canyon was "Hades Canyon."[1]

FIGURE 3.1. Outlaw Cave interior view. Photo by Bob Brennan (2021).

On August 16, 1933, Harold H. Leich pulled his punt that he named the "Dirty Devil" ashore from the Colorado River at the Denver & Rio Grande Railroad Pumphouse near Cisco. Leich had just completed running the rapids in Westwater Canyon, which had once been considered unnavigable and at the time were only known to have been successfully boated once before by Ellsworth Kolb and Bert Loper in 1916. A recent graduate of Dartmouth College, Leich chose a temporary nomadic life instead of joining the workforce struggling through the Great Depression. His newest adventure was a solo boating excursion down the length of the Colorado River.

At the landing, Leich met the pump station engineer Roscoe C. Hallett. A longtime resident of the region, Hallett arrived as a small child with his parents to homestead land near the former railroad town of Westwater in 1892. Later, his family moved downriver to Cisco. Hallett was well versed in the region's history and spent most of the following morning talking with Leich about Westwater Canyon. Curious about the cave that he discovered midway in the canyon, Leich inquired about it and was told that the cave was manmade and was dug out in the 1860s or 1870s. This would have happened ten to twenty years before Moab or Grand Junction was settled and the region was populated mostly by Utes. Hallett and other local residents called it "Counterfeit Cave" because they claimed there was a gang of counterfeiters living in it during the 1880s. When discussing the river, other than the boating exploits of Kolb and Loper, Hallett mentioned only one other party attempting to traverse the canyon by boat. He said, "Another party of 2 men & a woman tried the canyon some time ago in a big boat & came to grief. The woman was drowned in the whirlpool."[2] The story of a woman drowning was known by other local ranchers.

The story of the boating incident does not appear to have been reported in Moab's newspapers, and according to Hallett he said that it followed Kolb and Loper's exploits. Attempts to locate the boating incident in Grand Junction newspapers also failed. Fortunately, looking at earlier dates I found an accident reported in several newspapers in 1887 that may reveal the source of the story.

A Woman Drowned Near Cisco,

> The first of the week information was received of the drowning of Mrs. Mary Osborne, of Delta, in the Grand river, near Cisco. Mrs. Osborne was traveling by boat down the Grand river with her husband, Jos. Osborne, and two other men. Their destination was opposite the Cisco pumphouse, and when within three miles of this point Mr. Osborne tied the boat to the bank and went down the river to investigate the rapids which they were approaching. Mrs. Osborne remained in the boat and the two other men of the party remained near her in another boat. While Mr. Osborne was absent Mrs. Osborne's boat broke adrift and was carried down the river, finally striking a rock with great violence and upsetting. Mrs. Osborne rose to the surface, clung fast to the keel of the boat and cried for assistance but before it could reach her she was swept off and disappeared. This occurred on March 17th, and up to the present time the body has not been discovered. Mrs. Osborne is well-known at Delta, where for some time she had charge of a hotel. Her husband is a trapper and is well known throughout the reservation. Mesa County Democrat.[3]

Two years later Frank Clarence Kendrick was conducting a railroad survey in the Westwater valley for the DCC&P RR, and in his notes dated April 10, 1889, he wrote, "Ran line down through Box X ranch to Sta 2207 at mouth of 'Hades canon' where the woman was drowned."[4] The "Box X" Ranch is an earlier name for Westwater Ranch. It appears that the stories and the legend of a woman drowning refer to Mary Osborne. Could the shoe belong to her?

There are no known efforts by the BLM or other parties to date the woman's shoes in Outlaw Cave. In 1973, Dee Holladay of Holiday River Expeditions invited BLM archaeologist, Richard E. Fike to join him on a river trip down Westwater Canyon in an effort to record and preserve the relics found in the canyon, including Miners' Cabin (Wild Horse Cabin) and Outlaw Cave. Mr. Fike recorded artifacts found at both locations; however, he did not mention the shoes. Based on his observations the earliest date given for the artifacts was 1887, and according to BLM Archeologist Don Montoya, of Moab, the only other date given in Fike's report was 1910.[5]

To assist in efforts to date the shoes John Magill, former curator of Historic New Orleans Collection, was contacted. Among other expertise John is recognized for being proficient with identifying and dating historical clothing. His first impression upon seeing photos of the woman's shoes was that they were anywhere from 1880 to 1910, matching the date range given by Fike. John asked for better pictures of the shoes to be certain.

On one of his final river trips as a BLM Westwater ranger, Alvin Halliday assisted in obtaining detailed photographs of various angles of the woman's shoes for Mr. Magill to research.

In his reply, Magill referred to them as women's boots. Working from better photographs of the boots, he recalibrated the timeframe for them to the early twentieth century and noted that they likely would fall "somewhere between 1905 and 1920." He wrote that several of the "lace-boot" styles from a 1908 Sears catalogue were very similar to those found in the cave. Magill appeared to dismiss an earlier age for the boots when he wrote:

Those Darn Woman's Shoes Found in Westwater's Cave | 61

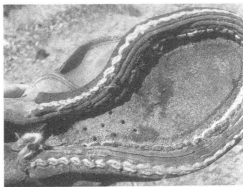

FIGURE 3.2. Tabletop that includes a woman's shoe found at Outlaw Cave. Photo by author (2009). Woman's shoe found in Outlaw Cave. Photos by former BLM Westwater ranger Alvin Halliday (2015).

Earlier women's boots from the 1880s tended to be button boots, rather than lace-up, made of very soft leather, very tight fitting and quite pointy in the toe. Indeed, very feminine and not a bit masculine looking.

Some later boot models showed rounded toes and were more like a tailored man's shoe only with a high heel. I feel that is where your boot fits.[6]

Another clothing specialist who offered to research photos of the shoes came up with a similar date of around 1920.[7] Without further conclusive research, it would appear from these evaluations that the shoes do not date back to when Mary Osborne was in Westwater Canyon.

There are many stories surrounding Outlaw Cave, but few document the names of individuals who resided in it. Except for Mary Osborne a woman's name has not been associated with anyone in Westwater Canyon until 1950, when two women and their spouses and two other men were trapped in the canyon after damaging one of their boats.[8] There is a report from 1908 that five "tramps" stole a boat in Grand Junction and that the next day it capsized in rapids sixty miles downstream killing three. It appears that they may have been all men; however, they were unknown to Westwater resident Joe Harris, who retrieved the boat and reported that the other three bodies weren't recovered.[9]

The earliest named resident of the cave was John Warren, of New York, who moved into it around 1904. He was an elderly man who also owned a small dwelling on the bank of the Grand/Colorado River downstream of the current Westwater boat launch. Warren may have been hustled to come to Westwater by the cave's previous occupants, who promoted it as a quicksilver mine.[10] For income, Warren delivered mail to the railroad. Each morning John hiked from the cave to the post office at Westwater Ranch, where he picked up the mail by 9:00 a.m. and delivered it less than a mile away to the Denver & Rio Grande Western Railroad Depot. After delivering the mail, he would get into his boat, cross the river, and hike back to the cave to work it. He did this for five years until he lost his job at the post office and disappeared from the region.[11]

A former Westwater resident, Elwood Malin, told a story of a one-armed man named Rich McGrooder, who with another man bought a boat at Westwater for a prospecting trip in the canyon. They "lived in Counterfeit (Outlaw) Cave for some time" as they tried to interest parties in New York to invest in mining equipment for them. When their offer was rejected, they left their equipment in the cave and never returned. Malin recalled the incident occurred approximately 1908 or 1910; however, there are Westwater news articles from 1917 and 1919 indicating "R. W. or R.A. McGruder" had a claim in the canyon that he was working. He is likely the same man who Malin recalled living in the cave. Each time Mr. McGruder entered the canyon by boat, he was accompanied by different individuals.[12]

Likely the last-known occupant of Outlaw Cave was L. D. "Luke" Hummel. Several boating parties in the 1950s and early 1960s reported mail found in the cave. Some of the parties said that they could not read the names or did not remember them. Others brought some of the mail back to Moab or to Salt Lake City, where it was deposited at the Utah Historical Society to be preserved.[13] Unfortunately, the mail and envelopes have not surfaced to be examined. Most of the reports of the mail had them dated in 1903, just prior to John Warren's occupancy of the cave. In 1962, the first-known group of kayaks traversed the canyon and reported finding letters. On a slide register for the photos that were taken of the trip, Joe M. Lacy referred to the cave as L. D. Hummel Cave. Forty years later when he was asked in an interview about the name, Mr. Lacy did not recall where it came from. However, a letter written by Walter Kirschbaum revealed that they "Found one of the two envelopes dated 19 Dec 1902, and addressed to Mr. Hummel at Westwater, Utah, in the cave."[14] Luke Hummel was a popular trapper throughout the region making headlines in local newspapers from 1908 to 1928. He held property in Glade Park and at Westwater near Bitter Creek.

Outlaw Cave was extremely remote, with difficult access. As a trapper, Hummel could live off of the land to support himself; however, Warren lasted only as long as his final paycheck for delivering the mail. What information that can be found about these individuals does not provide any evidence of women involved with them. The news article that named R. W. McGruder in the canyon in 1919 has his middle initial wrong; his full name is Richard Adolphus "Rich" McGruder. Born in Colorado, McGruder lived a relatively short distance from the Utah border, residing in Cedaredge and Glade Park during the time when he was inspecting his claims in Westwater.

Rich McGruder married at the age of twenty-two in 1904 and divorced three years later. According to a descendant, McGruder, a miner, lost his left arm while he was working on the Gunnison Tunnel in the Black Canyon near Montrose, Colorado. On May 30, 1905, the tunnel collapsed, killing from four to ten persons and burying thirty-five others who were expected to be rescued. McGruder's left arm was amputated from the incident, and it prevented him from serving in World War 1.[15] In 1919, he remarried Ida Merkt; this was during the same time frame that he was working his claims in Westwater.[16] Ida had children from a previous marriage who may have preoccupied her from visiting the cave, and she was not named in either of the articles about McGruder and his partners visiting the claims in Westwater Canyon; however, the time period is correct for the shoes. Perhaps it was their honeymoon location?

Unless there is someone who can place the woman's shoes on Mary Osborne or Ida Merkt's feet, we do not have an answer to the mystery of who belongs to the shoes found in Outlaw Cave. Although the shoes do not appear to fit the time period for Ms. Osborne, she, her husband, and two other men would appear to be the first-documented boaters in Westwater Canyon. Perhaps one day we will learn of another party of boaters in the early part of the twentieth century where a woman drowned... without her shoes.

4
DENTISTS' SABBATICAL ON THE GRAND RIVER IN 1897

It's been two decades that Westwater Lost and Found *(2004) was published, and since then I am only aware of a handful of historical river books that continue to contribute to our knowledge of Westwater and the Upper Colorado River regions. One in particular that I was anxious to see published was Harold H. Leich's solo boating journey down the Colorado River in 1933. In the mid-1980s, I located one of several manuscripts Harold H. Leich wrote; it was being edited by noted river historian Otis Reed "Dock" Marston. The manuscript was located in Marston's exhaustive historical files held at the Huntington Library in California. Before he died, Marston helped Leich identify locations along the river and assisted with edits of his detailed diary that describes his river journey from the source of the Colorado River to Cataract Canyon, where he wrecked his boat. It is a chapter in the Upper Colorado River history that was lacking until Roy Webb was able to receive authorization from Leich's two surviving sons, Harold M. and Jeffrey R. Leich, and have it published as* Alone on the Colorado.[1]

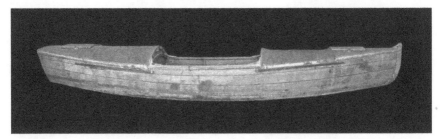

FIGURE 4.1. Galloway-style Cataract boat used on the Stone expedition in 1909. Grand Canyon National Park Collection, photograph by Kai Little, courtesy of the American Southwest Virtual Museum (https://swvirtualmuseum.nau.edu/photos/picture.php?/6750/categories).

Another book of interest is Brad Dimock's The Very Hard Way: Bert Loper and the Colorado River, *published in 2007.*[2] *Brad's indefatigable research contributed to our knowledge of the "Grand Old Man of the Colorado River," and he included a chapter on the role that Loper played in Ellsworth Kolb's boating efforts down the Grand and Gunnison Rivers in 1916. Last, it is refreshing to finally get something in print regarding Denis Julien, with James H. Knipmeyer's* The Life and Times of Denis Julien: Fur Trader.[3] *Denis Julien's tie to the Upper Colorado River involves his trade activity along the Old Trapper Trails and the North Branch of the OST coming north out of Taos, New Mexico, into the Rocky Mountains to trap along the Green and Colorado Rivers.*

An issue that frustrated me while researching *Westwater Lost and Found* (2004) was a note located in Marston's massive collection at the Huntington Library. The note, ascribed to Marston's handwriting, indicated that Frederick S. Dellenbaugh received a letter from James E. Miller describing how he and O. D. Babcock made a river trip down the Grand River from Glenwood Springs in 1897. Before my first book was published, I spent considerable time and effort trying to locate the letter without success from several locations where Dellenbaugh's papers were housed. It was through an internet search that I found Miller's letter with Robert Brewster Stanton's records located at the New York Public Library. The letter Dellenbaugh received from Dr. Miller provided information about their recreation excursion to boat the Grand River and why they did it. The research that I received back from the library included an attachment of a letter that Stanton subsequently wrote to Miller. I felt that the content of Miller's letter is an important historical addition for the Upper Colorado River and Westwater Canyon. Both Dellenbaugh and Stanton were aware of Miller and Babcock's river trip: however, the dentists' excursion down the Grand River doesn't appear in any of their writings. Other than newspaper accounts, Miller's letter is the only personal account that we have regarding the event.

In the early years of boating on the Green and Colorado Rivers, there tended to be jealous rivalry among a number of the river men who made history. Each of them wanted their boating excursions documented according to their perspective, while often questioning the exploits of others. Examples include whether James White truly was the first man to float through the Grand Canyon in 1867. The ongoing controversy over whether the Howlands' and William Dunn's departure at Separation Rapid was due to cowardice or divisiveness from John Wesley Powell's geological survey in 1869, and whether Frank Clarence Kendrick portaged around Westwater (Hades/Granite) Canyon out of fear when he surveyed the Colorado (Grand) River from Grand Junction, Colorado, to Green River, Utah, for the Denver, Colorado Cañon and Pacific Railroad (DCC&P RR) in 1889.

Their experiences in the Grand Canyon caused a few of the early boaters to become Colorado and Green River historians as they diligently gathered considerable information while it was fresh from living boaters, and sought sources for those who could not be located, or who had died. The preeminent early historians were Frederick S. Dellenbaugh and Robert Brewster Stanton; both men were part of two of the earliest boating expeditions down the Grand Canyon, in 1871–1872 and 1889–1890 respectively. Later, Otis Reed "Dock" Marston would assume the role as the Colorado and Green River authority, when he took up the mantle and gathered volumes more data that are commonly used as a source by numerous authors and historians researching the Grand Canyon and its tributaries today.

Dellenbaugh was the ripe young age of seventeen when he joined Powell's second expedition to survey the Green and Colorado Rivers, which ended at Kanab Creek in the Grand Canyon in 1872. He admired Major Powell and defended his reputation regarding controversies

Robert Brewster Stanton (1846-1922)   Frederick Samuel Dellenbaugh (1853-1935)

FIGURE 4.2. Robert Brewster Stanton (1846–1922). Image courtesy of Miami University Libraries, Walter Havighurst special collections. Frederick Samuel Dellenbaugh (1853–1935), Collection of Photographs and Drawings of the Colorado River Region, Yale Collection of Western Americana, Beinecke Rare Book and Manuscript Library.

that surfaced about the first expedition in 1869. Dellenbaugh would write two historical publications about the Green and Colorado River; *The Romance of the Colorado River*, published in 1902, and *A Canyon Voyage*, published in 1908. Stanton's experience on the river began in 1889 while he was the chief engineer surveying the plausibility of building a railroad along the Colorado River to the Gulf of California for Frank Brown, president of the DCC&P RR. Stanton died before he could publish a large volume of the history and exploration of the Colorado River that was to be titled *The River and the Canyon*. Two books he wrote were edited and posthumously published: *Colorado River Controversies* (1932) and *Down the Colorado* (1965).

In the early 1900s, both Dellenbaugh and Stanton were made aware of a previously unknown voyage beginning at Glenwood Springs down

FIGURE 4.3. Dr. James Edwin Miller DDS (1857–1945). Permission obtained from Martin Sperry, Ancestry.com

the Grand and Colorado Rivers that didn't make it into their publications (see appendixes C and D). Unknown to these men, the 1897 river trip by dentists James E. Miller and O. D. Babcock was reported in newspapers as far east as Chicago, New York, and Virginia.

After reading Dellenbaugh's *The Romance of the Colorado River*, James E. Miller wrote a letter to the author dated November 2, 1906. In it Miller described a boat trip that he made on the Grand (Colorado) River with fellow dentist O. D. Babcock in 1897. Dr. Miller was surprised that Dellenbaugh wasn't aware of the doctors' excursion before his book was published. He surmised that Major John Wesley Powell would have informed Dellenbaugh. Sometime after Dr. Miller's Grand River trip ended in September 1897, Major Powell arrived in Glenwood Springs to give a lecture at the "Colorado Hotel" about the lower Colorado River.

He led both the first and second historical expeditions down the Green and Colorado Rivers in 1869 and 1871–1872 respectively. While in Glenwood Springs, Powell became acquainted with Dr. Miller, and they spent nearly an entire day together discussing and viewing negatives of the dentists' boating excursion down the Grand and Colorado Rivers. Powell must have been impressed by the story and while he was delivering his lecture that evening, he cut it short and invited Dr. Miller to join him and present his story to the public.[4] Dr. Miller seemed perplexed that Major Powell did not inform Dellenbaugh about the excursion before he died on September 23, 1902.

It appears that nothing came of Dr. Miller's letter to Dellenbaugh. We probably wouldn't have known about the existence of a letter except for a note that was found among Otis Reed "Dock" Marston's exhaustive volumes of river research. The note reads:

> experiences of Dr. O. D. Babcock and myself in the summer of 1897
> Dr. J. E. Miller of Yampa, Colo, to FSD
> left Glenwood—18' long 3 ½ beam
>   (probably [fiction or pictures])[5]

In parenthesis at the bottom of note regarding the event there appears to be the comment "probably fiction." It is not entirely legible, and the characters could possibly read "probably pictures" because there were photos taken of the event and Dr. Miller offered to show them to Dellenbaugh.

A few years later, in 1909, Dellenbaugh shared Dr. Miller's letter with Robert Brewster Stanton, who was accumulating material for a book that he intended to write. A note scanned at the bottom of the letter indicates that Dellenbaugh was suspicious about the distance that the doctors' claimed to have traveled by boat.[6] Dr. Miller indicated that they had "nearly lost our boat about 150 miles below the mouth of the Green," and a statement that Dellenbaugh may have questioned most was what Miller wrote about Cataract Canyon. Dr. Miller wrote that they found the canyon "not so disastrous. We never stopped to even look the thing over but went right through." Cataract Canyon presents difficulties even today, and it would seem unheard of for someone from the dentists' era using cumbersome, less-manageable wooden boats to survive the canyon without stopping anywhere to scout rapids. At least there isn't any implication that they scouted or portaged any of the rapids. There is a reason that the canyon is referred to as the "Graveyard of the Colorado River." Not many of the early expeditions through Cataract Canyon were able to avoid portaging or lining their boats around at least some of the rapids. Moreover, the doctors began their river excursion in mid-August, when the river is generally running low and many of the rocks are out. Without their stopping to scout Big Drop 3 (Satan's Gut), it seems improbable they could have made it through the rock-clogged rapid. It is no wonder that both Dellenbaugh and Stanton questioned part of the letter's contents.

The plan to boat down the Grand (Colorado) River was a spontaneous decision made shortly before the excursion started. Dr. James Edwin Miller was forty years old in 1897. He was born in Canada on February 23, 1857, and moved to the states in 1864. He spent time in Minnesota, South Dakota, Utah, and Chicago before arriving in Glenwood Springs, Colorado, around 1896. He was married with children when he arrived in the town. Dr. Miller had established a chain of dental offices in Leadville, Aspen, Rifle, Telluride, and Glenwood Springs before his death on April 18, 1945.

Oro Degarmo Babcock, who went by O. D. Babcock, was fourteen years younger than Miller. He was born on August 27, 1872, in Wisconsin, and at the age of two his family moved to Minnesota. Dr. Babcock appears to have remained in Minnesota until at least 1894, when his name appears in a College of Dentistry yearbook at the University of Minnesota. It is unclear whether the two doctors were previously acquainted when they resided at Minnesota before they began a dental business venture together. Their business association appears to have lasted until March 1900, when Dr. Babcock, with his physician wife, Helen, moved to the state of Washington, where he earned a medical degree at the University of Oregon in 1907. He died the same year as Dr. Miller in Seattle, Washington, on December 5, 1945.

Dr. Miller wrote that the dentists decided one day that they wanted to quit their work and let a coin flip determine what they would do with their time off. His description for abruptly quitting their work may have been stress related or for other health reasons. Miller wrote, to cause two men of stomach troubles we one day decided to quit work, pitched up a half dollar in the office to decide whether we were going into the hills, or down the river. The River trip won and in an hour we had rented a carpenter shop & tools and the boat was under construction before evening.[7]

The boat took about one week to build. One newspaper described it in this way:

> They have a boat about 18 feet long, strongly put together with two large airtight compartments, one in the bow and one in the stern, in which they expect to store those things they desire to keep perfectly dry. The boat is built with two sets of oar locks and arranged to carry quite an amount of sail. They will have a canvas cover to protect them from the sun and rain. In the stern they have put a heavy piece of timber in which a rope is attached to be used in case it becomes necessary to shoot the rapids. By the means of the rope the boat will be guided over the rapids while the excursionists take to the shore.[8]

The doctors were reportedly excellent oarsmen and were not dissuaded by reports of others' failures and reported deaths in the rapids below. They planned to boat down the Grand (Colorado) River to Cataract Canyon, then return up the Green River to the railroad town at Blake (Green River). The excursion was unusual for the era and appeared to be mostly recreational, undertaken for the thrill of boating and scenery; they also intended to search for cliff dwellings and collect artifacts along the way. The newspaper continued, "Picks and shovels constitute a part of the outfit and the pleasure seekers expect to do some excavating in the hopes of discovering some interesting and valuable relics. They have a camera and will bring back some of the choicest views."[9]

Two days before the boat launched, Glenwood Spring's newspaper, the *Avalanche* reported, "Drs. Miller & Babcock's offices will be closed until the first week of September."[10] Then at 10:00 a.m. on August 13, 1897, as a crowd reported to be as many as 500 or more onlookers watched, the boat christened *Little Gold Dust* was pushed off of the Grand River shore and the two dentists headed downstream.[11]

Dr. Miller wired his whereabouts and their experiences to his family whenever it was possible. Details of the excursion appeared in several newspapers located along the Grand River in Colorado and at Moab. The dentists arrived the following afternoon at Rifle and reported there were no serious mishaps. Up to this point their only difficulty was encountering shallow water in places where the river divided. The article read further that "they did not anticipate any more trouble from that source between Rifle and Green River."[12]

Sometime between August 23 and 26, 1897, the doctors docked at Moab and remained there for a few days to investigate cliff dwellings. They reported two primary obstacles between Rifle and Moab, at Palisade and Granite (Westwater) Canyon, with Palisade being mentioned as "one of the most dangerous runs." In his letter to the newspaper Dr. Miller described the rapid at Palisade:

> It was a quarter of a mile long, filled with boulders, and the water ran like a millrace. First, there was a very rough stretch of water through which it took all our skill to steer the boat; then there was a short stretch without a ripple, only it ran faster as it approached the drop. It was full of rocks, concealed by just enough water to make them dangerous. Once in this current, there was no stemming the rush—we went like the wind. How we got through is a dreamy sort of remembrance. It was one wild rush for a quarter of a mile. With set teeth we made the plunge. After we were once fairly in I do not think we minded it much. I imagine it's like a soldier going into a battle. The approach is terrible. I shall not attempt to tell you what a sensation comes over one when, after you have slipped by one rock by the skin of your teeth, you find another only a few feet ahead. To hit one of these rocks with the velocity we had attained could mean only one thing.[13]

Their reported experience at Palisade is unusual because there are no significant rapids in that area of the river. Today, some river companies offer "tame" Palisade Wine Country float trips. The Grand Valley Diversion Dam, Cameo Dam, was built upstream of Palisade in De Beque Canyon between 1913 and 1916. It is a low-level dam that would not likely have inundated a major rapid as described by Dr. Miller.

Moab's *Grand Valley Times* on August 27, 1897, wrote of the boaters: "They report having had some exciting rides over rapids; in some cases boat and passengers diving under the water. The worst places being

FIGURE 4.4. Westwater Canyon at the head of Skull Rapid.
Photo by author (2003).

through the Pallisades [sic] and the Granite Canon above Cisco. From Cisco down they found smooth sailing."[14]

There may be questions about whether the doctors traversed Westwater Canyon because of information presented in Glenwood Springs' the *Avalanche* on August 28, 1897, where after the article reported the difficulty that the dentists had experienced with a rapid at Palisade, it further noted that the party "wisely did not attempt the Black Canyon run, with its 15 miles of length between perpendicular walls of a thousand feet in height, through which two travelers have gone while a dozen have failed."[15] Could they have had their boat portaged around Westwater Canyon? The mileage corresponds to that of Westwater Canyon; even so, it does not make any sense for the newspaper to mention the "Black Canyon" unless it was a former name given for Westwater. The alternate names for Westwater Canyon that we are aware of include Hades and Granite Canyons. Otherwise, the Gunnison River flows through the Black Canyon and merges with the Colorado near Grand Junction.

A description in Dr. Miller's letter could describe Skull Rapid and corroborate them being in Westwater Canyon. In the letter Miller describes an experience that they encountered in Cataract Canyon; however, the description sounds uncannily similar to other early boaters when describing Skull (Whirlpool) Rapid. He writes:

> We came to one place in the Colorado that was strenuous for a moment, coming around a short bend. The river seemed to divide into two channels, one shooting under an overhanging rock and the other going over a fall of three or four feet. There not being room enough under the rock for boat and selves, we chose the falls. You know how quickly one has to decide some things, well, the water going over the falls had excavated a considerable hole, I was slung, my companion jumped back & sat down between my feet to lighten up the bow, but her stern went into the [bar] & for a moment it was a toss-up whether we were going end over end or not but we came out all right.[16]

Whether Dr. Miller's description of the rapid is Skull in Westwater Canyon, or one of those found in Cataract Canyon, may not be important. The description of the event does appear to give credence that the doctors did have sufficient experience to run the rapids that they encountered, and there is no indication in the letter that they made any portages. Dr. Miller described their boating skills: "Dr. Babcock & self use to make the boat spin when we saw the white water ahead I had a good [aim] & could generally put the boat through alright but not always."[17]

Little else of the trip below Moab was mentioned in the newspapers that followed. Dr. Miller provided a brief description that left both Dellenbaugh and Stanton questioning how far the dentists had floated. He wrote:

> We do not know how far down we went. We ran across a cowman, who came down to the river for water, he told us that we were then in what was known as Buckskin Canyon ... I do not see how Mr. Brown (Frank Mason Brown) in your account (*Romance of the Colorado River*) could of found the Cataract Canyon so disastrous. We never stopped to even look the thing over but went right through and I have a number of negatives in my possession to prove it.[18]

Dr. Miller mentioned in the letter that Major Powell recognized a number of locations from the negatives that he was shown. Major Powell would have been familiar only with photos taken below the confluence with the Green River. Dr. Miller wrote further, "We nearly lost our boat about 150 miles below the mouth of the Green, barely saving our lives, over 50 negatives were ruined but we didn't kick for reasons you would understand."[19] Then he described the incident in the preceding long quotation as occurring in either Cataract or Glen Canyon on the Colorado River.

One hundred fifty miles would have placed the adventurers well into Glen Canyon before they returned to Glenwood Springs.[20]

Needing to return to work, the dentists bypassed the Green River and returned on the Grand River to Moab. On September 17, 1897, the *Grand Valley Times* reported:

> Drs. Miller and Babcock of Glenwood Springs, who passed through Moab some weeks ago on their way down the river, having come down Grand river in a boat, returned the first of the week (Sept 12 or 13 at Moab). They went as far as Cataract canon. They concluded not to return via Green river as was on their program, hence rowed back to

FIGURE 4.5. Big Drop 3, often called "Satan's Gut," at lowest recorded level of 2,700 cfs during week of July 1, 2002. NPS, photo by Neil Herbert.

FIGURE 4.6. Cataract Canyon, also known as the "Graveyard of the Colorado River," which offers some of the largest whitewater in the United States. The Big Drops are formidable rapids at any water level and would have presented a difficult transit for Drs. Miller and Babcock in 1897. Photo by author (1980).

Moab and went home on the stage. They report having had a very pleasant trip and well repaid for their labor. The scenery is simply grand.[21]

They arrived at Glenwood Springs by September 13, 1897.

Few boaters on the Grand River were recognized by the early river historians. Their emphasis instead followed Major Powell's boat wake down the Green and Colorado River below the Confluence and through the Grand Canyon. Historian Otis Marston kept a running count of the first 100 and then the second 100 individuals who boated through the Grand Canyon. No such inventory exists for the Upper Colorado River. Even today there is sparse information about the early Grand (Colorado) River boaters, primarily because there were no major expeditions or surveys made on it, and it was good fortune when an early boater received recognition by appearing in a local newspaper.

Residents of the former railroad town at Westwater claimed to have intercepted and discouraged boaters from unknowingly floating past them into Westwater Canyon. This occurred when Ellsworth Kolb and John Shields attempted to boat from Grand Junction to Moab in August 1916. Recognizing their concerns, Ellsworth shipped his freight canoe to Cisco and instead hiked through the canyon to see what he was up against. He returned a month later with Bert Loper, and they became the first individuals credited with successfully navigating Westwater Canyon. In addition to Westwater Canyon, Kolb and Loper made numerous national headlines in 1916 that included boating parts of the Gunnison River and the Grand/Colorado River that began at Glenwood Springs and culminated at the end of Westwater Canyon. There are others who testified during the Colorado Riverbed cases that took place from 1929 to 1931, determining the navigability of Utah Rivers, that Elmer Kane and Parley and John Galloway had come down the Grand River, possibly transiting Westwater Canyon. Fortunately, local newspapers captured glimpses of others who attempted to boat down the Grand (Colorado) River through which we learn of Frank "Bunny" Barnes in 1921, Beppo Saeckler in 1930, Harold H. Leich in 1933, and others.

Prior to the rediscovery of Dr. James E. Miller's letter, only the 1916 transit by Kolb and Loper was documented. Although we are missing Miller's photographs, we have considerable information from his letter and local newspapers that supports their trip down the Colorado River in the summer of 1897. Notes from both Dellenbaugh and Stanton indicate that they mailed letters with clarifying questions about the dentists' excursion. There is nothing in their files indicating that they received a response, and their questions went unanswered.

5

ELLSWORTH KOLB

Losing His Boyhood

A lingering desire remained with me since the mid-1980s to somehow introduce the boating community and river historians to Ellsworth Kolb's unpublished manuscript describing his exploits boating the Grand and Gunnison tributaries of the Colorado River in 1916. Compared to the writings about and documentation of river journeys, surveys, and expeditions that traveled down the Green River tributary, there are minimal noteworthy parties who boated down the Grand / Upper Colorado River. Kolb had no other agenda but to make photographs and be the first individual to boat all of the primary Colorado River tributaries to the Gulf of California.

Although he was boating in a different era, his mindset is possibly more representative of today's recreational boaters and kayakers. In 1918, Ellsworth Kolb was writing a draft of his experiences descending the Grand and Gunnison Rivers by boat. He intended to submit the manuscript for publication in National Geographic Magazine; *nevertheless, for some unknown reason it wasn't completed and went unpublished. To prepare the reader for Ellsworth Kolb's unfinished manuscript, I feel a need to introduce, or reintroduce, him to the audience.*

https://doi.org/10.7330/9781646425457.c005

FIGURE 5.1. Ellsworth Leonardson Kolb. NAU.PH.568.3148, Cline Library, Northern Arizona University, Flagstaff, AZ: Emery Kolb Collection.

More readers are familiar with his younger brother Emery Kolb, who resided at the Grand Canyon until his death in 1976; however, Ellsworth dropped from the river scene after 1928.

Stopping at the small-railroad town at Westwater, Ellsworth Kolb and John W. Shields were warned by the residents of the dangerous Westwater Canyon below. It was late in the summer on August 25, 1916, when Kolb and Shields arrived at the town. A day earlier they had rowed their eighteen-foot canvas covered Peterborough freight canoe down the Gunnison River beginning at Delta, Colorado, and after merging with the Grand/Colorado River at Grand Junction they continued down the river toward Moab, where they didn't expect to encounter any significant whitewater. After their arrival at Westwater, they were told that the canyon below was unconquerable and that numerous individuals had lost their lives in it. One old-timer warned of Whirlpool Rapid, which "no person can go through and live; the fishes brains are spattered on the walls."[1]

Ellsworth Kolb was a well-known explorer and photographer primarily because of his 1911–1912 highly publicized photographic and filmed river journey that he made with his brother Emery, traveling in the wake of Major John Wesley Powell down the Green and Colorado Rivers. Ellsworth Kolb authored *Through the Grand Canyon from Wyoming to Mexico* (1914),[2] about their river journey, which was also highlighted in a lengthy article, "Experiences in the Grand Canyon"; the latter appeared in *National Geographic Magazine* in August 1914.[3] Although surprised by the news of a dangerous canyon below the town of Westwater, Kolb probably wouldn't have been fazed by the prospect of boating it. However, John Shields was a cowboy and felt more comfortable on land.

A month earlier Kolb and Shields with a fellow adventurer, Julius F. Stone, and Nathan B. Stern made an unsuccessful attempt to boat the Gunnison River beginning at Cimarron, Colorado. At the time, a previously ordered Peterborough freight canoe was delayed and wasn't available, which left the party of four men with two collapsible canvas boats that Kolb said, "had a habit of collapsing at the wrong time" and an experimental inflatable life-raft that carried an Indestructo container filled with extra film magazines. In addition, the raft would be used as an experiment to line equipment past difficult rapids and avoid having to portage everything.

Beginning on July 26, 1916, in inclement weather, Kolb, Stone, Stern, and Shields began their journey through the Black Canyon during a heavier-than-expected flow of the Gunnison River. Before launching the two boats, the raft with its strapped-on container was put into the swollen river and it soon escaped from Kolb, who tried to control it with a rope, and floated downstream; it wasn't recovered until a few days later by fishermen two miles above the Gunnison Tunnel. Although Kolb questioned the durability of the canvas boats, they were all the men had. Giving chase to retrieve the life raft, Kolb launched one of the canvas boats at the head of the rapid below the Cimarron

FIGURE 5.2. July 26, 1916, L–R Ellsworth Kolb, John W. Shields, Nathan B. Stern, and Julius F. Stone pose with equipment along the Gunnison River near Cimarron, Colorado. NAU.PH. 568.5859a, Cline Library, Northern Arizona University, Flagstaff, AZ: Ellsworth Kolb photo found in Emery Kolb Collection.

Railroad Bridge and immediately got into trouble because one of his oarlocks wasn't secured. Before Kolb could replace the oarlock, his boat turned sideways and hit a rock crushing the frame of the boat; then it sank. Stone didn't fare much better in the other canvas boat and upset in the rapid. Fortunately, he held onto the boat as it dragged him downstream into an eddy, where both were rescued. That was their first day and, as Kolb described it, "was our introduction to the Black Canyon."

Having not gone far, they returned to their hotel at Cimarron and waited out the rain for two days before returning to the river. The canvas boat could hold only two men and their supplies. Stone rowed the boat while the other men took turns with him as a passenger, or they swam alongside the boat holding onto its sides. They covered approximately eleven and a half miles in four days before having to climb out of the canyon due to Stone being seriously ill and needing to get back to his business, inclement weather, and the high water. It also didn't help that the group did not have a dependable boat. Julius Stone credited Ellsworth for saving his life "by carrying him to the top of the canyon."[4]

After Stone and Sterns returned to their businesses back East, Kolb returned to where they left the canyon, repaired the canvas boat, and completed the remaining stretch of river to the Gunnison Tunnel. Shortly afterward, the Peterborough canoe arrived and Kolb and Shields used it on what was expected to be a leisurely trip from Delta, Colorado, to Moab, Utah. Understandably, when Kolb and Shields were warned about their imminent death if they were to attempt Westwater Canyon, they hesitated taking the risk and instead had their boat hauled to Cisco while Kolb and Shields hiked Westwater Canyon to investigate the rapids. The canyon was impressive and reminded Kolb of the Grand Canyon, where he and his brother Emery ran a photographic studio on the South Rim—only this canyon was smaller. Kolb acknowledged that Whirlpool (Skull) Rapid would be difficult to run at its current stage (10,100–12,100 cfs), but he felt confident it could be run at a lower water level.[5]

Ellsworth Leonardson Kolb was born December 27, 1876, in Smithton, Pennsylvania, to Edward and Ella Nelson Kolb. He was their oldest child, and his brother Emery was born five years later in 1881. Although there was a five-year age difference and another brother born between them, they developed a close relationship. Ellsworth got into mischief and brought his little brother along to take the blame. One episode that could have cost both of them their lives was during a flood of the Alleghany River and its tributaries in May of 1889. Ellsworth was twelve and Emery was eight, and being amused with all of the rain and the flooding of Buffalo Creek near their home the two boys decided to play Pirates and build a raft. The heavy rain, downed trees, and turbulent water during the flood didn't detour them as they pieced together slabs of unused lumber from a nearby planing mill, and then jumped aboard the raft. Initially gleeful, the boys' demeanor soon changed as the boards of their raft began to separate. Neither of them could swim. With no ropes or anything to hold the boards together, Emery laid his body across the boards with his belly facing down, and like a human vice he gripped one edge with his fingers and the opposite edge with his toes keeping the raft intact while Ellsworth steered the raft to shore before the creek merged with the much larger and dangerously flooding Alleghany River. Except for getting into mischief, few other detailed events of their childhood are recorded. Their family was poor, and the children had to go to work at an early age. Ellsworth worked at several jobs and didn't graduate from high school.

In 1896, at the age of twenty, Ellsworth left home and headed to the West. He was described as a wanderlust and had to keep moving. By September 1901, Ellsworth had already operated a snowplow at Pike's Peak, worked on roads at both Yellowstone and Yosemite Parks, and was a carpenter's helper in San Francisco, when his thoughts entertained crossing the Pacific Ocean and going to China. Just before boarding a ship for China, he began having second thoughts after he saw an advertisement by the Santa Fe Railroad to come and "See the Grand Canyon." He didn't board the ship to China, and the rest is history. After working for a year at the Bright Angel Hotel on the canyon rim, he was given a vacation and returned to Pittsburgh, where he invited Emery to join him at the Grand Canyon. During Ellsworth's absence, Emery had taken up photography and a business plan developed between them to take scenic views and photos of individuals and groups entering the Grand Canyon on mules. Their parents refused to allow Emery to leave home until Ellsworth found a job for his little brother. In October 1902, Ellsworth found a job for Emery (that fell through); even so, they reunited at the Grand Canyon and eventually began their photographic business.

Late Kolb Brothers historian William C. "Bill" Suran, suggested that Ellsworth Kolb may have envisioned running a boat through the Grand Canyon as early as 1901, when he first looked over the canyon rim at the Colorado River below and learned stories about Major John Wesley Powell and the dangers that his party encountered. According to Suran, the word *fear* was unknown to Ellsworth. It was Ellsworth's idea to make photographs and movies using a "newfangled motion picture camera" on their excursion down the Green and Colorado Rivers in 1911–1912. He is also credited with working out an installment plan

FIGURE 5.3. Kolb Brothers in the Grand Canyon. NAU PH 568.5787, Cline, Library, Northern Arizona University, Flagstaff, AZ: Emery Kolb Collection.

to purchase an existing photographic studio for $420 in Williams, Arizona, which the Kolb brothers eventually moved to the South Rim of the Grand Canyon. The brother's pictorial and motion-picture river journey made them celebrities that would be the catalyst for their early careers, and Emery's lifelong one.

Following after Major John Wesley Powell's historic survey of the Green and Colorado Rivers, the Kolb brothers likewise began their "Big Trip" at Green River, Wyoming, on September 10, 1911. They felt the need for a third person to help with camp, cooking, and portages and were advised to consider Nathaniel Galloway. That's not the kind of help the brothers sought. Ellsworth wrote,

> But . . . we may as well be frank about it . . . we did not wish to be piloted through the Colorado by a guide. We wanted to make our own trip in our own way. If we failed, we would have no one but ourselves to blame; if we succeeded, we would have all the satisfaction that comes from original, personal, exploration.[6]

With little to no experience, Ellsworth and Emery Kolb, the Kolb Brothers—began their river journey like many of their predecessors by learning along the way. Ellsworth was in his element. Having described himself as not having the sense to be scared, Ellsworth attempted something no one had reportedly done before in the Grand Canyon. Contrary to the advice given them by Julius Stone and Dave Rust to portage Soap Creek Rapid, the brothers instead decided to run it. Enjoying a challenge, Ellsworth most likely influenced the decision and volunteered to run the rapid.[7]

Entering Marble Canyon on November 8, 1911, the Kolb brothers stopped above Soap Creek Rapid to scout it. No previous party through the canyon had documented even attempting to run Soap Creek Rapid; instead, they portaged their boats around it. Not so with the Kolb brothers. After a thorough scouting of the rapid, the brothers decided it could be run; Ellsworth positioned his boat *Defiance* to the right side at the head of Soap Creek Rapid. Before starting, he directed Emery that no matter what happens he should take the picture. Ellsworth managed to get past a pivotal first rock at the head of the rapid and nearly made it past a second one, when the stern of his boat caught the rock and tipped the boat sideways, spilling Ellsworth into the Colorado River. He clung to the side of the boat which shortly afterward righted itself, and he climbed back inside the water-filled cockpit and finished the run.

Undaunted by the upset, and appearing confident that he could successfully run Soap Creek Rapid, Ellsworth coaxed his younger brother to allow him to take his boat, the *Edith*, through the rapid. Emery wanted to wait until morning; however, Ellsworth reportedly responded, "If I wait 'till morning, I'll lose my nerve."[8] It was getting dark, and they made plans for a rescue should something similar happen. It did; only this time, the *Edith* turned over completely and filled with water. Emery was in position in the *Defiance* to rescue Ellsworth but couldn't see him at first. Between trying to hold onto the heavy water-filled boat and trying to rescue part of Ellsworth's life jacket, he struggled getting to shore. As Emery attempted to direct the nearly submerged boat to shore, he viewed Ellsworth behind it holding onto a rope. Emery couldn't retrieve his brother from the river as they floated downstream in the direction of the riffle where railroad president Frank Brown had drowned in 1889. Ellsworth followed behind the *Edith* holding onto the rope and called out to his little brother, "Now Emery keep your nerve as we are being drawn into the rapid where Brown was drowned."[9] As the boats traveled a little further, they both were brought to shore and the men camped downstream from their gear.

Both brothers were adventuresome; however, Emery was more cautious than his older brother and initially was swayed at times by Ellsworth to take risks. He also had a family to consider.

The brothers' personalities sometimes contrasted along with their degree of comfort with the natural world: Emery is described as having an autocratic attitude that caused some individuals to intensely dislike him. He was a shrewd, yet honest, businessman and fought hard against Fred Harvey and the National Park Service (NPS) to keep Kolb Studios at the Grand Canyon. This is something Ellsworth was happy to oblige his younger brother.

Despite Ellsworth's support for his brother's struggle, he avoided the confrontations with Fred Harvey and the NPS and was diplomatic and likable. As Michael Harrison described him, "Ellsworth was the type anyone can get along with. He was a gentle gentleman. Very much a loner, very shy. He would keep in the background, would almost only speak when spoken to. Emery was always out front."[10]

Although shy, Ellsworth did manage to show up in a lot of the Kolb trail photos with women. However, he didn't enjoy working at the studio and giving lectures and was happiest when he was off on an adventure. This dichotomy and other differences between the brothers initially helped them to establish their photographic business at the Grand Canyon. However, after their successful river trip and subsequent lecture tours back East, their behavioral differences began to divide them. Ellsworth didn't have the business acumen Emery had. His element was in the adventure, and perhaps his shyness made it difficult to promote the results. This played out in the winter of 1914, when Ellsworth scheduled a number of small venues for their river lectures in the Midwest without obtaining any guaranteed fees. Unfortunately, many of the shows were during inclement weather conditions, were not well attended, and lost money. The events that Emery scheduled in the larger venues in the East, with guaranteed fees, helped them to recover some of the losses.

During the business trip Ellsworth wrote Emery's wife, Blanche, from Toledo on January 29, 1914:

> Poor Emery. I guess I got him into a box when I booked these shows. It looked like such a good chance and he can see nothing but failure and worries accordingly. As it is we will just about break even but he [loses] his time and all his hard work. He has eight clubs booked after this which are sure money... and if you and Emery want to sell the Canyon studio I am willing to take it with all the uncertainties... Don't think that Emery and I are quarreling. We were never getting along better. We simply can't see things in the same way. Emery gets to worrying, then I am affected by his attitude. He can't help it, neither can I. As soon as I am alone I am as carefree as ever, and happy whether I am making money or not as long as my health is good. That is all that matters.[11]

Quarreling or not, they brought up the subject of selling the ownership of their business at the Grand Canyon a number of times as they traveled together. The day following Ellsworth's letter to Blanche, Emery wrote and told her that he won the business from Ellsworth during a coin flip to determine who was to remain at the Grand Canyon. Ellsworth lost the coin flip three times. It wouldn't be until 1924 that their partnership was completely dissolved and Ellsworth left the Grand Canyon and moved to Los Angeles. During the decade between the coin flip and dissolution of their business, they took turns renting the studio at the Grand Canyon to each other; the terms were that for two consecutive years the renter had sole use of the studio. The brothers rarely worked together after 1914.

No one knows exactly what caused the split. Ellsworth's poor judgment booking lectures in 1914 is the first indication that something was wrong; however, there appeared to be more to it. Ellsworth did not enjoy doing the lectures and hanging out at the studio, which may have upset his more responsible brother. He wanted to be more physically active. He wasn't built to run a business like his brother was, and had he won the coin toss the business would likely have failed.

Roger Naylor wrote,

> Away from civilization, the brothers were a great team, always watching out for each other and balancing their more extreme tendencies. They brought out the best in one another. Without Ellsworth, Emery would never have experienced a fraction of the adventures he enjoyed. And without Emery, the business would not have thrived, giving Ellsworth the means to go gallivanting off on this next adrenaline junket whenever he felt the urge.[12]

Sometime between nearly being drowned on an ill-advised adventure on the swollen Buffalo Creek that he experienced as a youth and the travels that brought him to the Grand Canyon, Ellsworth Kolb entertained desires of running rivers. He must have also learned to swim. Whether it was in 1901, when Ellsworth first viewed the Colorado River from the South Rim and learned about Major Powell; or perhaps in 1911 and 1912, when he and his brother ran the Green and Colorado Rivers; or perhaps in the spring of 1913, then alone, he returned to complete boating the Colorado River from Needles, California, to the Gulf of California—one of these scenarios catalyzed his desire to be the first to traverse by boat all of the major tributaries of the Colorado River. Only three parties had previously accomplished the entire distance on the Green and Colorado River to the Gulf of California; however, no one had previously done it coming down the Grand River.[13]

In 1916, the Colorado River started at the confluence of the Green and Grand Rivers. As mentioned in chapter 1, it wasn't until 1921 that Congress officially changed the name of the Grand to the Colorado River to unite it with the state where its source originates. Ellsworth Kolb identified the Grand, Green, and Gunnison Rivers as the primary tributaries of the Colorado River. Of the three tributaries, Kolb expected the Gunnison River through the Black Canyon to give him the most problems. He had heard that the Black Canyon had "wonderful photographic possibilities," but he was mostly intrigued that reportedly the river "disappeared into a natural cave, to reappear further down." Kolb could not believe the story and went "for to see."[14]

The Gunnison River derives its name from Captain John W. Gunnison, who saw parts of the upper Black Canyon during his 1853 central route survey for a Pacific Railroad.[15] At the time that his party surveyed the region, they identified the Gunnison as the Grand River. It wasn't until around 1861 that the river received its current name as a tribute to Captain Gunnison, who was killed in Utah Territory by Pahvant Utes on October 26, 1853. Prior to its current name, the two primary branches upstream of Grand Junction took on several names and at one time or another both were given the name Grand River.[16]

The Black Canyon is a narrow and deep fifty-two mile slit in the earth. The cliffs are made up predominantly of gneiss, granites, and schists that were primarily eroded by the Gunnison River. The canyon bottom at one point measures forty feet wide, at the Narrows, with a 1,725-foot cliff that rises nearly vertically from the Gunnison River. Geologist Wallace R. Hansen wrote, "Several western canyons exceed the Black Canyon in overall size. Some are longer; some are deeper; some are narrower; and a few have walls as steep. But no other canyon in North America combines the depth, narrowness, sheerness, and somber countenance of the Black Canyon."[17]

Hansen further described the gradient of the Gunnison River:

> The Colorado in Grand Canyon—a much larger stream—averages 7 ½ feet per mile. To be sure, the Gunnison drops considerably less than 43 feet per mile through some stretches, but in the monument section it drops much more. The overall fall through the monument is about 95 feet per mile, the greatest drop being in the 2-mile stretch from Pulpit Rock to Chasm View. In that stretch the Gunnison falls nearly 480 feet and locally drops as much as 180 feet in a half a mile.[18]

In preparation for the historic Green and Colorado River photographic expedition Ellsworth made with his brother in 1911–1912, he read in advance the accounts of Major John Wesley Powell's 1869 expedition, *The Exploration of the Colorado River and Its Canyons* (1895), and the subsequent 1871–1872 expedition by Frederick S. Dellenbaugh's, *A Canyon Voyage* (1908). He also became friends with Julius F. Stone, who could

FIGURE 5.4. Black Canyon of the Gunnison National Park taken upstream from the Narrows overlook on the North Rim. Photo by author (2021).

have advised him about the canyons from his journey with Nathaniel Galloway in 1909. It likely was no different with the Black Canyon that he attempted to research what little was available about it. Ellsworth wrote that he was aware of at least two previous parties who did important work in the Black Canyon of the Gunnison. Although he did not name who they were, it's likely that he was familiar with the highly publicized first descent through the canyon that was done on foot by Abraham Lincoln "A.L." Fellows and William W. "Will" Torrence to survey for a location for an irrigation tunnel in 1901. Also, an earlier party in 1900 made up of five men headed by John Pelton unsuccessfully attempted to survey the Black Canyon using boats. Starting at the confluence of the Cimarron River with the Gunnison River, the party didn't get very far into the canyon before they lost one boat and most of their supplies to the river. The Pelton party continued downstream with the remaining boat until they reached the Narrows and conceded defeat at what they named the Falls of Sorrow and climbed out of the canyon.

Undaunted by Pelton's outcome and his having used boats that were impractical for the canyon, Kolb continued with his plans. Although Kolb did not name the parties, it is clear that he was familiar enough with those individuals mentioned to recognize several landmarks they gave names to during their surveys. Whether Ellsworth Kolb worked from Fellows's survey maps (1901–1902) or Torrence's photographs (1900–1901) he doesn't say; however, among the photos located at the Cline Library at Northern Arizona University (NAU), several are titled Flat Rock Falls (aka Day Wrecker, Class V+) and Torrence Falls (Great Falls, Class V+, U). Flat Rock Falls was named by the Pelton survey in 1900, and Torrence Falls was named by Fellows in 1901.[19]

According to Bill Suran, "Ellsworth preferred to be first at everything, or if this were not possible, at least to approach the feat in an unusual manner."[20] Although the Black Canyon was conquered fifteen years earlier on foot by Fellows and Torrence, it had not been accomplished by boat. Ellsworth did not indicate whether he thought that he might be the first to transit the Black Canyon, only that the Gunnison River was part of his agenda to complete a transit of the primary tributaries of the Colorado River system. Kolb broke down his plan to dissect the Black Canyon by narrowing it into four sections to conquer:

- Section One—Lake Fork to Cimarron
- Section Two—Cimarron to Gunnison Tunnel
- Section Three—Gunnison Tunnel to Red Rock Canyon
- Section Four—Red Rock Canyon to Smith's Fork

At Moab, John Shields had had enough of rivers and returned to the Grand Canyon. Ellsworth Kolb remained behind with unfinished business in the Black and Westwater Canyons. Having tackled Section Two of the Black Canyon as far as the Gunnison Tunnel, he recruited Albert "Bert" Loper to help complete the Grand River to Westwater and to tackle the remainder of the Gunnison River below the Gunnison Tunnel.

Four months earlier Loper (July 31, 1869–July 8, 1949) had become a married man, wedding Rachel Jamison on April 29, 1916. The honeymoon took a brief intermission when Loper accepted Kolb's invitation to join him boating the Grand and Gunnison Rivers. On September 9, 1916, he joined Kolb at Glenwood Springs to begin their journey down the Grand/Colorado River starting shortly above Shoshone Falls. Although extremely experienced as a capable boatman, Bert Loper, aka the "Grand Old Man of the Colorado River," was personally tormented from an incident that occurred in 1907. Bert's reputation was tarnished by a newspaper article and by his friend Charles Russell, who branded him as a coward. It bothered Loper throughout his life, and for a long time he could only counter the reports in the media by explaining his version of the incident to others. Even a few months before Bert ran his last rapid in 1949, acclaimed historian Otis Reed "Dock" Marston was badgering him for the umpteenth time about the 1907 incident.

On September 20, 1907, Loper, Charles Russell, and Ed Monett departed on the Green River at Green River Station in Utah. Only Bert had any previous experience with boats on the San Juan, a far less difficult river. Because of Loper's previous experience with boating, he had the skills to naturally lead the group down the stream. However, after Russell and Monett gained experience rowing the flat waters of Labyrinth and Stillwater Canyons and the early rapids in Cataract Canyon, their confidence handling their boats in whitewater increased. Still, approaching some of the more technical and larger rapids, they sought Loper's experience to get them through. At Mile Long Rapids, Loper ran all of the parties' boats through the whitewater. Later, at one of the most challenging rapids at Dark Canyon, Loper turned down Russell's request that he run the rapid for him. Russell wound up successfully negotiating Dark Canyon Rapid. With increased confidence after successfully running the difficult rapid, Russell began to question the leadership of the party and conspired to promote himself as the leader.

In Glen Canyon, Loper found that his camera's shutter was not working and he had to order a new part at Hite. Nothing was expedited in 1907. Russell and Monett went ahead to Lee's Ferry and planned for Loper to meet them there. A few days before the camera part arrived at Hite, Loper damaged his steel boat in a boating accident and needed parts to repair it. Again, there were no materials in the vicinity to repair steel boats, and he had to send for parts. Loper showed up twenty-three days late at Lee's Ferry, and Russell and Monett had already continued without him downstream through the Grand Canyon. Russell intimated that Loper was stalling and didn't want to proceed down the Grand Canyon with them.

Interestingly, Charles Russell again approached Loper in 1914 to make another photographic journey through the Grand Canyon. Although Loper wasn't his first choice to go down the river, it speaks volumes that Russell would ask at all given the slanderous statements he had made regarding Loper from the 1907 trip. Beginning again at Green River, Utah, the two men rowed what Loper described as inadequate steel boats for Cataract and the Grand Canyon. The boats had a low draft, and they were fortunate to have gotten as far as the Big Drops in Cataract Canyon when Russell's boat sank. According to Loper, Russell was exhibiting odd behavior throughout the journey even before they arrived at Cataract Canyon. He said that Russell would get into arguments and talk to himself. Russell continued with the odd behavior until eventually the party lost both boats and hiked out of the canyon at Hite. Sometime around 1919, Charles Russell was institutionalized.

Ellsworth Kolb didn't appear concerned that Loper was branded a coward, and he was excited to have someone with his experience join him in what he expected to be difficult and demanding boating attempts through Westwater and the Black Canyons. Kolb and his brother Emery first met Loper on the Colorado River in Glen Canyon on November 2, 1911, where Ellsworth wrote in his journal "Loper tells his side of the story."[21] During Ellsworth Kolb's ambitious task of boating the Grand and Gunnison Rivers, he kept regular contact with his

FIGURE 5.5.
Bert Loper at Pierce Ferry in 1939. CN V160/0114, the Otis Marston Colorado River Collection. The Bill Belknap image was reproduced from the Otis Marston Colorado River Collection at the Huntington Library. Permission to use the image was granted by Cline Library Special Collections and Archives at Northern Arizona University. The Bill Belknap collection is housed at and all rights are managed by Cline Library Special Collections and Archives.

fellow canyoneer and friend Julius F. Stone and may have asked his opinion of Loper. Stone experienced a similar introduction to Loper when they met in 1909 and wrote in his journal, "From his statements [Loper], which seemed straight forward, we gained the impression that he did not desert Russell and Monet [sic] on their trip down the canyons last year, as they claimed, but that instead they deserted him."[22] According to one newspaper report, Ellsworth Kolb didn't approve of the hype that they wrote about his own exploits. Then why should he accept the medias' opinion of Loper? It's likely that just meeting Loper in Glen Canyon was enough to convince Kolb that he could handle the job. Besides, there really weren't many qualified river people to hire in 1916. Kolb would write, "Much of the success of this trip, as well as the

FIGURE 5.6. Ellsworth Kolb filming Shoshone Falls above Glenwood Springs. NAU.PH.568.5977a, Cline Library, Northern Arizona University, Flagstaff, AZ: Ellsworth Kolb photo found in Emery Kolb Collection.

trip on the Grand River was due to Loper. He was the most enthusiastic rough-water man I have ever been associated with, not excepting my brother and Mr. Stone, which is saying a good deal."[23]

In 1939, prior to his seventieth birthday, Burt Loper joined Laphene "Don" Harris, William Gibson, and Chester Klevin to become the sixty-ninth documented individual to successfully navigate the Grand Canyon.[24] He finally made it! Afterward, Loper and Harris committed to run the Grand Canyon again in 1949. It was on the later trip that, just prior to his eightieth birthday, the "Grand Old Man of the Colorado River" died while running his boat through 24 ½ Mile Rapid.

Working with the Peterborough canoe that was used to boat from Delta to Moab a month earlier, Kolb and Loper began their Grand River excursion at Shoshone Falls above Glenwood Springs. Looking like an old-time football player, Ellsworth Kolb was garbed in what he described was a Kapo suit and padded helmet, probably anticipating an attempt at the falls.[25] Although fearless, Kolb was wise enough to

FIGURE 5.7. Westwater Station, 1902. George Edward Anderson Collection. Courtesy L. Tom Perry Collections, Harold B. Lee Library, Brigham Young University, Provo, UT 84602.

reconsider and portaged the canoe instead. The huge boulders that they portaged their boat over unknowingly prepared them for what was in store for them in the Black Canyon. Shoshone Falls no longer exists: "In 1985 construction of the highway moved the entire river channel a good distance to the south, rendering the rapid much more channelized and easier to run—but also making the runout below the rapid more dangerous."[26] There are now two significant rapids that replaced Shoshone Falls, named Upper Death (Class V to VI) and Barrel Springs (Class IV-NR) Rapids. The men experienced no other noteworthy events on the Grand River until Westwater.

National news preceded Kolb and Loper as they made their way down the Grand River to the small community at Westwater, Utah. Nearby towns along the Grand River at Moab and Grand Junction, and so forth reported that Westwater Canyon was a death trap and impossible to navigate by boat. Reportedly, an elderly Swiss man had taken a boat down the canyon in the spring and hadn't emerged from it. There were a number of similar stories reported in the newspapers. A month earlier, Kolb had hiked through the canyon to scout the rapids and terrain to determine the feasibility of taking a boat through. His primary concern was at the rapid that the Westwater residents named Whirlpool Rapid, or Big Whirlpool, which is currently named Skull Rapid. There was also the Double Pitch Rapid (Funnel Falls) to contend with. Kolb's mindset might be best gleaned from a letter that he wrote to John Shields in which he said, "I don't accept anybody's [sic] statement regarding impassible places."[27]

Among his preparations to document the first transit of Westwater Canyon, Ellsworth Kolb hired professional photographer Frank E. Dean, of Grand Junction, to assist them. Kolb wanted to secure both photographs and movie footage of the event. Westwater town's deputy sheriff Harvey Edward "Ed" Herbert and rancher William Stubbs accompanied them from atop the cliffs with long ropes to rescue the boaters should they encounter any trouble. Kolb and Loper took turns rowing the Peterborough canoe and filming the event. Loper ran the first portion of Westwater Canyon to the Double Pitch/Funnel Falls Rapid. It was late in the afternoon that Kolb was photographing Loper and lost track of him at Double Pitch Rapid. The plan was to stop short of Double Pitch Rapid the first day and wait to boat it and Whirlpool Rapid the following day. Dean and the two cowboys had gone ahead following a worn cattle trail to set up camp on a slope overlooking the big whirlpool (Room of Doom). Kolb had remained behind as the only observer when Loper inadvertently proceeded toward Double Pitch Rapid, where he disappeared from sight. After dropping into a steep entry into Double Pitch/Funnel Falls Rapid, the whitewater continues at an angle toward the north cliff; this is the same side of the canyon that Ellsworth was taking photographs from, and he likely wouldn't be able to see Loper from the 200-foot cliffs that rise vertically up from the river. Thinking Loper might have tipped over in the canoe, Kolb searched as best he could for signs of him, or the boat, until it was too dark to see. Frustrated and worried, Kolb returned to camp only to find that Loper had survived the rapid and was already there waiting for him.

The following day was assigned to Ellsworth Kolb, who said that he tipped over a couple of times but righted his boat and concluded the

FIGURE 5.8. Kolb and Loper camp above the Big Whirlpool aka Room of Doom in Westwater Canyon. Special Collections, J. Willard Marriott Library, University of Utah, Salt Lake City, Utah Albert Loper Collection, P11 36 n01.13.016.

historic run. Huge headlines followed: "Death Canyon of Grand River at Last Conquered by Daring Party Led by Kolb and Bert Loper," "Trip thru Westwater Canon Was Like Tickling Dynamite with a Lighted Match—WOW!," "Kolb Wins Over Westwater Canon: Outdares Death," and so on. Kolb wrote of their experience in Westwater Canyon, "We regard it as the 'sportiest rapid running' we have experienced."[28] And it still is.

Although Kolb made national headlines over several months while boating both the Black and Westwater Canyons, he expressed frustration with how the media reported his efforts. He sought credit for his achievements; however, he disapproved of them being exaggerated. One newspaper wrote about Kolb,

> He always keeps so far within conservatism in his own accounts which can be extracted from him, that a newspaper man realizes he will have to use his own imagination because Kolb will not boast of his experi-

ences nor will he describe them in such a way that a person feels there is anything extraordinary about the different stunts he has pulled off in the canyon.[29]

After navigating Westwater's infamous Canyon, Kolb and Loper set their sights on completing the Gunnison River through the Black Canyon. Ellsworth Kolb intended to continue where he left off in August at the Gunnison Tunnel and begin at Section Three. However, Loper had other plans and insisted that they redo the upper Black Canyon. This time the two river men ran the Peterborough canoe and completed Section Two below Cimmaron in a day and a half. They were then granted permission to be the first men to take their boat through the nearly six-mile-long Gunnison Tunnel. This they did using an oil lamp. Afterward, on October 13, 1916, the fun began as they entered the third and most dangerous section of the Black Canyon beginning below the Gunnison Tunnel.

The third section of the Gunnison River, which today lies within Black Canyon of the Gunnison National Park, begins at East Portal and is only eleven and a quarter miles to Red Rock Canyon, in which the riverbed gradient drops 1,050 feet in elevation. At one point below the Narrows, the river drops nearly 480 feet in a two-mile stretch. Fortunately, Kolb and Loper received two new fourteen-foot Galloway-Stone–designed boats with a three-and-a-half-foot beam from Julius Stone; unfortunately, each boat weighed about 250 pounds.[30]

Kolb and Loper hadn't gone two miles before the canyon significantly narrowed and the rapids became un-runnable for their heavy boats. They had to line or portage most of the Gunnison River during the eleven days that they were in the canyon. Kolb would write to Julius Stone that "there is not two miles of boating between the tunnel and Red Rock. It is all work on shore. It is seldom a boat can even be lined with safety."[31] Two and a half miles into the canyon, shortly after Flat Rock Falls (aka Day Wrecker, Class V+), one of the boats was caught in the rocks while it was being lined. It took four days and a stick of dynamite to release it from the rock's grasp so that they could continue. Kolb and Loper would make it approximately six miles before they would both be injured, and they limped out at probably Echo Canyon on October 24, 1916. Upon

FIGURE 5.9. Portage of one of the boats in the Black Canyon of the Gunnison River in Section Three. NAU.PH.568.5935, Cline Library, Northern Arizona University, Flagstaff, AZ: Ellsworth Kolb photo found in Emery Kolb Collection.

reaching Montrose, Bert learned that his wife was deathly ill and he wouldn't be able to complete the canyon so returned home.[32]

After two weeks recovering from his knee injury, Ellsworth continued with his dauntless pursuit to complete Section Three and invited Montrose resident William "Billie" Wright to assist him. They returned to where the boats had been left downstream of the Narrows. With only a week to work with before Wright needed to return, the party only made a quarter of a mile in what Kolb described as "the most dangerous quarter in the gorge." Once they were in the canyon, he said, "it snowed and rained, and snowed again. Even on those days when the sun shone, we had but twenty minutes between sunrise and sunset."[33]

Ten days later, Lawrence Coats replaced Wright and this time Kolb brought with him boat hooks to help with the ice while "portaging our boat and equipment under the worst conditions." The boat hooks weren't enough; the men needed more help and returned to the rim to recruit Lawrence's brother Adrian and their friend Jay Hall. Returning to the Black Canyon on Thanksgiving Day, November 30, 1916, the four men portaged the remaining boat until shortly after completing the last major obstacle at Torrence Falls. After the falls, the landscape widened and the river was running extremely low. It appeared that there were several locations in which the men could cross over to the south side. Tired of portaging the boat, Kolb decided to run a rapid and wrecked it. They saved the boat but lost the remainder of their provisions. Trying to once again salvage the boat to make a final crossing of the Gunnison River, Kolb tied the boat together with ropes where it had split open and covered it with a tarpaulin. Shortly afterward while he was lining the boat, it got away and crashed into a rock and sunk. They were near Red Rock Canyon and crossed the river and climbed out of the canyon on December 8, 1916. According to Kolb it took eighteen days comprising parts of three months for him to complete Section Three.

After the Black Canyon and Grand River boating trips ended in 1916, Ellsworth's exploits became few and far between. Losing the use of the Kolb Studios, and eventually his residency at the Grand Canyon, and selling his part of the Kolb Brothers partnership must have left an emotional impact on him.

In 1917, Ellsworth began presenting colored slides and motion-picture lectures of his Black Canyon and Grand River exploits. His most important presentation was made to *National Geographic Magazine* in Washington, DC, on March 16, 1917. It was a busy year, and Ellsworth had an interest in learning how to fly; he traveled to New York to take an aviation course, and partway through the course he returned to Colorado in late September to complete Section Four of the Black Canyon. The United States entered World War I on April 6, 1917, and Ellsworth intended to join the army as a pilot. Understandably, the war affected tourism and the brothers' business at the Grand Canyon.

The following year, on September 12, 1918, Ellsworth registered for the army and was denied entry because of his age. Disappointed by the rejection, and wanting to prove himself healthy despite being older, he prepared for three days to run in a marathon that was sponsored in New York. Of the 1,200 entries to the race, Ellsworth placed 378th.[34] Nevertheless, he was still depressed from being rejected by the army. Sometime in 1917 or 1918, Ellsworth began writing a manuscript that described his Grand and Gunnison River experiences for *National Geographic Magazine* that would go unpublished.

FIGURE 5.10. Between 1910 and 1924, Ellsworth Kolb next to biplane. NAU. PH.568.6384, Cline Library, Northern Arizona University, Flagstaff, AZ: Emery Kolb Collection.

Ellsworth retained his interest in flying, and on August 8, 1922, he hired R. V. Thomas, a daredevil stunt pilot, to fly him into the Grand Canyon and land on a plateau. It was considered impossible to land or take off in a plane in the Grand Canyon proper; however, we know how Ellsworth handled the impossible. Because it was a short landing, Kolb was advised by the pilot to keep his seatbelt loose in case he needed to jump. Upon landing, the plane stopped ten feet short of the edge.[35]

As Ellsworth and Emery's partnership deteriorated, they worked with each other only on a few occasions, such as the 1921 Cataract Canyon Survey, investigating the disappearance of the lost honeymooners, Glen and Bessie Hyde in 1928, and their historic hike to Cheyava Falls in the Grand Canyon in 1930. Otherwise, Ellsworth worked alone or explored with others.

Ellsworth was selected as the head boatman for the 1921 Cataract Canyon Survey. There are questions why he was not also selected to lead the Grand Canyon Survey in 1923. Emery instead got the nod, and Ellsworth was left off of the expedition. Emery thought his big brother may have suffered a mental breakdown possibly in 1922, when he and Blanche received a twenty-two-page letter from Ellsworth that left them believing that he had suffered a nervous breakdown from the business pressures. Between 1922 and 1928 Ellsworth exhibited moments of unusual behavior, and at times he was heard conversing with imaginary or deceased persons. It was during this period that Ellsworth's youngest brother, Eric, said that "he wasn't the boy he was before."[36]

What caused Ellsworth to have a mental breakdown in 1922 is mostly unknown. It may have been the business pressures that Emery alluded to from the letter that he and Blanche received that year; however, there likely were more reasons stemming from 1914, when friction between the two brothers first surfaced and continued to fester as they attempted to work separately at the Grand Canyon. According to Bill Suran, Emery Kolb never discussed what happened, and sometime during the last year of his life he considered the correspondence between the two brothers too personal and destroyed the letters. Many of Ellsworth's letters were also lost from an accidental leak of chemicals and water seeping onto a box where they were stored below the darkroom.[37]

Leaving the Grand Canyon in 1924, Ellsworth moved to Los Angeles, where he took up drawing and painting. His primary subject was women, clothed and unclothed. Ellsworth tried marriage and married Ella J. Shonsbye of South Dakota on June 30, 1924. Their marriage lasted only two months.[38] Much of the time Ellsworth lived off a monthly payment of $150 that was his payoff for selling his share of the business. Although Emery complained about paying the amount each month, especially during the Depression, he didn't miss making a payment to his older brother.

In 1942, shortly after the bombing of Pearl Harbor and the United States' entrance into World War II, Ellsworth attended trade school in Los Angeles to become a machinist. Soon thereafter, he was hired by Douglas Aircraft and was with them for ten years. His parents eventually moved near him to Los Angeles. Again, World War II affected tourism at the Grand Canyon, which left Emery's business struggling. Ellsworth signed over the royalties to his book *Through the Grand Canyon from Wyoming to Mexico* to help Emery get through it.[39]

During the 1950s Ellsworth experienced a number of health issues. In 1952, he had a serious episode with his heart, high blood pressure, and kidneys that put him in the hospital. He recovered; however, the health problems and accidents continued. His little brother Eric helped Ellsworth locate a hotel to live in near two movie theaters and a cafe. This was the extent of Ellsworth's final years: to attend movies almost daily. Except for the infrequent excursions mentioned before, his presence at the Grand Canyon disappeared. The wandering spirit had left him.

Suran wrote,

> Ellsworth died apparently in his sleep in 1960 at the age of eighty-three. His maid found him two days after his death. The family buried him in the Pioneer's Cemetery at Grand Canyon on 13 January 1960, a cold day with the temperature hovering in the low 30's. Dark gray clouds covered the sky and a light snow fell on those few who gathered at the gravesite to pay their respects. Ellsworth died almost an unknown. As one of the greatest rivermen to run the Colorado he should have received more credit for his deeds. During his years at the Canyon he had hiked more of the gorge than any other man though Emery often made this claim for himself. He reached and explored Cheyava Falls, hiked to Sockdolager Rapid and climbed Diana Temple before anyone else. Ellsworth made these trips either alone or with someone other than his brother, but they were soon forgotten.[40]

After the difficulty Kolb encountered in the Black Canyon during the fall and winter of 1916, he had a reasonable excuse not to return. However, determined to complete Section Four of the Black Canyon, he returned to Montrose in September of 1917. He had a lot on his plate and was taking aviation classes in New York with hopes of enlisting in the army during World War I. On September 14, 1917, Ellsworth Kolb and Albert Miller, a motion-picture operator from Montrose, reentered the Black Canyon at Red Rock Canyon. With a one-man collapsible canvas boat, they completed the sixteen miles through the Black Canyon and continued to Delta, Colorado. Although Kolb portaged most of five miles of the inner gorge below the Narrows, he was the first to take a boat through the Black Canyon from Cimarron to Delta. He was not done though.

After taking a few days off and making photographs at Ouray, Colorado, Kolb returned to the Black Canyon on September 29, 1917, and hiked down Echo Canyon (where he and Loper hiked out in 1916) to secure additional photographs of the region that had given him nearly five weeks of turmoil the previous year. This time he went alone and brought with him a small raft to float his camera and equipment on the river. Like Fellows and Torrence in 1901, Ellsworth Kolb clamored over the huge boulders and swam portions of the Gunnison River for approximately five or six miles, leaving the canyon again at Red Rock. He did it this time in one day.[41]

During the early years of boating the Green and Colorado Rivers, many of the participants recognized that they had a place in the history of the rivers. It helped with the likes of Frederick S. Dellenbaugh, Robert Brewster Stanton, and newcomer Otis Reed "Dock" Marston, who aggressively solicited their stories to be published one day. Marston started to number each individual who successfully ran the Grand Canyon with lists of the first 100, then moved onto the second 100. Ellsworth Kolb and Loper are listed at twenty-six and sixty-nine respectively. Both men would contend to be the first to boat the Grand and Colorado Rivers and through the Grand Canyon. Marston didn't credit either of them for the historical effort that they made. He appeared to disbelieve that Loper boated the stretch of river between Cisco and Moab, and Kolb acknowledged that he didn't complete the flat water from Moab to the Confluence. It may have been Kolb's mindset that flat water didn't count.

It appeared that the flat water counted in 1913, when Kolb completed the stretch between Needles, California, to the Gulf of California. Then again, in addition to his desire to complete the mostly placid stretch to the Pacific Ocean, he may have been enticed by other dangers in the region. He wrote, "I was told of the outlaws along the border, of the firearms and the opium smugglers, who shot first and questioned afterward, and the insurrectos of Lower California."[42]

He continued, "Many people had gone into these swamps and never returned, whether lost in the jungles or killed by the Cocopah Indians, no one knew. They just simply disappeared. It was all very alluring."[43]

What changed? When he planned to boat the Black Canyon in 1916, he split it into four sections. Thinking there was nothing significant in Section One, from Lake Fork to Cimarron, he wrote it off and traveled by train to Section Two, which began at Cimarron. Bypassing Section One by boarding a D&RG train at Lake Fork, he took the tracks that followed the Gunnison River, where Kolb observed. "We were not interested in doing any boating in this section. It was too easy of approach. But we did realize that we were up against a pretty hard proposition when we saw the rapids and cascades of this first section from the car."[44] In the end the flat stretches did count.

At the age of fifty-two, Ellsworth Kolb ran his last rapid. Having learned of the missing honeymoon boaters Glen and Bessie Hyde, Ellsworth wired his brother Emery to volunteer and help search for the missing couple. Traveling from his home in Los Angeles, he arrived at Peach Springs in time to assist Emery and Jimmy Brooks repair an abandoned boat that they would use to locate Hyde's sweeping scow. The search party launched their boat on December 24, 1928, with Emery Kolb manning the oars. Along the way they stopped to look for signs of the honeymooner's tracks and call out hoping for a response. After a lengthy time off the river, Ellsworth was itching to row a boat again and persuaded Emery to allow him to run 232 Mile Rapid. The episode had a hint of seventeen years earlier at Soap Creek Rapid, where Ellsworth tried to run the rapid twice and failed both times. The Colorado River was running below 4,000 cfs, and the rocky fangs at the bottom of the rapid were exposed. It did not go well: Ellsworth missed his run, and their boat crashed into the rocks. It put a scare into Emery and Jim; however, Ellsworth would write, "I haven't sense enough to be scared when I should be."[45] Fortunately, the boat remained upright; the men were able to extricate themselves from the rocks and stopped to camp for the night.

The following day, on Christmas, the men located Hyde's scow in an eerily quiet spot above river mile 237. The bowline was presumed to be lodged in the rocks below, restraining the boat from continuing downstream. Still seeing no sign of John and Bessie Hyde, the men searched their belongings for evidence of what might have happened to them.

FIGURE 5.11. Ellsworth Kolb, Gulf of California in 1913. NAU.PH.568.3601, Cline Library, Northern Arizona University, Flagstaff, AZ: Emery Kolb Collection.

With a lot of their belongings still on the scow—including Bessie's diary, a camera, a pistol, and so on—it has led to an unsolved mystery. After transporting all of the evidence from the scow to their boat Ellsworth wanted to test the sweeping scow on the river; he took it through a riffle, then let it loose.

6

FELLOWS AND TORRENCE

Overcoming the Narrows

I feel strongly that as we learn the history of the Upper Colorado River, Ellsworth Kolb's experiences might be the most important historical boating event. What better source for us to receive it from than his own writings. Kolb's herculean efforts getting past the Black Canyon of the Gunnison National Park section of the Gunnison River cannot be comprehended by today's river community. Where approximately 10,000 individuals annually boat Westwater Canyon's rapids, there is an estimated annual average of approximately fifty-nine kayakers over the past fifteen years who have been adventurous enough to kayak the fourteen miles of the inner Black Canyon.[1] It is not a canyon that lends itself to rafting. The few who experience the Gunnison River bottoms through the Black Canyon of the Gunnison National Park are hikers, fishermen, and adventure kayakers who brave class IV and higher rapids. The hikes into the canyon are steep and difficult.

Personally, I struggled to write about the Black Canyon. It was made clear to me that you can read all of the books there are about a subject such as the Black Canyon of the Gunnison River and not be able to comprehend it until you go there. Although hampered by a tender knee and unable to hike to the Gunnison

River bottom, I needed to at least view it from both the North and South Rims. Similar to the Grand Canyon and other special places on earth, you need to experience it in person. Fortunately, to get a glimpse of the Gunnison River from the river-level perspective, I located a website titled Black Canyon the Next Generation that provided me with a narrative and video that along with the writings from early explorers helped me to conceptualize the National Park section of the Gunnison River.[2] Clearly, Ellsworth Kolb had his work cut out for him.

Information on the Black Canyon is included for the reader to better grasp the efforts that Kolb made to successfully boat what he designated one of three primary tributaries of the then Colorado River that began at the confluence with the Green River. Having no experience other than peering over the cliff's walls, I borrowed freely from Abraham Lincoln Fellows's narrative to describe his and William Torrance's first decent of the Black Canyon of the Gunnison River in 1901.[3]

After completing the first documented transit of the Black Canyon on foot, Abraham Lincoln "A.L." Fellows remarked that "the enterprise was not attended by any unusual dangers, and that the timidity of previous explorers arose from their lack of knowledge rather than any real danger."[4] It doesn't sound like something someone would say who had nearly starved, was sick, and had lost approximately fifteen pounds from exhaustion, as well as sustaining numerous cuts and bruises from clamoring over huge boulders and, intermittently, swimming seventy-six times in the sieve-infested cold waters of the Gunnison River. The newspaper article also states that Fellows was modest.

Like Westwater Canyon, the chasm of the Black Canyon is comprised primarily of Precambrian rocks of gneiss, granite, and schist; only they are more dominantly displayed in Black Canyon, with cliffs rising from the Gunnison River bed to as high as 2,250 feet. The canyon is an extremely narrow and much deeper canyon; there is no record of early trappers exploring it. There is evidence of Indigenous people along the North and South Rims, and they developed trails in the vicinity of East Portal and Red Rock Canyon to travel between the rims; however, there is no evidence of them in the Black Canyon of the Gunnison National Park river bottoms. The North Branch of the Old Spanish Trail (OST), Old Trapper Trails, and Father Domínguez and Father Escalante's

FIGURE 6.1. The Black Canyon of the Gunnison National Park at Painted Wall taken from Chasm View on the north rim. Photo by Cory Milligan (2021).

expedition all bypassed the Black Canyon. In 1853, Captain John W. Gunnison was at the east end of the Black Canyon near Lake Fork making a central route survey for a Pacific Railroad, and he understandably avoided it. The first attempt to survey the Black Canyon came in 1873, when Ferdinand V. Hayden's party made a geological and geographical survey of the territory of Colorado. It appears that most of the work was done from the rim; however, some of the surveyors reportedly were let over the ledge by rope for 1,000 feet and reported back that the canyon is inaccessible. The Black Canyon of the Gunnison River was so steep and deep that there was no redeemable need to access it until the early 1880s, when the Denver & Rio Grande Railroad (D&RG RR) sought to extend its narrow-gauge tracks beyond the railroad town at Gunnison further west to the silver and gold mines in western Colorado, and because there became a developing need for additional irrigation water from the Gunnison River for the Uncompahgre Valley.

By 1881 and 1882, a number of settlements sprung up along the west side of the Rocky Mountains in Colorado because of mining activity and the recent removal of Utes to the Ouray and Uintah Indian Reservation in Utah. The removal of the Utes made lands available for settlement in the Uncompahgre and Grand Valley regions. General William Jackson Palmer and the D&RG RR went to work immediately to lay narrow-gauge tracks to the new and upcoming settlements west of Gunnison. He first surveyed the eastern region of the Black Canyon and built a railroad between Sapinero and Cimarron, Colorado, where it left the canyon. Men were lowered over cliffs to perform a survey of the canyon. Some died performing the survey, and others died later when laying down the railroad tracks. The extremely scenic and popular fifteen-mile Black Canyon route was hampered by rock, snow, and mud slides and was discontinued in 1949.

Not done, in December of 1882, General Palmer assigned his top surveyor, Byron Bryant, to survey what was then called the "Grand Canyon of the Gunnison River" from the Cimarron River through the Black Canyon to Delta Station, near the confluence of the Uncompahgre and Gunnison Rivers. Twelve men began the survey, and after a few days only four men remained to complete it. Bryant estimated it would take twenty days to survey the entire canyon, and instead it took sixty-eight days. The men did not go through the canyon but instead climbed down with pack animals and their survey instruments each morning and worked for three hours; then they stopped at 1:00 p.m. to climb back out of the canyon. It took approximately six hours to go roundtrip from top to bottom each day. Understandably, the results were negative; a railroad could not possibly be built through the Black Canyon.[5]

It is little wonder that few individuals desired to enter the steep confines of the Black Canyon. Geologist Wallace R. Hansen wrote, "In many places the Black Canyon is as deep as it is wide. Between The Narrows and Chasm View in the Black Canyon of the Gunnison National Monument (now Park) it is much deeper than wide."[6] One's first impression of the canyon can be intimidating. Initially, the Black Canyon cannot be detected when approaching it from the north rim through sagebrush, scattered piñon pine, and juniper trees, then suddenly, dramatically, the top of the sheer cliffs emerge, leaving one with a sense of awe and anticipation of what to expect once the edge is reached. Once you are there, you see that the canyon drops off so suddenly and deep that it is

FIGURE 6.2. Utah juniper found on south rim of the Black Canyon of the Gunnison National Park at Dragon Point overlook. Photo by author (2021).

both spectacular and daunting. Instinctively, you are inclined to step back from the edge and not chance slipping into the abyss. David Halpern wrote, "This is an awesome canyon by virtually every measure that

I can think of—rugged, wild and impressive in the extreme, inspiring, frightening, spellbinding, breathtaking—and at least one description that you are not likely to find in your dictionary."[7]

The Gunnison River is more than a half mile below the rim, and when the river is observed from this height, it resembles a brook running over small river rocks; in reality, it is a river with thunderous rapids and falls that can be heard by onlookers viewing the canyon from the rim.

The issue of irrigating the Uncompahgre Valley initiated a need to access water from the Gunnison River. There was insufficient water in the Uncompahgre River for the regional settlers' agriculture. In 1890, an early settler, F. C. Lauzon, envisioned accessing the Gunnison River to help irrigate the Uncompahgre region. The problem was that a mountain separated the river and valley. Lauzon conceived that the water could be retrieved by running a tunnel through the mountain. The Uncompahgre side was surveyed for a tunnel in 1894, and there remained a need to survey the interior of the Black Canyon for a practical location where the river was at a higher elevation than the valley. It wasn't until 1900, when John Pelton, M. V. "Frank" Hovey, and William W. "Will" Torrence, of Montrose; and J. A. Curtis and E. B. Anderson, of Delta, attempted to survey the bottom of the canyon in order to locate a site for a tunnel. As in Ellsworth Kolb's 1916 effort, the five men departed downriver at Cimarron, taking two 300-pound boats, the *John C. Bell* and *City of Montrose*, which carried thirty days of provisions for the men. On the morning of the second day the *John C. Bell* sunk in a rapid with the majority of their supplies. The men continued deeper into the Black Canyon with the remaining boat until they came to an impasse while approaching the Narrows that they named the Falls of Sorrow.[8]

In 1901, Abraham Lincoln Fellows, a resident hydrographer with the US Geological Survey (USGS) living in Denver, Colorado, was assigned to survey the Black Canyon and find a location within the canyon to build the Gunnison Tunnel. The tunnel would become one of the first major projects tackled by the newly formed U.S. Reclamation Service, established in 1902. Not satisfied with the earlier surveys mentioned before, Fellows needed to perform one of his own. Deciding to forgo the need for a boat to carry supplies, Fellows spent two months during the spring on Vernal Mesa searching for trails into the canyon where supplies could be brought down to the river, which would be critical to success when traveling afoot through approximately thirty-five miles of the Black Canyon. Montrose resident Asa W. "A.W." Dillon was hired to deliver food and supplies for the survey at three critical locations in what Fellows considered the most "dangerous miles" in the canyon at Trail/Nyswonger Gulch, Echo Canyon, and Red Rock Canyon. Hiking down to the locations, Dillon would be able to report on the surveyors' safety, and whether they made it to the specified drops. Traveling light, Fellows planned to hike and swim the entire canyon and take as few provisions with him as possible. He brought an inflatable mattress to use as a raft for carrying his equipment and provisions that was protected in rubber bags, when crossing the Gunnison River. The mattress was also used for bedding down on the rocks.

Fellows was warned by numerous individuals that he would be "killed if I undertook the trip"; however, "I made up my mind to at least make the effort."[9] To accomplish the survey, it required that he hire an assistant. Recognizing the potential risk of death, among other attributes, Fellows conscientiously solicited to employ someone who was "unmarried and have no one entirely dependent on him."[10] Among other job requirements Fellows also emphasized the need for candidates to be strong, athletic, and good swimmers. From the numerous applicants that applied, Will Torrence, from the previous year's failed Pelton survey, was hired to assist him with the survey. Torrence was already knowledgeable about the Black Canyon as far as the Falls of Sorrow and was anxious to return to it.

On August 12, 1901, carrying packs that weighed approximately thirty-five pounds each, the two men embarked on the survey on foot beginning at the confluence of the Cimarron River with the Gunnison River. Three days into the survey they reached the first food drop at "Boat Landing" at the mouth of Trail/Nyswonger Gulch. Their shoes badly worn, and the men exhausted from climbing and swimming, they asked Dillon to return to Montrose and purchase new shoes and obtain fresh supplies. Fellows wrote, "It was frequently necessary to swim through deep water, and all walking was along boulders which formed the talus of the canyon walls. Easy walking was never to be found unless it was a very few feet upon some gravel bar."[11]

FIGURE 6.3. Will Torrence and Abraham Lincoln Fellows. Courtesy of the Black Canyon of the Gunnison National Park, NPS.

While waiting for Dillon to return, Fellows and Torrence mostly slept to recover from being exhausted. They resumed the survey on August 16. The Gunnison River was contaminated at the time from pollutants coming from Lake Fork, and they relied on springs in the canyon to provide them their drinking water.

FIGURE 6.4. A. L. Fellows using an inflatable mattress when swimming in the Gunnison River in 1901. Courtesy of the Montrose Historical Society.

Describing the Black Canyon, Fellows wrote,

> Our surroundings were of the wildest possible description. The roar of the water falls was constantly in our ears and the walls of the canon towering half mile in height above us, were seemingly vertical.

FIGURE 6.5. Carrying the boat around rapids in the Black Canyon in 1900. Z-7384 9–1900, Will Torrence photo, Denver Library. Location currently identified on Milo's list of rapids as vicinity of Ramp w/ S-Turn.

> Occasionally a rock would fall from one side or the other, with a roar and crash, exploding like a ton of dynamite when it struck bottom, making us think our last day had come. At times the canon would become so narrow that it would almost, but never quite, be possible to step across the river. At times, great gorges of rock that had fallen in from the sides would hem in the water to such an extent that it would be nearly concealed... Our most dangerous work, possibly, was that of clambering along the sides of precipices, traversing old mountain sheep trails, at points where it was impracticable to swim without too great danger to life and limb.[12]

He continued,

> The canon, heretofore comparatively open with walls having slopes of about 1 to 1 and covered with spruce and pine timber, with here and there groves of aspen and an undergrowth of oak brush, now became more and more rugged. The geological formation was of gneiss and mica schist and the apparently vertical cliffs, instead of being met

with occasionally, now became almost continuous. At times we would traverse along reaches looking like mill ponds with the sky and canon walls reflected in the depth of the blue water, but again we would come to rapids and water falls as turbulent as the waters of Lodore. The canon walls appeared more and more to be hemming us in from the outer world.[13]

Fellows proceeded with his narrative:

On the morning of the 17th, we again started out upon what we expected would be the most perilous portion of our journey. Others had been as far as this point and escaped with their lives, but no one had ever gone far beyond. We had made good time the preceding day and were farther along than I had expected, so I thought it best to make great bonfires of the huge piles of driftwood which lined the stream, to indicate to Dillon above that we had passed this point. We made an early start, for we expected the day would be a hard one, and about 11 o'clock that morning we reached what had hitherto been the Ultima Thule of other explorers.[14]

The "Ultima Thule" is defined as "a distant unknown region; the extreme limit of travel and discovery." Two miles below the boat launch at East Portal of the Black Canyon of the Gunnison National Park begins a nearly six-mile stretch of Class V and VI and un-runnable rapids and falls. The Narrows lies in the heart of a sequence of rapids beginning at Day Wrecker (V+). The historical name for this rapid was Flat Rock Falls, named by the Pelton party in 1900. Continuing downstream, rapids have such contemporary names as Ramp-S Turn (V), Double Drop (V), Lower Intestine (V), Triple Drop (VI), Principals Office (V), and others until the Narrows Boulder Garden shortly above the forty-foot-wide Narrows.[15] Pelton's party struggled significantly to get past these rapids with the added burden of portaging the remaining boat around one difficult fall after another until eventually their food supply was exhausted. Not knowing what to expect beyond the Narrows, they conceded in defeat. Disheartened, the party located a potential, and dangerous, exit from the canyon, abandoned their lone boat, and began their treacherous climb out, leaving the Falls of Sorrow behind them.

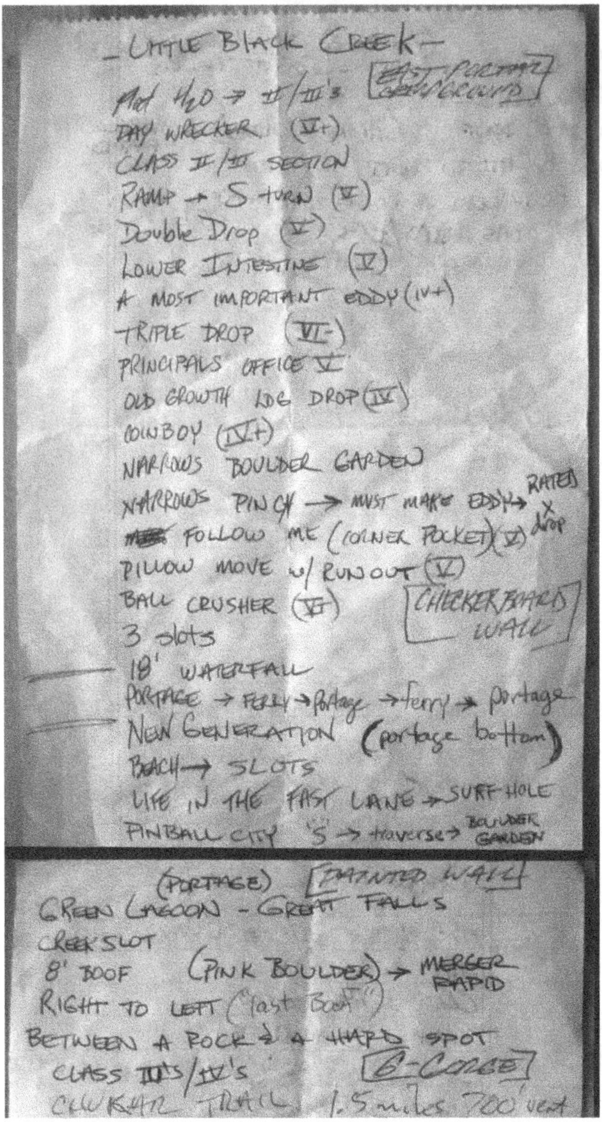

- LITTLE BLACK CREEK -
Red H_2O → II/III's [EAST PORTAL CAMPGROUND]
DAY WRECKER (V+)
CLASS II/III SECTION
RAMP → S-turn (V)
Double Drop (V)
LOWER INTESTINE (V)
A MOST IMPORTANT EDDY (IV+)
TRIPLE DROP (VI-)
PRINCIPALS OFFICE V
OLD GROWTH LOG DROP (IV)
COWBOY (IV+)
NARROWS BOULDER GARDEN
NARROWS PINCH → MUST MAKE EDDY → RATED X DROP
FOLLOW ME (CORNER POCKET) (V)
PILLOW MOVE w/ RUNOUT (V)
BALL CRUSHER (VI) [CHECKERBOARD WALL]
3 slots
18' WATERFALL
PORTAGE → FERRY → portage → ferry → portage
NEW GENERATION (portage bottom)
BEACH → SLOTS
LIFE IN THE FAST LANE → SURF HOLE
PINBALL CITY "S" → traverse → BOULDER GARDEN
(PORTAGE) [PAINTED WALL]
GREEN LAGOON - GREAT FALLS
CREEK SLOT
8' BOOF (PINK BOULDER) → MERGER RAPID
RIGHT TO LEFT ("last Boof")
BETWEEN A ROCK & A HARD SPOT
CLASS III's/IV's [G-GORGE]
CHUKAR TRAIL 1.5 miles 700' vert

FIGURE 6.6. Milo Wynne aka Captain Black's second edition standard list of rapids and drops between East Portal and Chukar Trail in the Black Canyon of the Gunnison National Park. Image courtesy of Milo Wynne aka Captain Black.

Unencumbered by a boat, Fellows and Torrence proceeded deeper into the Black Canyon, until the steep canyon walls appeared to hem them in and the river became more turbulent and violent from increasingly dense large boulders that had fallen from the cliffs and settled in the river bottoms as they advanced toward the Narrows.

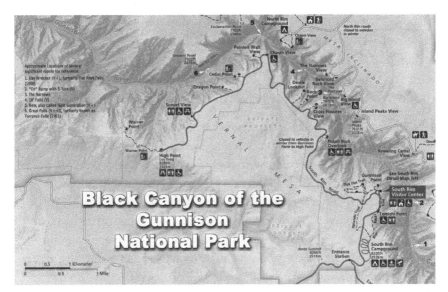

FIGURE 6.7. Modified NPS map of the Black Canyon of the Gunnison National Park. Author added several current rapid names and their locations.

When hiking to get through the Narrows, the hiker encounters a gravel bar immediately upstream of it on the south side of the river. Because of cliffs and other obstacles, most travel up to this point is done from the north shore. There is limited access to the gravel bar except by making a dangerous upstream swim near rapids in order to cross the Gunnison River and avoid being swept prematurely into the Narrows. As the two men approached the Narrows from the north (river right) side and considered crossing the river to the gravel bar, Fellows said,

> we reached the lowest point attained by earlier explorers and saw before us the mighty jaws, past which there was to be no escape, a feeling of nervousness and dread came over me for the first time. I said to Torrence, "Will, your last chance to go out is to the right. You can make it there if you wish, but if we cross the river at this point there can be no return: we must go on."
>
> Torrence replied, "Here goes nothing!" And he commenced to pull off his coat. Nothing further was said. We swam the river, reaching a similar point of rocks on the other side, but still above the gorge.[16]

In the fall of 1998, Robb Magley and his friend Michael attempted to retrace what Fellows and Torrence accomplished on foot. Perhaps others have also attempted the trek, however. Magley documented his effort in the book *Deep Black*. They encountered a similar dilemma in this area of rapids as Fellows and Torrence did, and Magley wrote,

> The issue, as we now saw, was not so much the Narrows itself, but the approach. We stood on a tidy sandbar on the north bank, and from the lowermost point we could see right through the chasm to a few giant boulders in the river down-stream. Once we were directly upstream of the Narrows on the south side, there would be an easy float for fifty feet or so to a gravel beach along the same side. But our little sand bar paralleled only about half the length of a difficult and complex rapid system, which gave up probably thirty feet of elevation along fifty yards of river. Crossing to the south side for our Narrows float was going to be the hard part.[17]

As they swam across the Gunnison River to the south side, their equipment was snagged in rocks and was irretrievable. Without any provisions, the men had to make a dangerous return swim to the north shore, where they exited the canyon at either Long Draw, previously known as Devil's Slide, or possibly Slide Draw.

Prior to 1901 the Narrows of the Black Canyon of the Gunnison River is where rational men were tested. John Pelton's survey party was thwarted at the Narrows. The Narrows hindered all earlier attempts to transit the canyon because of the uncertainty of survival beyond it. An old trapper and hunter, Moccasin Bill, spoke of this point in the canyon and said, "It was impossible for mortal man to go through the canyon and live."[18]

The Narrows is a mere forty feet wide and approximately 140 feet long with nearly vertical cliffs rising 1,750 feet above the Gunnison River.[19] There is no shoreline where the river squeezes through the small opening. Before the upstream dams were built, a surge of 19,000 cfs of the Gunnison River once forced its way through the Narrows. The annual discharge was approximately 12,000 cfs. Currently, most of the Gunnison River is diverted through the Gunnison Tunnel to the Uncompahgre Valley for agricultural demands, and rarely will the Gunnison

FIGURE 6.8. The Narrows taken from the Narrows overlook. Photo by Cory Milligan (2021).

River below East Portal run higher than 2,000 cfs. Even so, whether one is on foot or by boat, there is no escaping the Narrows. Unable to climb the steep walls to circumvent the Narrows, adventurers are left

FIGURE 6.9. Black Canyon rapids at the Narrows. Image Z-7398-1900, Will Torrence, photo courtesy of the Denver Library.

with the decision to either quit and climb out of the canyon, or gamble, possibly with their lives, and chance getting past the unknown rapids beyond the Narrows. A rapid can be heard and partially seen on the far end of the Narrows. It can also be seen and heard a half mile above on the North Rim. It's a point where all the early parties recognized that if they challenged the Narrows, there was no turning back. It was a "do or die" decision for Fellows and Torrence. Irrational, risk-taking men moved forward and learned what was beyond the Narrows. Torrence reported, "At the 'Narrows' the fun began."[20]

Shortly beyond the Narrows, Dillon was waiting for them at the second planned food drop. He had hiked a difficult route from the south rim down Echo Canyon and arrived early to build a fire to make his presence known. Dillon's instructions from Fellows at the onset was "to convey supplies of food to these three points, waiting at each one in turn until we should have arrived, or until there was no longer hope that we would ever arrive."[21] His presence in the canyon provided a "wonderful inspiration" for Fellows and Torrence that helped motivate them to swim through the "jaws of the gorge," where they arrived safely in a small eddy that formed along the south side to another gravel landing, and avoid a large boulder-strewn rapid on the opposite side of the river. It was low water, and they surmised the depth of the river was ten feet through the Narrows.

The nearly vertical cliffs rise up to 2,250 feet above the Gunnison River at the Painted Wall in the Black Canyon of the Gunnison National Park. The bottoms are primarily sliced through by the river, leaving them with mostly a steep and narrow talus slope, especially for the five-mile section that gave Ellsworth Kolb considerable problems portaging his boat(s) in 1916. As boulders of all sizes fall from the cliffs and crash to the bottom, they congregate in and along the Gunnison River. Some boulders, described as being the size of busses, clog the riverbed, and in some areas completely bury the river.[22] Because of the numerous stacked boulders clogging the Gunnison River through this section, it is described by kayakers as sieve infested. The nearer one gets to the river, the larger and denser the boulders.

Fellows continued,

> We were soon obliged to cross the river again, where we clambered along gigantic boulders, often as large as a good-sized house, the peculiar characteristic of which was that the nearer the water the larger and more impassable the boulders seemed to be. In consequence we

FIGURE 6.10. New Generation Rapid and Painted Wall taken from SOB Gulch by Milo Wynne aka Captain Black (2016).

kept ascending the side of the talus until, when darkness fell, we were a long way above the water, and we made camp under a huge shelving rock against which the roaring of the river reverberated and echoed like demons howling over their prey. We were so far above the water

FIGURE 6.11. Buried Gunnison River, taken from the South Rim Chasm View overlook. Photo by author (2021).

that it took an hour to make a trip down for a coffee pot full, the distance being augmented by the difficulties in climbing.[23]

On the morning of the 18th, we hoped that our greatest difficulties were passed, but we were doomed to disappointment, for on that day we encountered some of the most trying experiences of the trip. At the very start we came to a gorge where gigantic boulders had fallen in from the cliffs, the water flowing 100 feet or more beneath these boulders. They were packed closely enough, however, so that they formed a dam in high water. The boulders were smooth and polished to such an extent that it was only with the greatest difficulty they could be surmounted. It took us six hours to traverse less than a quarter of a mile. At times it would be necessary for one of us to climb on the shoulders of the other, clamber to the top of some huge rock and draw our supplies and the other man up by means of the rope which we carried with us. Again on the other side there might be a deep pool where we were obliged to swim, into which the water boiled from the caves above and sucked out again through the crevices between the boulders below. In one of these

FIGURE 6.12. A. L. Fellows in the Black Canyon of the Gunnison River looking up from transit point #44 at Torrence Falls in 1902. Photo courtesy of Abraham Lincoln Fellows Papers, Western Americana Collection, Beinecke Rare Book and Manuscript Library, Yale University.

pools I was drawn completely under water in an eddy. I fully expected to be drawn down into the crevices of the rocks below, but by dint of the hardest kind of swimming, succeeded in getting into still water. At this time Torrence felt that he would never see me again.[24]

FIGURE 6.13. Great Falls Rapid as seen from the South Rim's Painted Wall overlook. Based on Ellsworth Kolb's photographs, this rapid appears to be the one A. L. Fellows named Torrence Falls. Photo by Cory Milligan (2021).

> Soon after this we came to what, in my opinion, is the most beautiful part of the entire canyon. The river pitches down over a succession of falls which I named in honor of my companion Torrence Falls.[25]

On August 19 Fellows and Torrence reached the final food drop at Red Rock Canyon. Their survey was complete at this point, and they could have climbed out of the canyon but chose to finish the remainder of the Black Canyon and continue to Delta. Below Red Rock Canyon, the rapids were less frequent and there were longer stretches where the men were forced to swim often because the cliffs were "very straight up and continuous, and right to the edge of the water."[26] Torrence commented that they could have used a boat through it. It was the only time a boat was mentioned during their ordeal.

Abraham L. Fellows's survey for the Gunnison Tunnel was successful and in a real sense contributed to the survival of settlements in the Uncompahgre Valley with a welcome source of additional irrigation water. Construction of the Gunnison Tunnel began in 1905, was the first major undertaking project by the U.S. Reclamation Service, and was completed in 1909. Just shy of six miles long, it was, at the time, the longest irrigation tunnel in the world.

Today, the upper section of the Gunnison River above the Gunnison Tunnel is inundated by the Blue Mesa, Morrow, and Crystal Reservoirs. The late renowned kayaker Walter Kirschbaum considered the lost section of the Gunnison River between Cimmaron and East Portal as "one of the classic great runs in North America."[27] Ellsworth Kolb designated this as Section Two on his 1916 Black Canyon expedition, where he, Julius F. Stone, John W. Shields, and Nathan B. Stern had difficulty with their ill-advised collapsible boats on a swollen river. Two months later Kolb returned with Loper, and they ran this section in a day and a half to the tunnel with no incidents. What was once a popular whitewater section of the Gunnison River is gone.

Below the dams is the Black Canyon of the Gunnison National Park, where river trips predominantly using kayaks begin at East Portal of the Gunnison Tunnel. There are a number of hiking trails for fishermen and hikers to enter the canyon throughout this section that are rated as difficult or very difficult. Ellsworth Kolb designated this as Section Three on his 1916 list to tackle in the Black Canyon. It took several attempts in the early 1900s to realize that heavy boats below the East Portal are not welcome. Even traveling on foot can be hazardous and physically taxing. In many instances, swimming may be required and is dangerous, particularly at the Narrows, where there isn't a safe way downstream but a swim on the south side along the cliff where the swimmer cannot see what is ahead of them.

Kayaks can be run down the Gunnison River through parts of the Black Canyon of the Gunnison National Park; however, it is not advisable for novice or moderate kayakers and is geared more toward expedition kayaking. One kayaker's feedback on the American Whitewater website describes kayaking the Black Canyon National Park section:

> The description posted here is deceptive to say the least. I ran the Black Canyon last year at a medium/low level, and nothing about this run is Class IV in nature. Until the relative flatwater near the end, there are numerous class V rapids, and the portage is very strenuous, it took our

group quite a bit longer than what the description indicates. In addition these rapids are some of the most sieved out pieces of shit I have ever seen. This is a true multi-day class V run, and while not as difficult as the stuff in the high sierra, it definitely deserves a V+ rating when taking the remote nature into account.[28]

Eleven years later, in 2020, another kayaker posted,

> I want to iterate the comment from Nick David 11 years ago. By all standards this is a Class V run and the description is misleading. Sieves are endless in the Black Canyon, portages are mandatory and arduous and any rescue would have to come from the air as the walls are sheer. I am positive consensus amongst the state is this is for seasoned class V+ boaters.[29]

Kayakers begin their journey at East Portal and for the next fourteen miles downstream to Chukar Trail; the river is rated Class V. Some sections are un-runnable where the Gunnison River disappears at points below huge boulders, and, as mentioned above, deathly sieves are numerous.

Although Fellows and Torrence were in the Black Canyon for ten days and received at least three meals and supplies delivered to them by Dillon, they wrote of nearly starving because of the exertion of clambering over huge boulders and constant swimming. At one point they were fortunate to have an injured mountain sheep literally delivered to them for one of their meals. Still, they lacked sufficient food and nourishment and each of them lost weight.

Possibly only those who kayak the canyon can imagine the difficulty John Pelton's survey party and Ellsworth Kolb's efforts portaging heavy boats over huge rocks that stood above their height. Kayaker Tom Michael Janney wrote of Kolb's efforts, "I have no idea how they portaged that with those boats and all that ice."[30] Another kayaker, Tom Chamberlain, wrote, "Those were some hard men."[31] More portaging than any boating, Kolb telegrammed Julius Stone stating that there wasn't a two-mile section that could be successfully boated between East Portal and Red Rock Canyon. Shortly after the Narrows, many kayakers take a two-mile "Hell Portage" along the talus slopes to

FIGURE 6.14. Tom Janney kayaks Next or New Generation Rapid while Janson Stingl looks on. Photo by Nick Abrams (2010)

avoid a section of the Gunnison River considered un-runnable. This is where the largest rocks are, and it's easier to hike around them on a path that is infested with poison ivy that grows over six feet tall than to scramble over boulders carrying their kayaks. Some have attempted to run whatever pools are exposed in this un-runnable section and probably find that it's not worth it, because of the numerous sieves. On August 14, 1997, a sieve in the upper section of the river that is generally portaged took the life of internationally known rodeo competitor and world-class kayaker Chuck Kern.

The portage begins on the north side for one mile to where Cave Camp is located, and then crossing to the south side the portage continues the next day for another mile. It is in this section of river that Fellows and Torrence advanced a quarter of a mile in one day. Ellsworth Kolb reported a similar experience of taking a full day to move his remaining boat the same distance. Whether in summer or winter the rocks are extremely slippery. Will Torrence described the region just past the Narrows: "The canon is full of great boulders, which form bridges across the stream. Over these we must scramble, one getting on top and pulling the other up. These rocks were slick as grease, and hard to climb. We spent a day in going a quarter of a mile."[32]

Given that there are sections of the Gunnison River that are buried beneath boulders, no individual will likely ever boat the entire stretch of the river through the National Park. Ellsworth Kolb portaged most of this section. In 1949, Ed Nelson, of Montrose, used a one-man raft using ping pong paddles for control and boated, hiked, and fished this section in five days. Kayakers have boated more parts of the river than Kolb could have dreamed of going. According to Fletcher Anderson, Walter Kirschbaum was the first to successfully kayak the entire Black Canyon in 1961 or 1962. Incredibly, he did it solo.[33] Kirschbaum had a mindset similar to but more than Ellsworth Kolb's and had a goal to paddle all the whitewater stretches of the Colorado River and its major tributaries. The late world-class champion slalom kayaker Kirschbaum is credited with other firsts, including running Gore Canyon in 1962, and he was credited as the first to run Cataract Canyon (1959) and Grand Canyon (1960) without portaging. In August 1962, Kirschbaum, Joe M. Lacy, Ulrich Martins, and Ted Young were the first to kayak Westwater Canyon. The next successful group known to kayak the Black Canyon of the Gunnison National Park was the renowned Ron Mason, Filip Sokol, Bill Clark, and Tom Ruwitch, in 1975.[34]

FIGURE 6.15. Walter Kirschbaum kayaking through a rapid on the Colorado River in the Grand Canyon in August 1960. Photo from Grand Canyon Museum Collection.

Improved kayaks and their maneuverability have introduced more adventurers to the sport. Kayaks are now made of much more durable material, are lighter, and are shorter than those used by Kirschbaum. The Black Canyon of the Gunnison National Park has attracted a new breed of adventurous kayakers to test their skills. Beginning with one individual in the early 1960s, the boating population rose to four

FIGURE 6.16. Tom Janney kayaking 18' waterfall below the Narrows in the Black Canyon of the Gunnison National Park. Photo courtesy of Jim Janney (2010).

kayakers in the mid-1970s, and today NPS ranger Paul Zaenger, claims that he likely underestimates that there is an average of fifty-nine kayakers that annually boat the National Park section of the Black Canyon.[35] Although equipment has improved, there remains significant risk for kayakers. It is not an easy canyon to kayak or hike. Milo Wynne, who has kayaked the National Park section of the Black Canyon fifty-two and a half times, his fiftieth being in 2012, said, "I've gone gray, I've lost sleep, I've lost skin, I've been knocked out, I've almost drowned but it's worth it." He said further, "I do not recommend going in there for any fun at all. If you want 'fun,' buy a mountain bike and adjust your derailleur."[36] A description of this section of the Black Canyon from another source reads, "Paddlers who seek the Black Canyon solely for its whitewater will be disappointed, but those who seek challenge and adventure will long to return."[37]

Where kayakers generally end their run at Chukar Trail is where other boaters, including rafters and hikers and fishermen carrying pack rafts arrive to run the lower section of the Black Canyon through the Gunnison Gorge aka Gunny Gorge. This is the section where Torrence wished he'd had a boat to finish their 1901 survey. It's runnable. Ellsworth Kolb didn't complete this section of the Black Canyon until the fall of 1917 in a one-man collapsible boat with Albert Miller of Montrose. A few days after completing the run to Delta, Kolb returned to Section Three of the Black Canyon and hiked down Echo Canyon to below the Narrows to obtain additional photographs. This time, like Fellows and Torrence, he brought an air mattress to float his equipment when needed to cross the Gunnison River and traveled to Red Rock Canyon in a single day.[38]

Reverend Mark T. Warner is primarily credited with getting the Black Canyon designated as a national monument, on March 2, 1933, and later it became a national park, on October 21, 1999. However, long before he appeared on the scene national news and magazine coverage of both Fellows and Torrence's Gunnison River tunnel survey in 1901, and Ellsworth Kolb's boating accomplishments in 1916 and 1917, brought considerable national recognition to the Black Canyon of the Gunnison River. Regarding Kolb's exploits, the *Delta Independent* reported that "Montrose has been given some wonderful advertising through Kolb's trip through the roughest of all deep canyons."[39] The stark beauty of the Black Canyon prompted Fellows to predict, "When the people realize what has existed unknown in their midst," then, "I believe there will be a demand for a view of its beauties."[40]

Reverend Warner wrote,

> The Black Canyon of the Gunnison has always held a strange fascination for those who have had the privilege of peering into its abysmal depths with the eye following the course of the roaring Gunnison River as it tumbles and foams and dashes its way over and among great boulders to be found strewn along the narrow river bed at the base of the precipitous canyon walls. But this fascination and the thrill of the Black Canyon is greatly intensified for those who have been privileged to traverse the rough river bed and view the rugged canyon walls from below.... One will never have seen the Black Canyon in its more majestic and thrilling aspects until he sees it from the bottom.[41]

Ellsworth Kolb had no idea how difficult the Black Canyon would be when he set out to run a boat through all of the primary tributaries of the Colorado River. What lies beyond the Narrows became known through the efforts of Fellows and Torrence, and a boat cannot get through it without portaging parts of the canyon. However, for three miles above and approximately three miles below it took a heavy toll on Kolb. Where it took ten days for Fellows and Torrence to transit the canyon on foot and swimming, it took Kolb and his assistants parts of six months between two years to accomplish the same distance with a boat(s). Regarding this section of the river, Will Torrence said, "It is a perilous trip and I would not advise any one to try it, unless they were prepared for accidents."[42] Nothing has changed.

EPILOGUE

I did return again on a private trip to run Westwater Canyon with an old river friend, Doug Guest, and my daughter Lindsi on August 26, 2022. Not knowing when I'll be able to enjoy Westwater Canyon again, I approached the private trip differently. I wanted to conscientiously absorb everything about Westwater that makes it special. We arrived at the ranger station in the evening before dark and set up our tents. It was a basic trip: we brought our own food and split the costs for gas and the permit fees.

We camped upstream of the launch next to the Colorado River. For quite a while, there were just four of us camped, and it was extremely quiet and serene. I watched the river flow past us and observed the reflections that appeared on its surface. There was a potential for rain, and although I put the rain fly over my tent I left one of the side doors completely open so that I could breathe in the fresh air and listen as the nearly silent current passed by. During the night I had to get up twice to attend to business at the public latrine, and each time when

I returned to my tent, I took time to observe the wonderful canopy of stars and reflections that continued to be present on the Colorado River. A train had gone past us earlier in the night, which tied together some of my favorite memories of camping at Westwater. Then as the sunrise approached, a pack of coyotes yelped from the opposite side of the river.

On the river I continued to absorb each mile as we continued downstream. Goats have now replaced the sheep, which replaced the cattle and wild horses over the years at Westwater Ranch. Canadian geese nearly carpeted much of the shorelines above the entry to Westwater Canyon. In the upper and lower canyon, Great blue herons intermittently flew ahead of us along the river. Unfortunately, we did not see a bald eagle.

At 2,850 cfs, sleeper rocks are prevalent and are scattered about in rapids and the straight sections. Some are jagged and can damage a raft for the unwary. Razor Rock in Skull Rapid is one of them. One must be observant on the river at all times. For those who want respite from the sun, a short cliff corridor preceding Little Hole has seemingly always provided shade relief. I'm reminded at the upper Little Dolores Rapid of possibly the first time I ran a boat through Westwater Canyon and was trapped in the eddy on river right. It took me several attempts to break through. Fortunately, that was the only difficult time I had in an eddy in Westwater Canyon and was able to avoid the Room of Doom during medium and high waters. Today, we purposely rowed into the Room of Doom to take photographs of the kayaks that were with us run Skull Rapid. Our run through Skull Rapid was left of Razor Rock, which intermittently displayed its sharp point within the turbulent whitewater. It was a route that was rarely considered when I guided rivers in the late 1970s and early 1980s.

Except for Skull Rapid, I hadn't contemplated researching the other rapid names. The earliest given names from former Westwater residents for Skull Rapid and Funnel Falls were Whirlpool and Double Pitch Rapids respectively. I generally prefer names that have a history behind them that can be researched, but Sock-It-To-Me, Surprise, Funnel Falls, Staircase, and Big Hummer? These names remind me of names that might be found at an amusement park ride. Dee Holladay wanted to change the name of Big Hummer to "Hunters Rapid" after the three deer hunters who overturned their raft in it and died in 1972. Perhaps naming rapids after tragic events isn't such a good idea; otherwise, we'd have to change the name of Skull Rapid regularly, or just call it Death Falls. In August 1962, when the first-known kayakers—Joe M. Lacy, Walter Kirschbaum, Ulrich Martins, and Ted Young—ran Westwater Canyon, they assigned their own names to the rapids such as Luscious, Big Hole, Delicious, One More Time, and Fat Lip. It appears likely that the history of the rapid names came from someone's experience with them that stuck. During today's run, the drops and splashing waves throughout our trip in the whitewater did remind me of an amusement park ride. Perhaps the current names are appropriate.

Reveling in Westwater Canyon has brought me to a new perspective of it. In the early years of boating Westwater Canyon, there were considerable angst and uncertainty about what to expect each trip. Over the past forty years we've experienced the highest and nearly the lowest water fluctuations, and we are becoming more familiar with the canyon's personality. With each fluctuation of cfs, it is a different river to experience; even so, we now know considerably more about the canyon to have a general idea about what to expect.

Beginning at the ranger station and launch site, boaters and kayakers are constantly reminded that the 500-foot massive Wingate sandstone cliff three miles away marks the passage into Westwater Canyon. At that point, Precambrian metamorphic rock made up of gneiss, schist, and granite emerges from beneath the much younger Wingate and Chinle formations and continues to rise until it reaches heights of 200 feet in the inner canyon; then, as gradually as it appears, it is buried again eleven miles downstream approaching Cottonwood Wash. The feelings and scenery that are experienced from beginning to end are indescribable, particularly for such a short canyon. Ellsworth Kolb described Westwater Canyon as a miniature Grand Canyon. He added, "This kind of water compared well with the rapids of the Colorado River and was entirely to our liking."[1] Those who are waiting on the long list to obtain a permit for the Grand Canyon may want to consider glimpses of the Grand in the meantime by boating Westwater Canyon.

Trying to describe the scenery of Westwater Canyon is impossible for me to do. As much as one might try, some of the beautiful places on earth are simply ineffable and may be partially because there is an experienced feeling associated with it. When I view a sunrise, sunset, clouds, Westwater Canyon, and other special places or scenes, a photo, painting, or other descriptions don't do them justice—they are simply images that attempt to remind us of them but cannot replace them.

Completing *Westwater Lost and Found: Expanded Edition*, I reflect on what motivated me to expand upon my first book. After all, author Roy Webb wrote in his forward notes for *Alone on the Colorado* that my first book *Westwater Lost and Found* (2004) was an "encyclopedic history."[2] Nothing more might have been expected? Shadows of unanswered questions troubled me after the first book was written. For instance, there had to be some supportive evidence about the story of outlaw brothers living in Outlaw Cave, which is found in the middle of Westwater Canyon, and there was evidence of a letter written by Dr. James E. Miller to Frederick S. Dellenbaugh about a historical boat trip with fellow dentist O. D. Babcock down the Grand River in 1897. Newspaper articles that followed their journey reported that they took a great many pictures.[3] If Miller's letter and photos could be located, they might document conclusively their experience in Westwater Canyon and the distance below Moab that they traveled on the Grand River.

Furthermore, after learning about the possibility of Westwater being a significant camp along the North Branch of the Old Spanish Trail (OST) and knowing that findings related to that location would be of historical significance motivated me to research the trail further and share my findings. This said, what motivated me most to continue researching Westwater and the Upper Colorado River was a desire to somehow share Ellsworth Kolb's unpublished manuscript about his exploits on the Grand and Gunnison Rivers in 1916. The manuscript by itself is too short to be published and needed to be couched with other related material in order to share it with the river community and historians.

Given that most historically important river journeys followed down the lengthier Green River to the confluence with the Colorado River and through the Grand Canyon, there are volumes of books written about that tributary. However, my interest in first researching Westwater included a desire to set the groundwork for research that would include the historical Grand / Upper Colorado River. After all, whoever managed to boat down the Grand River as far as Westwater could possibly be credited with the first descent of the Upper Colorado River? The establishment of small towns with newspapers that cropped up along the Grand River in the early 1880s became a primary source of identifying some of the successful boaters. Any individuals' reportedly attempting Westwater Canyon was newsworthy. In addition, the Colorado Riverbed cases that were held from 1929 to 1931 to establish navigability of Utah Rivers revealed other historic boaters who otherwise would have been forgotten. In 1869, attempting to compete with Major John Wesley Powell's expedition down the Green and Colorado Rivers, Captain Samuel Adams began an attempt that was ill planned and disastrous to replicate Powell starting on the Blue River at Breckenridge, Colorado. Struggling downriver for thirty-one days, Captain Adams had to quit because of the loss of all four of his poorly designed boats that he had begun the exploration with, then the loss of four rafts, and because all but two men had departed prior to completing Gore Canyon on the Grand River. Other than Samuel Adams's attempt, until Ellsworth Kolb arrived in 1916 there was no evidence of anyone else having attempted any significant portion of the Grand River.

Except for a few exceptions—such as Miller, Babcock, Kolb, Loper, Elmer Kane, Frank "Bunny" Barnes, Beppo Saeckler, and Harold H. Leich—knowingly or unknowingly challenging the whitewater on the Grand River, many of the tributaries that drain into it have more recent boating histories. With the arrival of world-class European kayakers—such as Walter Kirschbaum, Roger Paris, and Ulrich Martins—coming to Salida, Colorado, to compete in the FIBArk whitewater competition on the Arkansas River in the 1950s and 1960s, some remained and left their historical marks on the Green and Colorado Rivers and their tributaries. A book that documents many of the first descents on southwest rivers is *Rivers of the Southwest: A Boater's Guide to the Rivers of Colorado, New Mexico, Utah and Arizona*, by Fletcher Anderson and Ann Hopkinson.[4] Unfortunately, biographical information about these later historical kayakers is lacking.

One might say that Westwater's popularity began with recreational boaters. Most commercial outfitters shunned it until the mid-1960s. Of Westwater Canyon, recreational boater William Davis wrote, "This

FIGURE 7.1. Grand Canyon, with Jack Brennan, Don Harris, and Bert Loper scouting a rapid in 1939. Special Collections, J. Willard Marriott Library, University of Utah, Salt Lake City, Utah Albert Loper Collection, P11 36 n02.01.069.

is a canyon that many river men say that they are going to run one of these days, but generally never get around to."[5] A few exceptions were river men James P. "Jim" Rigg Jr., Laphene "Don" Harris, Ed Hudson, and possibly the Woman of the River, Georgie White. Perhaps Jim Rigg, co-owner of Mexican Hat Expeditions, ran his cataract boat through Westwater Canyon several times in the early 1950s to determine whether it was feasible for commercial river running. Thirty-seven years later, his partner J. Frank Wright offered his opinion about why their company and others didn't offer Westwater trips to their customers. He wrote that

> preparations and travel distances were extensive. The time spent in rapid running was relatively short and risky and ... the type of boat and other equipment that was being used at the time we were running rivers was not adequate, and ... prospective passengers were not

interested enough to pay for a trip of this kind when other runs were available that offered more for their money.[6]

Don Harris became familiar with Westwater Canyon when he and Jack Brennan did a water survey through it for the USGS in 1946. Thirteen years later, in 1959, they traded their cataract boats for two hard-hull outboard motorboats, and beginning at Glenwood Springs they piloted them downriver through Westwater Canyon. To earn a little extra money and gain more time on rivers, Don started a commercial river company. In an interview he spoke about his business: "We didn't get rich. We made extra dollars on the side. But we weren't doing it to get rich. The enjoyment was half the reason. And if we could make a few dollars on the side while doing something we enjoyed, why so much the better."[7]

Harris and Brennan commercially ran boats four additional times through Westwater Canyon, in 1962, 1964, 1966, and 1967. Wright's opinion may have proved correct about running Westwater trips, that they likely were not cost effective, and Harris and Brennan's business stopped running them. When Dee Holladay reported that either Holiday River Expeditions or Ron Smith's Grand Canyon River Expeditions may have been the first commercial companies to regularly run Westwater Canyon in 1966, he might not have been aware of the few infrequent trips made by Harris and Brennan. Until commercial river outfitters established locations nearer to Westwater, the distances and expenses for the short canyon jaunt were likely not cost effective. Westwater may not have been feasible and attractive in the early stages of commercial and private river running; however, recently *National Geographic* reported that it is "considered by many to be the nation's best overnight whitewater river trip."[8] The canyon can also be run in a single day.

If not for a rescue attempt of two men who overturned their boat in Cataract Canyon on the Colorado River, we might not have known that Georgie White may have boated Westwater Canyon in 1956. The *Times Independent* reported that it was hoped that her party might have rescued one of the men after departing from Grand Junction enroute to Hite.[9]

Ed Hudson appeared to be seeking historical recognition for boating the most miles on the Colorado River when he and Ed Nichols ran a converted river boat with a 65 HP engine from Glenwood Springs to Glen Canyon in 1955. Upon reaching Music Temple in Glen Canyon, he claimed on the register located there to have completed nearly 1,400 miles of the 1,450-mile Colorado River. Of the "canyon of mystery," he wrote on the register, "Westwater canyon was roaring fast and rough."[10] The contrast between Hudson's motorized accomplishment and those of Ellsworth Kolb's efforts in 1916 is glaring.

The late 1940s introduced more recreational boaters to the rivers and Westwater Canyon. Paul Geerlings led a group of University of Utah students through Westwater Canyon in an inflatable raft in 1950. That same year, another party of young celebrities—including Dick and Margaret Durrance, Florian and Beatrice Haemmerle, Theodore Steinway, and John Corley—unknowingly attempted the canyon, and after losing one of their two Bavarian Klepper foldboats wound up hiking through the canyon and exiting it near Big Hole. In 1951, avid whitewater enthusiasts from Chicago, William and his daughter Mildred Davis, successfully navigated Westwater Canyon. In a decision that was formulated while skiing in Aspen, inexperienced rafters Earl Eaton and Charles Bolte started on the Roaring Fork River, and after converging with the Colorado River they ran their motorized pontoon boat past Westwater, past Cataract Canyon, and through the Grand Canyon in 1954. John L. J. "Jerry" Hart and friends ran a ten-man neoprene raft through Westwater Canyon two consecutive days, July 4 and 5, 1958. John wrote the first-known article introducing Westwater Canyon to a larger audience for *Trail and Timberline* in 1964.[11] The popularity for private boating was expanding.

The seventeen miles of turbulent whitewater in Westwater Canyon inadvertently made a huge historical impact along the approximate 450 miles of the Grand / Upper Colorado River. Without the canyon obstructing river traffic, there likely would have been a significant gap in our knowledge of the boating history on this stretch. Westwater Canyon, once known as Hades Canyon, had a sinister reputation that prevented wary boaters from attempting it, and there were numerous reports of deaths of the unwary. In 1955, Ed Hudson wrote, "It was a canyon of mystery to us all we could get about it was that it was all bad, but all stories were vague and ominous."[12] Until the

1950s there were a handful of boaters who managed to make their way downriver through Westwater Canyon. Even until 1956, when Leslie "Les" Allen Jones with a group of friends ran Westwater Canyon to make a river scroll map for boaters, Kolb and Loper's 1916 transit continued to be recognized by locals at Cisco as the only successful individuals to survive the rapids.

Westwater Canyon not only hindered early river navigation but also was a barrier that caused historical land trails and surveys to bypass it. An exception was that the open valley separating Ruby and Westwater Canyons was an integral location to historical developments along the Grand River shores, where grass, wood, and water were critical to early trappers, surveys, and eventually settlers moving between Utah and Colorado Territories. The Salt Lake Wagon Road that was developed in 1858 by the military led by Colonel William Wing Loring improved a preexisting historical North Branch of the OST. Some settlers remained in the Westwater Valley, where a small settlement was established along the D&RGW Railroad tracks. Entering into Utah Territory from Colorado, there were only a few locations where traveling parties along the North Branch of the OST had access to the Grand River: Westwater and Cisco were the two primary locations in Grand County where water and grass could be obtained before travelers made the precarious journey across the Cisco Desert to converge with the main OST near Crescent Junction. The introduction of Frederick Kreutzfeldt's less-known journal notes (see appendix A) is an invaluable addition for the study of Captain Gunnison's 1853 central railroad survey.

Researching *Westwater Lost and Found: Expanded Edition* took me to places that I hadn't been before. I learned about the Old Trapper Trails, the North Branch of the OST, and the Black Canyon region. It also reintroduced me to a time in my youth when I was fascinated with mountain men and trappers. Except for my familiarity Kit Carson, I had not heard of many of the trappers who worked in the Southwest and am especially surprised that I did not know about Antoine Leroux.

On April 26, 2022, Westwater ranger Bob Brennan with his son Bobby drove Roy Christenson and me in his 4Runner on the preexisting back roads of Westwater Canyon to a location near Big Hole where Three Spanish Crosses are chiseled on a sandstone wall in an alcove

FIGURE 7.2. Author and Westwater ranger Bob Brennan at the Three Spanish Crosses inscription in Westwater Canyon, April 26, 2022. Photo by Bob Brennan.

that drains into Cottonwood Wash. I've wanted to view the crosses since 2019, when Bob first discovered them, and I wanted to understand where they were situated in the landscape. The crosses are much smaller than I envisioned them from the photo that Bob shared with me and fortunately they are not on a cliff face, where they could be easily seen and defaced or used as target practice by local cowboys and hunters. Throughout my research, I had not previously heard of the Three Spanish Crosses and can only guess what their significance is. Their likely dating and location would not appear to be related to the reported Spanish counterfeit gang who resided in Outlaw Cave in the 1880s.

After visiting the Three Spanish Crosses, we drove further southwest toward Big Hole and stopped our vehicle at a point that was a two-mile roundtrip hike to a Westwater Canyon overlook above Skull Rapid. Scheduled for a knee replacement later in the year, I was slow but anxious to see the canyon from on top again. Bob was most helpful, keeping close to me and allowing frequent stops along the way. At some point during what is mostly a walk with a few dips and inclines, Bob asked me a question that I rarely talked about over the past thirty-nine years since my mother died in Skull Rapid. It also took me back to a letter that I received in 1984 from a friend and former Westwater ranger, Karla VanderZanden, in response to a letter that I had written to her. She wrote, "As I'm sure you struggle with mixture of feelings for Westwater. I am also glad that you have retained your interest in the history of the canyon—I felt exceptionally bad that someone who loved Westwater so much should suffer there a personal tragedy."[13] Bob is possibly only the second person to genuinely ask about how I am able to love and study a canyon that caused me so much trauma, guilt, and heartbreak.

To a certain degree, I explained one of the reasons that I continued to research Westwater in the introduction to this book; however, there remain other reasons that are unclear to me. In the beginning of my professional river guiding career, as I delved into historical books on the Colorado and Green Rivers, the title of Frederick S. Dellenbaugh's book *Romance of the Colorado River* always impressed me. The title succinctly says a lot of how I feel about the rivers that I have traveled. Perhaps during all of these years performing research, I've simply had a romance with Westwater and the Upper Colorado River.

APPENDIX A

FREDERICK KREUTZFELDT (CREUTZFELDT)— PARTIAL JOURNAL NOTES FROM 1853

The existence of Frederick Kreutzfeldt's (Creutzfeldt's) original journal from 1853 is mostly unknown. There are four different copies of his journal at the Smithsonian Institution Archives covering the period of June 18 to October 23, 1853. Surprisingly, the handwritten German version goes only to October 12, 1853. On October 26, 1853, Frederick Kreutzfeldt, Captain John W. Gunnison, and six other members of their survey party were killed by Pahvant Utes along the Sevier River in Utah Territory.

Although this appendix of Kreutzfeldt's journal from September 17 to October 1, 1853, is included to highlight a little-known third source of biographical information regarding Captain John W. Gunnison's proposed central route transcontinental railroad survey along the thirty-eighth and thirty-ninth parallel to the Pacific Ocean, it also unintentionally highlights the author's disdain for the captain. The provided journal notes include parts of the North Branch of the Old Spanish Trail (OST) as far as the Westwater region.

Little has been written about German botanist Frederick Kreutzfeldt. One source claims he was a gardener turned botanist from St. Louis, Missouri. He is

https://doi.org/10.7330/9781646425457.c008

described as "being tall, strong, active man, weighing 180 or 190 pounds."[1] His name, under the spelling of Creutzfeldt, first appears as the botanist with Colonel John C. Frémont's ill-advised initial attempt to perform a railroad survey in the winter of 1848–1849 that would have generally followed the same route as Gunnison. Kreutzfeldt probably would have remained anonymous along with most of the thirty-three men who accompanied Colonel Frémont, except that he volunteered with trapper and guide "Old Bill" Williams, Tom Breckinridge, and Henry King to leave the stranded party at Camp Hope and travel ahead to the nearest New Mexico settlement to obtain relief.

Frémont and his party were warned several times that there was already more snow than usual in the mountains, and a severe winter was predicted as the men worked their way from Bent's Fort to the foot of the Rocky Mountains. Frémont wrote to his father-in-law, Senator Thomas Hart Benton, "Still, I am in nowise discouraged by the prospect, and believe that we shall succeed in forcing our way across."[2] When the survey entered the Rocky Mountains on November 26, 1848, it had 120 mules carrying instruments and supplies. Twenty-four days later, only 59 famished mules remained; the heavy snow blanketed the ground and vegetation and to survive the mules ate blankets, ropes, pads on saddle bags, and eventually the hair off their bodies, their manes, and tails. The remaining mules became frozen dinners for the men, who were not faring much better, enduring heavy snows, winds, freezing temperatures, and frostbite.

On December 26, 1848, Henry King led the small party of Williams, Breckinridge, and Kreutzfeldt in the deep snow and headed toward the Rio Grande River and settlements to obtain relief. Within three days the party hadn't advanced far, and they had already exhausted all of their food supplies. They were slowed down by frostbitten feet, hunger, and fatigue. Replacing their boots with blankets that they wrapped around their feet to walk, the men roasted their leather shoes and belts and subsisted on them for several days. With the heavy snows, game was sparse and they only managed to shoot a hawk. Fortunately, they found the carcass of a dead otter on the ice next to the river and devoured it as the only other sources of food.

Eventually, to avoid following a large bend in the river and possibly confronting hostile Utes, the party chose a fifteen-mile shortcut over barren land, where the men were exposed to the elements without any shelter or wood to make a fire. At some point near the end of the trek as they neared the river, King sat down to rest and directed the three men to continue ahead to make camp. Williams,

Breckinridge, and Kreutzfeldt continued walking and reached the river, where there was wood to make a fire and camp. After the three men built a fire to get warm, Kreutzfeldt insisted on returning to where they had left King to help him get to camp and instead found him dead. According to several sources, "The shock affected his mind." Breckinridge wrote,

> Kreutzfeldt now became very despondent. His mind seemed to dwell upon the poor fellow's death. When he had approached King he thought the latter was asleep, and was much startled at finding his old companion dead. I could see that the shock was affecting his mind. He could talk of nothing else.[3]

The following morning the remaining members moved down the river, and by evening "Kreutzfeldt played out entirely, and lying down refused to go further."[4] Williams and Breckinridge were reluctant to leave him but had no choice for their own survival. Fortunately for Kreutzfeldt, not far from where the two men planned to leave him, Breckinridge shot and killed a deer. They returned with the fresh meat, which revived Kreutzfeldt, and between the three of them they feasted on the deer meat for two days before they were located by Frémont, who also sought help for his stranded men. Frémont rescued the three men seventeen days after they had left Camp Hope. Breckinridge claimed to have shot the deer that saved their lives; however, some members of the main party alluded to having cannibalized King's body. After he was rescued, Kreutzfeldt continued with Frémont and a number of other survivors, taking an alternate route on the lower Spanish Trail along the Gila River to California in 1849.

Kreutzfeldt doesn't appear again until he signed on as botanist for Captain John W. Gunnison in 1853. It is unclear where Kreutzfeldt's animosity for Gunnison is derived from unless it possibly developed from his previous experience working with Colonel John C. Frémont. We don't know how Frémont may have reacted to the men if he suspected Kreutzfeldt and the other two of cannibalism. He allowed Kreutzfeldt to continue with him to California; however, in a letter to John Torrey dated March 28, 1850, Frémont wrote of an incident in which he may have revealed his feelings toward him: "I had collected many fine plants along the Gila and in Sonora but the man to whom I entrusted their collection although professing to be a botanist, permitted them to get wet repeatedly and many are ruined & the rest he did not even label."[5]

Because there is no known journal that he kept for the 1848–1849 expedition, we can only base such an assumption from what has been written by others.

There were reported conflicts between Frémont and his guide, "Old Bill" Williams, especially as the severe weather hit the party hard and Williams suggested they travel a more southerly route, contrary to the object of the survey. Kreutzfeldt might have had a conflict for his safety between his superior's agendas and the experienced guides they hired. He spent considerable time with "Old Bill" Williams during the Frémont Expedition, and he appeared to have complete confidence in Antoine Leroux during the Gunnison survey. He also harbored hostility toward Indigenous people, particularly Utes, when they traded with Captain Gunnison. With Kreutzfeldt on the Frémont Expedition were the three Kern brothers—Dr. Benjamin J. Kern (1818–1849) and artists and topographers Richard H. Kern (1821–1853) and Edward M. Kern (1823–1863)—who became embittered with Colonel Frémont and laid the blame for the failed expedition on him. Could their criticisms of Frémont have affected Kreutzfeldt's opinion of him? During the spring of 1849, "Old Bill" Williams and Dr. Edward M. Kern returned to the mountains with a small party to retrieve items that were cached by the Frémont Expedition, and were killed by Utes. Richard Kern accompanied the Gunnison survey and was killed with Captain Gunnison, Kreutzfeldt, and five others.

FREDERICK KREUTZFELDT'S JOURNAL ENTRIES FROM SEPTEMBER 17 TO OCTOBER 1, 1853

September 17, 1853. A very pretty journey is made to day, the Campagre down, over desolated, waste plateau to the Grand river,[6] which though wide has here a shallow bed; we cross it, leave behind us good grass water and wood, travel on in dreadful deserts till late in the night, and encamp without pasture, water, wood, supper and c. in beautiful stone fragments pert cactus peeping out in order to disturb also the sleep of the tired. All this is a natural consequence of *Rohrle's* energetic arrangements;[7] LaRoux had advised him to encamp near the river, because the nearest water is 30 m. distant.

Weather good but very windy. On account of the many cavities and the heavy sandy and stony soil we do not make more than 20 m. In the morning we had been detained till 10 o'cl., by nearly 100 Indians, who had surrounded our camp last night, [and] had to get their presents from our coward who soils his pants at their sight. He allows the coppy dogs all liberties, which they use with impudence, looking all over, molesting by begging and finding the most convenient opportunity to propagate their lice. In the sandy soil are found: Cactus, as yesterday, Oenothera, Erigonum inflatum and much crippled [Artemisia] Messemb. and Lenos. On the river Pop. canad. is growing and equistum in abundance. Our new constructed cart pole is like a see-saw either above the heads of the mules or in the ground [and] has to be unpacked and changed repeatedly and is finally balanced by the captain's own sublime body.

September 18. Though it is Sunday to day and after the opinion of our resurrectionists a criminal offense to travel, still we are obliged to obey in preference the command of the grumbling stomach and hungry and thirsty with ditto mules to set out and look for better luck. We travel along our Saharah-soil for 8 ½ miles, find, what we badly needed water, grass and wood and encamp of course glad enough to get something warm in the stomach having been deprived for 30 hours. The weather is good. In the East of us is the range of the Elk mountains, cut off abruptly and showing nothing but barren yellowish sides, consisting of sand stone, slate, gypsum and sandy soil. In the West are similar mountains but smaller.

September 19. Having been visited again by a couple of filthy Indians, we set out and reach soon the Grand river (Gunnison) again, cross a small tributary creek and continue our journey on the right bank through miserable sand-hills. In the afternoon these change into a flat desolate valley, where we, after 13 m. travelling meet a very considerable branch of the Gr. River, even larger than the river itself, called Bon Carre or Blue River,[8] which we traverse with great difficulties and then encamp between Indians: The water in the Gr. River is of a greenish color, but in this branch clear and beautiful. In the bed of the river are some places good wood of Canad. Pop. In the desert only poor Sage and Lenosyrus. Weather clear, quiet and hot; even mosquitoes visible on the river.

September 20. We follow on Indian path this river which soon joins the Gr. River and forms a considerable stream, in width equal to the Arkansas river, but with a changeable bed now deep and then running over flat stones in nearly W. direction. There must also be plenty of fish in it, since our men succeed in catching specimens of 1 ½-2 lb, but of same kind as have been observed before. The valley of the river, here about 4 m. wide is a hard loamy soil, producing only poorly Art. Lenosyr. Messembryanth and a few Opun phaecantha. But immediately on the banks are growing: willows and Canad. poplar trees, the latter of considerable size. Of birds are in this region: Raven, ground owls, Magpie, field sparrows, Sky and field larks, starling, falcons, Turkey buzzards and a few hawks, but they are all sparse. In an unmeasurable height we observe a flock of white cranes; we see also sometimes Sand-hill-Cranes but scared and not reachable. The Elk meat obtained from the Indians is extremely fat and has the taste of roasted greased boots.[9] The Old Dog captain traded for two more ponies, for himself of course; he had some difficulties with the Doctor to day the consequence of which only God knows. The weather clear, quiet and hot, therm. 90°. Our journey is somewhat over 9 m. and we have to encamp here at the advise of the Indians, because here the grass is good, and further down nothing to be found, as they say.

September 21. Having followed the valley of the river for 6–7 miles, we leave the river, since it is running in S. W. through canyons, and make our way through a Western Bottom where after a march of 14 m. we find a Creek with pasture and some driftwood. We encamp on this brook, called Salt Creek on account of its salty water. We have to do our cooking with water taken along from the Grand river. The whole region, valley and mountain, is a desert, producing nothing but poor Art. And Messemb.; the earth has in many places exudations of saltpeter that give a whiteness to the ground reflected by the sun and detrimental to eyes and lips. I find on the Salt Creek a single specimen of echino cactus spiralis (?), which would indicate a mild winter. Weather fine, but a little too hot, after the mountain temperature; the nights are cold. Thermometer in day time 90°, in the morning 40°.

September 22. We go on to day senselessly in a desolate waste land without an idea, where to get water or grass, in all directions of the compass, and finally stop in this Arabia late in the dark night, on a Creek with some little water trickling in, but for its salty and bitter taste unpalatable. Men and beasts are suffering dreadfully. One wagon is left behind, the mules fatigued to death being unable to go on. All this because of our great genius whom La Roux instructed not to procede [sic] with our journey before he explored the route for some days. We have of course nothing to eat but bacon and bread; this devil lives only for himself, uses ham, molasses, pickels, fresh butter, sardels and so on for himself and has the audacity to call it private property wereas we have to eat bread + bacon to keep body and soul together. La Roux having searched for us half the day and having used up his munition in signaling us to follow him, arrives in the evening very angry about Röhrles kind of management, and frankly pronouncing his opinion. The weather is hot to nearly 90°; in the morning 32°. We make about 22 miles.

At the right hand side or towards N. the Buck Mountains extend; in S.W. direction two isolated high mountain ridges, called by La Roux: Salt mountains; and in front of the chain of mountains from which the Green River flows.

September 23. Forced to refresh our mules, tired to death and ourselves, we are compelled to remain here, in a distance of 5–6 m. from the river in deep barren sand, seasoned with a little Sage, rattlesnakes, and scorpions; we drive the animals to the water and let them graze in the bottom lands where they find plenty of grass. La Roux and the captain are arguing all day long; La Roux's critic not too flattering; besides called him a picayune man but in the afternoon the captain gets his instructions, how to come out of this hell; since La Roux intends leaving us to morrow. How we will fare only Lucifer & company know. When this dog of a captain takes over who is too cowardly to make advance explorations of our route. On some of these sandhills Juniperus is growing. Ephedra, some dry grass, sage and Griswood. This region is described by the guide as god forsaken hot in summertime; and we have even now the best proofs of it; we have to day 91° of heat, and after a cold night the thermometer may be on the freezing point. The sky is cloudless and quiet. Did write a letter to Washington and then reposed. Some of the soldiers had gone to the river and had caught great many fishes, but all of one sort, called Pikerell by Sancho Pansa.

September 24. We remain here for the animals sake, they being much exhausted; we go to the river for fishing.

September 25. We spend the Sunday in the same way; our journey before us being long; fatiguing and without good water and grass. La

Roux left us yesterday. We had hot, clear and fine weather yesterday, but today thunderstorm, rain and cold air are alternating.

September 26. Being delayed by the driving in of the mules from the river, we set out pretty late and travel through barren sandy loam soil with nearly no vegetation, besides Cactus, Art, and on some places a little Bůlten Grass. We make over 16 m. and encamp after sunset on the Springs, a small creek with a little very dirty but sweet fresh water, and some poor grass on the hill. Heat and cold, thunderstorm and rain alternate in quick succession all the day, certainly a consequence of the equinox because the quality of the soil, partly pretty good, indicates good vegetation were it not for the prevailing drought in general. Our course for the day is mostly to the W., directed to the head waters of the Green River on the Western mountain side, where the Spanish trail is said to be running; we shall have to follow this trail to the Little Salt Lake.

September 27. Thunderstorm and vehement showers all the night and continue this morning, not until about 10 o'clock do we find a clear moment to harness the animals. But the returning thunderstorms soften the ground and make even the smallest waterrun swell; we encamp therefore, after a journey of 5 m. in the mud and find a little dry grass. Very little Art. is sufficient to make some coffee with pool water; dripping with rain and dirt and half benumbed with cold, our bowels find it very salutary.

September 28. All the night thunderstorm and rain; with sun rising the sky becomes clear and remains so all the day. We set out as soon as possible and find the travelling very fatiguing the ground in these hills being much loosened by the rain. Towards noon the country becomes more level, and the sun has graciously & sufficiently dried up the ground to enable us to proceed a little farther. The ground is as before a miserable desert and the mountains in sight bare and barren, but in Southern direction shaped in interesting forms. First appear in mighty height two prominent mountain ridges in beautiful formation, their summits covered with snow and looking quite winter-like. At their feet smaller chains are giving the appearance of Obelisks, Pyramids, Ruins of castels [castles] in all variations but with no trace of vegetation; they consist mostly of slate and sandstone. We live in the hope to see the Green R. soon, but after 16 m. travelling not a trace of it is to be seen; all is a continuation of the desert in which we might probably have lost all our animals, if not the rain had provided us with water, which though dirty, was drinkable, for nothing can be found between the so called Springs and the Green River. Our rascal captain calls it the commencing of the rainy season.

September 29. Continuing our journey in the S. direction over triste hills and valleys, we reach at noon the so called Spanish trail, which coming from the foot of the Salt mountains takes its course towards N.W. We follow the path hoping either to reach or to see the Green River; but disappointed in both we have nothing before us but broken hills and waste valleys and encamp with little dry grass and pool-water; small crippled Griswood merely sufficient to make some coffee. Of flowers and plants no trace. Weather clear and fine, even hot.

September 30. Having dragged along for 14 m. in this abject land following the Sp. trail, we reach at last the Green River so much longed for; we try to rod it, but find it too deep and sandy. The river is considerable; probably a couple 100 yards wide, rapid and as dirty as it could possibly be. On its banks we find sufficient grass, Cottonwood and willows, besides now and then a Helianthus, Erigonum, Aster, Solidago and small shrubs of Fremontia. I found in the desert a half grown specimen of Mammillaria cornifera, and Op. megacantha and phaeacantha, Rattlesnakes, crows, scorpions and some beetles are the other inhabitants of this sad country. Of prairie dogs numerous habitations are seen, but the animal itself is nowhere visible. The soil is clay mixed with sand and all over covered with small sand-flint and quartz stones between which quantities of gypsum are shining through, brilliant as diamonds. A few filthy Indians, roving about near us, come to visit us in the evening, but they do not carry anything to swap with. The weather in the night: thunderstorm and rain; in the day clear and good, alternately warm and cold.

October 1, 1853. Yesterday evening some Indians came across the river and did show us a ford, where we after some mendings of the road and the raising of our things in the wagon, easily traversed the river and encamped on the right bank, where our animals might become refreshed by the existing good grass. The river is pretty well overgrown with Cotton-wood, willows and Sumach, has extraordinary dirty water and a nearly S. course. Weather beautiful.

APPENDIX B

WESTWATER CAMP AND WATER STOP CHRONOLOGY

Based on their research William Lyman "Bill" Chenoweth and Lloyd M. Pierson identified a number of parties who camped or stopped at Westwater. A chronology of them follows, including any detailed descriptions they left and the mileage (if they provided it) they measured from the Grand River Crossing at Grand Junction to Westwater camp.[1] Discrepancies in the mileage may be the result of using different methods to make the measurements. Although listed, the other parties are speculative, as there are fewer historical records to go by.[2]

1848, June 4 or 5, Lieutenant George D. Brewerton and Kit Carson. It is uncertain which of the OST routes were taken. Brewerton lost his notes while crossing either the Green or Grand River. Because Kit Carson first stopped at his home in Taos, it seems likely that they would have traveled the North Branch before proceeding to Santa Fe. Chenoweth speculated that they camped at Westwater on one of the provided dates.[3]

https://doi.org/10.7330/9781646425457.c009

1853, July 22/23 (46 miles), Lieutenant Edward F. Beale. According to the journal kept by Lieutenant Beale's cousin Gwinn Harris Heap, their party "encamped late at night on the Grand River." The only description he gave of Westwater camp that night involved the mosquitos.[4] The next morning after following near the Grand River he wrote,

> at 10 A.M. rested for the last time on its banks. The scenery here was picturesque. On our side, the stream was overhung by high cliffs of dazzlingly white sandstone, against which it dashed with violence; whilst on the left shore were extensive meadows, ornamented with numerous clusters of trees.[5]

1853, September 22–26 (46.22 miles), Captain John W. Gunnison. Leroux was not with Captain Gunnison's railroad survey team when they stopped late at night to make a miserable camp on the desert at Bitter Water (Westwater) Creek, about four miles shy of Westwater.[6] Either on September 17 or 18, Leroux, because of a previous commitment with Lieutenant Whipple, took several party members with him in advance of the survey team to scout a route to the Main OST and to instruct them on how to reach it. Because there was a lack of water for approximately thirty miles, Leroux instructed Captain Gunnison to remain camped near the Grand (Gunnison) River until he returned. The botanist for the survey, Frederick Kreutzfeldt (Creutzfeldt), was not pleased when Captain Gunnison continued on his own without a guide, and he complained frequently about their camps and the lack of pasture, water, and wood.[7]

Leroux may have given the party instructions to go as far as Salt Creek, where Beckwith wrote, "We left Salt creek without a guide"[8]; however, beyond that it was all guess work to them. He continued,

> We determined, therefore to keep up the broad, roaming valley between Roan mountain on our right, and the cānon bluffs of the river on our left. The day was very hot and oppressive, and the soil friable, with the usual amount of sage and an increase of cacti; with numerous gullies to cut and fill. We found no point at which we could approach the river until too late an hour in the afternoon to reach it with our train, for it was impossible to travel at night with wagons without a road.[9]

Gunnison decided to camp where there was a small "intermitting creek of bitter water," Westwater Creek.[10] Beckwith wrote that many of their animals gave out and some didn't make it to camp that night. Kreutzfeldt wrote in his journal for September 22, 1853,

> We go on to day senseless in a desolate waste land without an idea, where to get water or grass, in all directions of the compass, and make finally halt in this Arabia late in the dark night, on a Creek with some little water trickling in, but for its salty and bitter taste disgustful.[11]

Further criticizing Captain Gunnison, Kreutzfeldt wrote, "After La Roux's order we should not continue our journey before he explored the route for some days."[12] Leroux located the party that evening and was "very angry" with Gunnison apparently for disobeying his instructions to wait for him to return.

When Chenoweth concluded in his writings that Gunnison made a camp at Westwater, he was unaware that German botanist Frederick Kreutzfeldt kept a journal (see appendix A for part of Kreutzfeldt's 1853 journal). In it Kreutzfeldt confirms what most historians believe: that the Gunnison party's primary camp was a few miles inland from the Grand River at Westwater. With only Beckwith's description to rely on, Chenoweth believed that they later moved their camp to the Grand River at Westwater where there was plenty water, wood, and grass. Beckwith wrote,

> We were here about four miles from the river, which, by following the ravine cut through the cañon wall by the creek, was easily reached by horseback, and only obstructed for wagons by a dry channel cut deep in the clay, at a narrow bottom of fine grass two or three miles in length, with shady groves of cotton-wood on the banks of the stream. The red sandstone cañon walls are nearly vertical, and two hundred feet high; beyond which smaller ledges rise above each other, terrace-like, for some miles towards Salt (La Sal) mountains, which bears south from our camp, some twenty miles beyond the river. The cañon narrows to the width of the river below the groves of cotton-wood.[13]

With the party's discovery of Westwater, the exhausted mules were herded to the Grand River to regain their strength. They remained there for three days. In the meantime, the members of the survey party that remained in camp were miserable, while others decided to "go to the river for fishing."[14]

Upon fulfilling his commitment and instructing Captain Gunnison on how to get to the main OST, Leroux left the Gunnison survey party on September 24 and returned to Taos.

Between 1853 and 1854, Colonel John Charles Frémont privately funded the fifth and final expedition. No record remains of camps and distances traveled during the winter expedition. Estimates are that Frémont's party arrived in Utah Territory sometime the first week of January 1854. Solomon Nunes Carvalho was an artist and produced daguerreotype pictures for the expedition; he also provided the only information. He indicated several times that the group's members generally followed the trail left by Beale and Gunnison. Regarding the distance between the Grand and Green Rivers, he wrote, "At the season that we crossed, there was no water between the two rivers, a distance of about forty miles."[15] This remark implies that they followed Beale's route through Grand County and left the Colorado River at Cisco.

1858, August 12–15 (42 miles), Colonel William Wing Loring: Colonel Loring's party camped at Westwater for three days to upgrade the road ahead of them. His description for Westwater is that "the valley we are in is some six miles in length and two or three in width, surrounded on all sides by high mural precipices. Soil good and covered with large cottonwood trees and sage bush, grass abundant and numerous fish in the river."[16]

Second Lieutenant John Van Deusen Du Bois also kept a journal, and his entry for August 12 reads,

> Left the river today & passing around a hill which comes to the water's edge in a bluff rocky bank we came to the river again. This camp is a pretty good one and as the road in advance is perfectly impractical we will be forced to remain here at least a day to dig a road of nearly a mile from the side of a hill. Fine trout are caught daily, but no deer or game of any kind seen. The men are in good health.[17]

In his next entry, August 15, he wrote, "We remained in our last camp two days; working parties of seventy men were digging from early daylight until darkness put a stop to their toil. Our animals needed the rest, however, & our toil is only begun."[18]

1860, June 24, Colonel Edward R. S. Canby. An important contributor to further establishing the Salt Lake Wagon Road came from Colonel E. R. S. Canby. In 1860, when D. C. Collier Esq. and the fifteen remaining Denver prospectors applied for assistance from the quartermaster at Fort Garland, they met Colonel Canby, who had just recently arrived from Camp Floyd, Utah, on July 28, 1860.[19] Similar to Colonel Loring two years earlier, Colonel Canby was commanded to go from Camp Floyd to Fort Garland, where he was ordered to contend with hostile Navajos. His command was additionally assigned to make road repairs along the way and investigate whether a route to Santa Fe via the Dolores River was shorter than the "Loring Trail" and practical for development. His command included the Fifth Infantry and companies A, F, and H of the Tenth Infantry.

Unfortunately, the records detailing Colonel Canby's work, camps, and mileage are lacking. Lloyd Pierson, in an article titled "The Salt Lake Wagon Road Across Grand County," appears to be the first to recognize Colonel Canby and his infantry's contribution to improving the Loring Trail aka Salt Lake Wagon Road.[20] Pierson places Colonel Canby at Westwater camp on June 24, 1860, where he waited for his lead scout Dan Jones, who was accompanied by a "sergeant and Indian," to scout the road ahead to the Grand River Crossing.[21] Being the only guide knowledgeable of the area, Jones, upon his return, was reassigned to Lieutenant Donald C. Stith and the Fifth Infantry to investigate the Dolores River as a possible shorter route to Santa Fe. Colonel Canby then proceeded to Fort Garland without his guide.[22]

1876 (50 miles), Henry Gannett of the F. V. Hayden Geological and Geographical Survey of 1875. Because Gannett's party was attacked by Utes while surveying near the La Sal Mountains in 1875, their work in eastern Utah and the Salt Lake Wagon Road was completed the following year. Gannett's 1875 *Map of Western Colorado and Part of Utah* brought attention to the Salt Lake Wagon Road through northern Grand County and western Colorado.[23] Gannett did not list dates but instead assigned numbers to stations or camps where he conducted his work; Westwater was assigned number 72. Of the area he wrote in the report,

"From the ford (Grand River Crossing) the road follows the Grand pretty closely for 20 miles" to Salt Creek.[24] After Salt Creek, he reported, the road continued for thirty miles bypassing Ruby Canyon before it again reached the Grand River. He observed,

> Where the river can be reached there is plenty of wood and a mile or thereabouts from it good grass, but little or none at the river. Then there is another drive of 15 miles before the river can again be reached (Cisco), and here wood and grass are both scarce. At this point the main wagon-road finally leaves the Grand, striking off in a course generally west toward the Green River.[25]

Gannett also wrote that he "examined this road from Ouray nearly to the crossing of the Green River."[26]

Two years later, in 1878, Rollen J. Reeves while surveying the Colorado and Utah Territory border mentioned one of two roads he encountered:

> The only other road we encountered was what is known as the old Salt Lake wagon road. This is in better condition, has been considerably travelled and worked. It was first built by US Troops, many years ago, and has been much used since. This road is the main thoroughfare between Colorado and Utah.[27]

APPENDIX C

DR. JAMES E. MILLER'S LETTER TO FREDERICK S. DELLENBAUGH, NOVEMBER 2, 1906

When Colorado River historian Frederick S. Dellenbaugh completed his comprehensive book The Romance of the Colorado River *in 1902, unbeknownst to him he left out a boating party of two dentists who claimed to have traveled a significant part of the Grand and Colorado River in 1897. On November 2, 1906, Dellenbaugh received the following letter from Dr. James E. Miller, which described a boating excursion him and a fellow dentist, Dr. O. D. Babcock, made in the summer of 1897.*

Yampa, Colo 11/2/06
F. S. Dellenbaugh

I have been reading an account of your trip down the Colo River as described in your book "*Romance of the Colo.*" Judging from the credit you have given to so many who have had more or less experience on the river, I regret that you never heard of the experience of a Dr. O. D. Babcock and myself, in the summer of 1897. I believe you would of been glad to have incorporated part of our run in your work. I do not quite understand why Major Powell did not mention it to you as he was acquainted with many of the features of the trip. He spent nearly all of one day at my office in Glenwood Springs, talking over the river & looking over the negatives I made of such points that interested me. He was to give an illustrated lecture at the Colorado Hotel, that evening on the lower river, but after talking to me he changed the program somewhat and illustrated the trip we made from Glenwood down.

Dr. Babcock and self made our own boat at Glenwood, the point of departure, where at least 500 people witnessed the start—and the trip was reported in some of the Chgo. & NY daily's and in one or two magazines.

In all probability such a trip was never before undertaken for such a purpose, viz.—to [cause] two men of stomach troubles we one day decided to quit work, pitched up a half dollar in the office to decide whether we were going into the hills, or down the river. The River trip won and in an hour we had rented a carpenter shop & tools and the boat was under construction before evening. It was 18 ft. long 3 ½ foot beam with a water tight compartment in either end. We do not know how far down we went. We ran across a cowman, who came down to the river for water, he told us that we were then in what was known as Buckskin Canyon, Major Powell recognized many of the places. I do not see how Mr. Brown in your account could of found the Cataract Canyon so disastrous. We never stopped to even look the thing over but went right through and I have a number of negatives in my possession to prove it.

We nearly lost our boat about 150 miles below the mouth of the Green, barely saving our lives, over 50 negatives were ruined but we didn't kick for reasons you would understand. We came to one place in the Colorado that was strenuous for a moment, coming around a short bend. The river seemed to divide into two channels, one shooting under an overhanging rock and the other going over a fall of three or four feet. There not being room enough under the rock for boat and selves, we chose the falls. You know how quickly one has to decide some things, well, the water going over the falls had excavated a considerable hole, I was steering, my companion jumped back & sat down between my feet to lighten up the bow, but her stern went into the [bar] & for a moment it was a toss up whether we were going end over end or not but we came out all right. We visited a number of cliff ruins, also found a number of arrow heads & two broken spear heads in the Arroyos on top. But you know so much more about all this than I do that I will not tire you if I haven't already.

I made one other trip long ago from Winnipeg to the James Bay in a Birch Back Canoe. I believe my experience on that trip made the Colo. River trip much safer. One claim I contend for is, that to run the Rapids with safety one should always have the boat going faster than the current. I learned this from Indians who [went] at it daily. Dr. Babcock & self use to make the boat spin when we saw the white water ahead I had a good [aim] & could generally put the boat through alright but not always.

I am here only temporarily going to West Palm Beach Fla. in few days for the winter. If you would come to see some of the pictures I will print a few for you. I am very glad to have read your account Mr. Dellenbaugh and would like to swap yarns with you if we ever meet.

Yours very truly,
Dr J. E. Miller

A note written by Frederick S. Dellenbaugh was included with the letter. It read:

Received Nov. 27th 1906
Wrote him for details.

The point 150 miles below the mouth of the Green where he had his only danger is smooth river—no rapids worth mentioning—at least compared with Cataract Canyon which he found so easy. FSD

APPENDIX D

ROBERT BREWSTER STANTON'S LETTER TO DR. JAMES E. MILLER, MAY 11, 1909

Too late to include James E. Miller's account of the 1897 excursion down the Grand and Colorado Rivers in his own book, The Romance of the Colorado River, *Dellenbaugh gave a copy of the letter to fellow historian Robert Brewster Stanton. At the time, Stanton was gathering historical information for his own comprehensive Colorado and Green River history that he was writing. Like Dellenbaugh, Stanton questioned the distance Miller and Babcock traveled and the ease with which they reported getting through Cataract Canyon. A handwritten note that is not entirely legible is included with the letter and appears to read "Letter returned."*

May 11th, 1909.

Dr. J. E. Miller,
Yampa, Colorado.
Dear Sir:

Mr. F. S. Dellenbaugh has handed me your letter of November 21st., 1906, in regard to your trip on the Colorado River with Dr. O. B. [sic].

https://doi.org/10.7330/9781646425457.c011

Babcock in 1897. As I am writing a more complete history of the navigation of that river I should like some further information from you and Dr. Babcock.

Taking up what you say in your letter

1st. Can you give exact date of your starting?

2nd. In what magazines—dates, etc was the account of your trip published?

3rd. You say you do not know how far you [went] below Glenwood Springs, but were told by a cowman you were in Buckskin Canon. Did you go out from there? And what <u>settlement</u> did you reach first after leaving the river?

4th. You speak of going through Cataract Canon with great ease and coming to grief "150 miles below the <u>mouth of the Green</u>." Can you tell me what canon you were in at that time?

As I made a railroad survey down the Colorado in 1889–90[.] I am familiar with the whole distance, and may be [able] to locate just where you went.

Sincerely yours,
Rob B., Stanton

APPENDIX E

ELLSWORTH L. KOLB'S NEWSPAPER ACCOUNTING OF SECTION THREE OF BLACK CANYON OF THE GUNNISON RIVER

Whether it is personal histories, diaries, journals, or letters, personal sources are important for documenting events. Factual or not, they tell a story from the author's perspective and they can generally provide the best details of an event. Newspapers are invaluable to discover leads to research, dates, and historical settings; even so, media sources can be exaggerated or biased. It was a newspaper article that denigrated Bert Loper for not joining Russell and Monett's boat journey through the Grand Canyon in 1907. The article only gave one side of the story of why he didn't continue downriver with Russell and Monett. Loper was left to address his reasons without the help of the media.

    Ellsworth Kolb expressed his concerns about newspaper reporting in the Montrose Daily Press *and said that he didn't like how they "exaggerated his stories and refused to tell the truth." Because of this view, he was reluctant to reveal any details of his experiences to them. He said further, "It is a relief to read an article which clings to unexaggerated facts and gives the essentials of interest to the people as they really are."*[1]

The article continues,

> to try and get Mr. Kolb to explain any of the hazards of the Canyon. He always keeps so far within conservatism in his own accounts which can be extracted from him, that a newspaper man realizes he will have to use his own imagination because Kolb will not boast of his experiences, nor will he describe them in such a way that a person feels there is anything extraordinary about the different stunts he has pulled off in the Canyon.[2]

To satisfy Kolb's qualms about the press, the Montrose Daily Press *conceded and allowed Kolb to write his own story for their edition reporting him and Loper's attempt at boating Section Three below the Gunnison Tunnel on October 26, 1916.*[3]

Kolb And Loper Have Thrilling Ride Down The Gunnison River (By Ellsworth Kolb)

The start was made Friday, October 13, at noon, at the tunnel. Reached great rocks and rapids which can be seen from near top of tunnel road. Great flat rocks 30 feet above the river, a 10 or 12 foot fall. Took boat up the rocks and camped. Next morning dropt boat into rapid and lined it thru narrow channel. Overlooked the fact that one third of river entered passage and most of water went under one rock. The boat caught on the rock in the channel and stern swung under side of rock. We worked all day with poles and ropes but failed to budge the boat. Sunday I climbed out thru slide and reached tunnel road and made my way to the tunnel. I secured some old drills and giant powder from the watchman,[4] W. Tupper, and retraced the route.

The next day Loper drilled the rock in the channel and dynamited the boulder. Ropes were stretched across the river, attached to the boat and an effort was made to pull it loose with a very small block and tackle. We were not successful this day but the boat was finally dragged loose after being held by the river for four days. We repaired the broken boards with a stave from a beer keg for a rib, the canvass being stuck with paint on the boards and all covered with tin from a cracker box.

We resumed the trip Wednesday morning at eight o'clock. Below the old State Heading, a sheer wall on each side with numerous rapids, makes difficult work, but the rapids were negotiated without mishap. We considered one-half mile from [each] day a good day's work.

Saturday, October 21, we reached Torrance [Torrence] falls. This afternoon Mr. Loper's boat received a similar break to the other one, while being lined or roped thru channel. Thirty minutes later Loper fell and injured his back. At present the attending physician is unable to say whether he has a broken rib or not. I acted as nurse all night, applying hot water bottle, the only remedy carried.

Things looked blue about this time. There was no chance to climb out on the north side, where we were camped. The most violent cascade of the series beside camp, and both escapes cut off with sheer walls. I was alone and unable to handle the 300 pound boats over the great boulders. We only carried sufficient provisions to reach Red Rock canyon. The four day delay had cut deeply into our supply.

On Sunday, Octoer 22, Loper was some better and able to get around with difficulty, but helped me with the ropes while moving boats and in some positions helped lift the boat by balancing it on his back and shoulders in the middle of the falls (over 100 feet fall in 500) three great rocks all but dam the river, and the only visible channel is 3 ½ feet wide. With ropes and poles the channel is bridged and the boats are lined to the other side, with great difficulty. We then worked down to the end of the falls and camped for the night. In the morning there were two inches of snow on the boats and seven inches on top of the canyon. The last provisions were eaten on the morning of the 24th. My boat was lined into a violent rapid, and all but tore loose, when it shot into the middle of the stream and turned upside down and filled with water. One rope was lost, but Loper snubbed the other to a rock, while I tumbled over the boulders down to the boat, which was heading toward the shore. My knee was wrenched, but the boat was secured at the very beginning of Box canyon.

Here the river fills the channel. A four-foot fall is fifty feet below and a second rapid has two rocks on one side, which may be caught before going into the cataract. There is still another fall below this. All are filled with huge granite boulders.

With no provisions, it seemed like suicide to attempt passage, so we two cripples turned to the snow-covered walls. A slide of rock aided what seemed to be a hopeless climb. Near the top the walls go sheer, but a break on the right offered a chance to escape.

Loper went first and I followed, but could scarcely drag my foot into Bostwick park.

A rig was secured at the Dunlap ranch and returned to the top of the cliff for me.

Upon arriving in Montrose Mr. Loper received a telegram saying that his wife was seriously ill and he left today for his home near Richfield, Utah.

This breaks the trip temporarily. Julius F. Stone, who was with my party last summer, supplied me with the boats used at present and was prevented by business from joining in on our trip. It is likely we will start with me at Cimarron in a canoe, and the run repeated down to Torrance [Torrence] falls.

APPENDIX F

ELLSWORTH L. KOLB'S 1918 MANUSCRIPT OF THE GRAND AND GUNNISON RIVERS

As I researched Ellsworth Kolb's highly promoted 1916 first descent of Westwater Canyon, there was evidence that he kept a journal or notes from when he hiked through the canyon prior to taking a boat through it a month later. Seeking to locate his writings, the late Kolb Brothers historian William C. "Bill" Suran assisted me with locating a diary or journal among the Kolb collection found at Northern Arizona University's Cline Library. Bill was unable to locate a journal or diary from 1916; be that as it may, he did locate a copy of Kolb's 1918 manuscript that he was writing of his experiences on the Black Canyon of the Gunnison, Westwater, and the Grand River.

In addition to the assistance Bill provided, I enjoyed the letters he wrote back to me. Included with the research he sent, his accompanying letters provided some details about the Kolb brothers that would later appear in his book *The Kolb Brothers of the Grand Canyon*,[1] *and in a web-based book* The Kolb Brothers Biography–With the Wings of an Angel.[2]

In April 2018, I visited the Cline Library at Northern Arizona University to make another attempt to locate a journal of Ellsworth Kolb's 1916 efforts on the

Grand and Gunnison Rivers, and to search for any of his photos or movies that are not found on their digital website at Northern Arizona University, https://archive.library.nau.edu/digital/. Unfortunately, I was unable to locate any new information that Suran had not already shared with me. If Kolb did keep a journal of his 1916 efforts, it may have been destroyed with personal letters and additional photos and film from darkroom chemicals and water that seeped through a rotted floor onto the box(s) that were stored below it. I'm aware that a few of Ellsworth Kolb's 1916 photos that are not found at NAU were shared with Bert Loper and can be located with the Albert "Bert" Loper Photo Collection deposited at the J. Willard Marriott Library located at the University of Utah.

The following is Ellsworth L. Kolb's unpublished manuscript, written in 1918, of his experiences on the tributaries of Grand and Gunnison Rivers. Kolb apparently was not sure what title to use for his manuscript and indicated that he intended to submit eighty photos with his submission to National Geographic Magazine.

THE LONG WATER TRAIL FROM THE ROCKIES OR EXPERIENCES WITH WESTERN SLOPE RIVERS AND CANYONS, BY ELLSWORTH L. KOLB.

My experiences with the Gunnison and Grand Rivers were a continuation of similar boating trips my brother and I had made in 1911–1912 through the canyons of the Green and Colorado Rivers—other divisions of the same watershed and rivers system. Other parties had duplicated the earlier trips and at least two parties had done important work in the Black Canyon of the Gunnison, but as yet no one person had made a complete exploration of the three tributaries and of the Colorado as well. This record was my goal.

The Black Canyon of the Gunnison being the most difficult and the least known, although surrounded by a ranching country, was my first objective for serious work. This does not take into account a week of preparatory work, while waiting for my equipment to arrive, at the headwaters of the Lake Fork, a branch of the Gunnison River. I wanted to follow one of the most rugged and picturesque branches down from the springs and snows in the mountains. All of this was to be found in the Lake Fork.

FIGURE 13.1. Waterfall at Lake Fork of the Gunnison River. NAU PH 568.5854, Cline Library, Northern Arizona University, Flagstaff, Arizona: Ellsworth Kolb photo found in Emery Kolb Collection.

The Lake Fork heads in Lake San Cristobal, at an elevation of somewhere near 9500 feet. The Lake is about three miles long, and is formed by a lava flow across the mountain valley. Its waters are crystal clear and of a numbing coldness, I found, on attempting a swim. It was the middle of July and the last snow was melting in the mountains. All the earth was oozing water.

Above the Lake are numerous streams and creeks coming down from the eastern slope of Mt. Ouray and other 14,000 foot peaks bordering on the San Juan mining district. The mining towns of Silverton and Ouray are just over the mountains.

Directly below the Lake is a 150 foot fall and cascade, a mile below that is another and the Lake Fork is shot on its tortuous and tempestuous way, to join the upper part of the Gunnison. Nearby is Lake City, once a booming mining camp, now given over to the entertainment of tourists and fisherman.

I came to Lake City by a narrow gauge branch that leaves the Denver and Rio Grande R.R. at the Junction of the Lake Fork and the Gunnison Rivers. It is considered a picturesque branch in that state which contains more miles of rugged mountain railway than any other two states in the Rocky Mountain region. A wooden bridge, 115 feet above the stream[,] is one attraction: the old Gunnison trail is another.

The branch boasts of one train a day; a combination of day coaches and any freight that may be destined for Lake City. It is run, the residents say, entirely for the benefit of the trout fishermen that line the stream, and, to quote one of them, "the crew will stop the train if you come to a likely looking spot and will sit on the bank, spit on your bait and pull for you while you whip the pool."

Two of my party joined me at Lake City, coming on horseback from Santa Fe, NM, possibly a 200 mile ride—through the mountains. One was John Shields, a cowboy and Grand Canyon guide; not yet a waterman, but ready for any adventure. The other was N. B. Stern, a New York business man who had learned of my proposed trip when on a mountain-lion hunt near our home in the Grand Canyon. His time was limited but he was anxious to join me for all of the trip he could manage. Stern afterwards proved to be the strongest and most daring swimmer that I have yet seen.

A missing member was Julius F. Stone, a manufacturer of Columbus, Ohio. Mr. Stone is a trustee of the Ohio State University, is an amateur astronomer of note, and is a lover of nature, especially of canyons. He enjoys adventure, though he says nothing himself about the last. Mr. Stone had headed one of the parties which had negotiated the entire series of rapids of the Green and Colorado Rivers. He was to join me for a limited time on the Black Canyon trip.

I expected to spend from four to six weeks on the two rivers, I allotted about three weeks to the Black Canyon. I smile now when I think of my plans. After re-outfitting three times that year there were still seventeen miles of the Black Canyon left for another season when I last saw it in December. But this is getting ahead of my story.

I made use of my week at Lake City to initiate my companions into the intricacies of the cineometograph [sic]. My principal injunction was "no matter what happens take the picture."

One of the two canvass [sic] boats, which I had ordered, arrived at Lake City. We launched it on the Lake, then made a ten mile run on the Fork. It was sporty boating, but we began, even then, to doubt if the boat was going to measure up to the job. It was of the collapsible type but it had a habit of collapsing at the wrong time: when running into a tree, for instance, which had fallen into the stream and was hidden by a sharp turn.

This was my first experience with canvass boats. Our main dependence was a cedar freight canoe, canvass covered and fitted with oars in addition to paddles. This canoe seemed to be lost in transportation. I had also included a buoyant life-raft to be used for a novel experiment. On other trips, when we came to unrunable [sic] cataracts, all material was portaged with a great deal of labor, along the sides of the canyon to quieter water below. I thought it possible to avoid much of this by placing this material in an oval receptacle attached to a float and by maneuvering it with ropes through the dangerous channels. The life-raft was the float, and indestructo trunk of the steamer size was decided on as the container.

On July the 24th, Mr. Stone wired that he would join us the next day, so our boat was loaded on the train and shipped to the station of Cimarron, where we intended to embark.

The D. and R.G. R.R. penetrates the first sixteen miles of the Black Canyon. An open observation car allows passengers an opportunity to enjoy the scenery. The walls, here, approach a height of 3000 feet, the river is a turbulent mountain torrent varying in size with the seasons.

In my opinion it is the most wonderful canyon in the US that is entered by a railway.

The line leaves the river below the Cimarron bridge, follows Cimarron Creek for a mile, then climbs the canyon wall where it slopes less abruptly and is only 1000 feet high. Then it drops down into a fertile ranching district irrigated by the Gunnison Tunnel and the Uncompahgre River. Montrose, Colo. is the center of this district. The road swings back to the river again at the town of Delta, twenty miles below the mouth of the Black Canyon. From this point it follows the river through an open valley and joins the main line at Grand Junction, Colo., where the Gunnison empties into the Grand River.

The Black Canyon has its head just below the mouth of the Lake Fork and is estimated to be about 70 miles long. It has never been accurately surveyed. For convenience we have divided it into four divisions, or sections, each division with certain characteristics of its own. The first division ended at the Cimarron Creek. This, as well as all the tributaries above are well known to the fishermen who come to lure the trout. We were not interested in doing any boating in this section. It was too easy of approach. But we did realize that we were up against a pretty hard proposition when we saw the rapids and cascades of this first section from the car.

"What will you do when you come to a cataract like that" a passenger asked, interrupting my picture making. "Oh! There will be ropes and things" I replied. "Perhaps we can fell trees and bridge the channel. Why worry until we reach it" and I went on cranking, dismissing the questioner but not the query. I had thought about the same thing myself and the question was yet unanswered.

The transparent or green tinted waters of the upper tributaries had given way to a muddy stream caused by violent rains which had swollen the river considerably above the ordinary stage for the season. We had picked a bad year, it seemed. The year before, for instance, the Gunnison Irrigation Tunnel, sixteen miles below Cimarron, entirely drained the flow of the river. Now it apparently made little difference, we were told, for a flow of 1600 feet was going past the tunnel.

Mr. Stone arrived on the 25th of July. All equipment except the freight canoe had also arrived as we planned on leaving at once. It rained all of

FIGURE 13.2. A swollen Gunnison River near Cimarron, Colorado. NAU. PH.568.5858, Cline Library, Northern Arizona University, Flagstaff, Arizona: Ellsworth Kolb photo found in Emery Kolb Collection.

that night and most of the next day we did not doubt that we would be wet most of the time but we were not keen about starting in a rain, and the pictures had to be taken in consideration, so we deferred starting until mid-afternoon. The events of that afternoon were typical of the trip.

On Thursday, July the 26th about 4 P.M. our party was assembled under the Cimarron bridge, a few hundred yards above the point where the Cimarron Creek joins the Gunnison River. Our equipment was scattered about us. Swimming suits of kapo, not forgetting head-protecting helmets of the same material, were adjusted, for the first rapid was bad. It was so swift that the center was rounded up about four feet higher than the shores; the rapid was a third of a mile long and about 75 feet across. Most of the bad rocks were covered by the high water but they made some nasty waves. Rocks projecting from the shores, turning the water this way and that, were the greatest danger.

A group of sightseers from the village, in addition to the usual small boys, was perched on the bridge above, waiting for the fun to commence. Most of them thought we were just staging a "movie" and had

FIGURE 13.3. Crew from 1916, L–R Ellsworth Kolb, Julius F. Stone, John W. Shields, and Nathan B. (N. B.) Stern, pose along the Gunnison River at Cimmaron, Colorado. NAU.PH.568.5859, Cline Library, Northern Arizona University, Flagstaff, Arizona: Ellsworth Kolb photo found in Emery Kolb Collection.

no intention of running that rapid. There [sic] judgement was better than ours as it happened. We did put on quite a show but we failed to cover ourselves with glory.

After the provisions and the duffle bags were tied into the boats, the trunk, loaded with the extra film magazines, was lashed to the raft. A light but strong line was played out as the raft, buoyant as a cork, floated into the currant. The scheme gave promise of working well. In a few seconds it had reached the end of the line and swung in towards the shore. I followed, scrambling over great, slippery boulders, taking in some of the line, but allowing the raft to float along as I did so. In a few minutes I was a hundred yards below the bridge.

Here there was a change. Reaching almost across the stream was what swift-water men call a pinwheel or perpendicular whirlpool.

Shields and Stern were busy with camera and cineometograph nearby. I was on top of a pointed rock [a] few feet from the shore. Mr. Stone, who had complained of not feeling his best that day, remained with the two canvass boats, under the bridge.

Over confidence on my part was to blame for what happened. I certainly did not anticipate any trouble. A pull on the line sent the float sailing down the stream towards me. It passed, and in an instant was caught in the breaking wave. Instead of plunging through, as I had expected it to do, it kept whirling over and over and shooting across the river at alarming speed. It lunged on reaching the end of the line like a bronc on the end of a lasso. I was being pulled off my perch, so turned it loose and leaped for the shore. The raft, by this time, had struggled through the breaking waves and was whirling down the rapid. Another big wave hit it and turned it over with the trunk underneath. In this manner it disappeared around a turn in the canyon a quarter of a mile below.

Here was action enough for any picture enthusiast. The camera men remained at their post. I ran back and told Mr. Stone what had happened. I proposed giving chase. We had decided on the opposite side as being the least dangerous. Mr. Stone proposed following in his boat a short distance behind. In about three minutes we learned what could and what could not be done with canvass boats in the Black Canyon.

We reversed the usual method of rowing and backed down the river. That is, we faced down stream and checked the speed of the boat by pulling against the current, dodging here and there to escape the hidden rocks.

An unsecured row-lock was the cause of my trouble. A high wave lifted the lock and the oar from the socket and the boat turned sideways to the stream while I was replacing the lock. Before I could get in a stroke we banged against a great rock projecting from the shore. There was a cracking of frail timbers, the sides were crushed together and the boat submerged, sliding downwards along the face of the rock. I was overboard hanging to the gunwale but saw that the boat had no intention of coming up so turned it loose and struck out for myself.

It is impossible to tell just what happened. I found myself swimming in a whirlpool below the rock. A filled rubber bag was floating nearby. I grabbed it and swam to the shore. My craft had gone to pieces; canvass, boards and cargo were being spewed up on all sides. I had a glimpse of Mr. Stone passing the first danger point, holding his boat true. I hurriedly secured another bag.

A shout from Stern, carrying above the roar of the rapid caused me to look up. There in the middle of the swift water was Mr. Stone hanging to the stern of his boat, which had overturned. It was the coolest thing I have ever seen. There were no futile efforts on his part to struggle with the waves. He calmly surveyed both shores as he sped past; his spectacles were riding serenely on his nose.

Stern leaped into the rapid and made a brave and powerful effort to overtake the boat, but the middle of the river was so much swifter than the sides that he was soon distanced and returned to the shore. This I took in as I ran pell-mell along the steep, rough bank.

A big, rather quiet whirlpool at the end of the rapid stopped Mr. Stone. He had made his fourth revolution when I arrived. He was trying to swim to shore with the boat but the current held him. He had no trouble in swimming out unencumbered with the boat. I tried it too, but had no better luck until he reached me with a pole from the shore. Everything in the boat was intact but weighted with water.

Shields, meanwhile, was chasing down the opposite side, salvaging what material came his way. He was stopped a mile below by a wall rising sheer out of the river. I was blocked in my last effort by a thirty foot slide down a wall which I tried to climb.

An inventory of our equipment showed that we were "out"; one boat, a life-raft and trunk, a metal container filled with film, both "still" and "movie," three film magazines, a camp bed and other personal effects. It might have been worse, we were still "in" four capable men, one boat and much of our equipment besides the cameras which were on the shore. This was our introduction to the Black Canyon. It was with aching limbs and heavy hearts that we returned to the hotel that evening.—all except Mr. Stone. He said he felt better.

Rain fell much of the next day so we remained indoors and held a council of war. Business demands placed a limit on the time Messrs. Stone and Stern could remain with us; in spite of this they did not fancy the idea of being left out of the trip altogether. No word of the freight canoe had been received. We finally decided to make an attempt to go as far as the Gunnison Tunnel—the end of the second division—with the canvass boat. It would carry one man and the equipment in quiet water. We planned on carrying it when bad water was reached. Judging by the little we had seen of the canyon we could expect to find a shore on one side or the other most of the way. We hoped to make our crossings between the rapids. I did not doubt our ability to climb out if we got cornered.

Provisions for five or six days was put into the boat. We took but one camp bed; there was a possibility of finding another downstream. If we did not, two of us decided that we could rough it for awhile.

There were no pyrotechnics at our second start. We got away early on the morning of the 28th. The boat was launched at the end of the first rapid-the lower end. Two sons of Italy, borrowed from the R.R., helped us carry our equipment along the steep, rocky bank, then returned to their hand-car. We made no attempt at shooting the rapids.

The boat was carried or 'lined' with ropes when we came to bad water. It was slow work but sure. The first difficulty was the sheer wall that had stopped Shields. Here, the water was comparatively quiet but there was a rapid just below. Life-preservers were adjusted and two of us swam. Shields trailed behind the boat, which Mr. Stone rowed. The water was icy.

There were other walls which we climbed, following a game trail. Signs of mountain sheep were plentiful. An air-compartment, floating on top of the water was found to be attached to my sleeping bag, which had sunk. The river was rising again and we camped under a great fir which protected us from the rain, which was falling again. We were well pleased with our first days work.

Opposite our camp was a talus slope, alternately bare and tree covered, between two ridges of rock, which I felt certain could be climbed if we were put to the test. In fact I could pick out one such place, on one side or the other, for each mile we had traveled. The river, here, was headed almost directly North. We were camped on the East side. The shore, we found, usually lay on this side. Montrose was some miles away over the ridges on the West.

The walls were now about 3000 feet high, of a grey, green color composed of gneiss and micacious [sic] schists; rather rotten or decomposed except in the sheer walls. There were occasional ledges of granite slashed with veins of quartz. Jagged pinnacles topped many of the sheer walls.

The color scheme of the rocks blended with the foliage. There were occasional balsam fir, clumps of long-leafed pine, and that most beautiful of all evergreens; the blue spruce. On top, the quaking aspen mingled with the pines. The undergrowth was dense in spots, and there was a musty odor of decayed vegetation. Berries were plentiful, and we expected to see signs of bear, which we knew were not far distant. But we saw no game. We regretted the frequent rains which made the stream so turbid. What trout there must be in some of those streams that were never fished!

July the 29th. was not our day of days. We started off bad. First, we had a spill as we lined a boat while Mr. Stone rowed. But for Stern he might have had a difficult time getting ashore. Again, it was advisable to cross the river. It was a hard job and took four trips. Then there was a difficult portage and another crossing. We estimated that there were from six to eight rapids to the mile, each long enough at this stage of water that the swift water was almost continuous. How we longed for such boats as we had used on the Colorado River, for with such boats nearly all these rapids could be run.

We made less than a mile that day and camped early in the rain. We were a little alarmed about Mr. Stone, for the fever which had bothered him before our start was increasing and we feared he was threatened with pneumonia. He made light of it and insisted on doing a little more than his share of the work. He and I had both remarked that no one ever got sick on our trips, and naturally he was pretty much disgusted with the turn matters had taken.

A note in my journal, written at this camp, reads, "There is a wall rising sheer from the river just below camp where some one will have to swim." We were up at 5:30 the next morning; the sun touched the tops of the cliffs at 6 A.M. The river had receded to its former stage, but everything was a little more than damp. Mr. Stone repaired some small tears in the boat with pitch gathered from the firs. We made our swim without trouble, then lined and portaged three rapids, and climbed over one sheer wall, all on the right or East side of the river.

FIGURE 13.4. Julius F. Stone, John W. Shields, and N. B. Stern at the great pile of driftwood in the Black Canyon of the Gunnison River. NAU.PH.568.3763, Cline Library, Northern Arizona University, Flagstaff, Arizona: Ellsworth Kolb photo found in Emery Kolb Collection.

At another wall we found a ledge under the water and made our way slowly over this.

About noon we reached another wall beside a good sized rapid, but with a dangerous rapid just a short distance below. A whirlpool eddied on the opposite side, at the end of the first rapid. Stern decided to swim the rapid and whirlpool, which he did in splendid style. I was to handle the boat and assist the others if needed. I soon joined Stern, and we were discussing the feasibility of the others climbing a ledge which we had discovered when we were surprised to find Shields had misunderstood our signal and was almost opposite us. I had a hurried pull to catch him and 'fumbled the ball' by throwing him the line attached to the bow instead of the stern. He had made a good fight but was badly strangled. On landing we found that the short wooden strips which took the place of a gunwale had broken and split. The boat was unloaded; Stern and I paddled and helped Mr. Stone to land—pretty rough treatment for a man with a temperature of 102°.

On account of the dilapidated condition of our boat, in addition to its unsuitability to our needs, we concluded to discontinue the trip for the present. As we prepared our camp on a great pile of drift-wood we discovered signs of a fisherman's camp. Some one had found a way into the canyon!

Without any well formed intention of climbing entirely out, and without telling the others of my intention of reconnoitering the situation from the higher walls, I pushed into the thicket behind the camp and began a scramble up what afterwards proved to be a 3500 foot ridge or hogs-back. There were occasional slides of trap-rock and a few small ledges with precipitous drops on either side a hundred yards away. The undergrowth near the river gave way to a heavy growth of evergreens, and patches of brambles and berry bushes, the red-raspberry predominating. The service or June-berry was still green; the Oregon grape-root acted as a thirst quencher. Near the top was a tangled timber-fall and a dense growth of small quacking aspen, soaking wet. Once on top, I found numerous cattle trails leading out of the dense thickets into open parks between groves of the largest aspen I have ever seen. Sleek, white-faced cattle were grazing on all sides.

I was lucky. The trail I picked out of all the lot led me by the most direct route to the Thompson Cattle-ranch and the only cabin on the top of the Black Canyon, two miles back from the rim. After a short talk with the Thompsons I trotted, tumbled and slid back to camp, arriving just at dusk. Shields and Stern had been without tobacco for two days and their hearts were made glad when I supplied them with a tin given to me by the Thompsons.

All equipment was cached above the high water mark. The ham and bacon was hung on a tree out of the reach of any animal but a porcupine or a bear ... Porcupine signs were numerous and the bear were here too, for the Thompsons had trapped one the day before I called.

We climbed out the next day, Stern and Shields going ahead to order a team. Thomson met us at the rim. Then we had a ranch meal that we will never forget and a glorious ride down the mountain side behind a pair of spirited greys, into the valley, then a fifteen mile drive over the Rainbow Trail into the town of Montrose. We had failed to reach the Gunnison Tunnel by four and a half miles.

Mr. Stone left for his business, promising to send me two boats similar to those we had used on the Colorado. Stern accompanied him. Men at the tunnel had telephoned out that the life raft and trunk had been rescued by some fishermen two miles above the tunnel, so Shields and I got horses and rode back to the canyon. An excellent road had been constructed by the Government leading by easy grades to the top of the canyon. The apex here is 2100 feet above the river, and the road into the canyon only intended for a down-hill pull, as it has a 20 percent grade.

The two care-takers, Walter Tupper and Wm. Comstock, together with Comstock's family consisting of Mrs. Comstock and two bright-eyed boys, made it very pleasant for us. We remained at the tunnel overnight.

The Comstock boys had an exciting story to tell of a black bear that had crossed the river, swimming towards them but indifferent to their presence. He was calmly eating the service berries and choke-cherries when Tupper arrived, armed with a Colt. He felled it with a shot in the neck, but it instantly leaped to its feet and scrambled into a thicket. Possibly he had been attracted by some angora goats that posed on the cliffs above. The goats were once domesticated, but the native mountain sheep are no wilder than these same goats, after a few years of freedom in the canyon.

I was pleased to see that for two miles above the dam the stream was comparatively quiet and the canyon walls were much less precipitous. The direction had changed and the river flowed to the N.W. Judging by the signs, the trunk had had a rough journey, descending about 450 feet. It had filled with water and remained under the float with the rope broken from one end. The fiber covering had a thousand scratches and cuts, but the frame was intact and uninjured.

I needed my equipment, left back in the canyon for other trips, and the favorable water in this section of the canyon gave me the idea of bringing it down on the river, instead of by trail.

Shields was stationed at the dam as a lookout and I returned by our former trail to our wrecked boat in the canyon, carrying the material needed for repairs. The work occupied me for an entire day; the repairs lasted about two hours. I had run three rapids and lined two; the biggest I had seen. At a side canyon called Pool Gulch, the walls were jagged and sheer; great fallen boulders all but dammed the torrent. I had lots of trouble here. Later, the boat wrapped around a rock in the middle of a rapid I was attempting to run. It took me half an hour to work

FIGURE 13.5. Nearly boulder-dammed Gunnison River probably found in Section 2. NAU.PH.568.5865, Cline Library, Northern Arizona University, Flagstaff, Arizona: Ellsworth Kolb photo found in Emery Kolb Collection.

it loose. This accomplished, I leaped on top of the wreck, a canvass rag and a board kept afloat by four air-bags. Duffle bags, held by ropes, streamed out from the sides. The end on which I kneeled was two feet under water, the other end floated on top. I held to the gunwales, swinging my weight from side to side when threatened with a spill. Twice again I was marooned on rocks and repeated my former exertions. It rained in torrents, but a little water, more or less, did not matter now. I was chilled to the bone.

Fortunately, none of these rapids were bad. Gradually they dwindled in size, the river made an abrupt turn toward the tunnel and the run was completed on a quiet stream. The second section of the Black Canyon had been traversed, but two boats were wrecked in the attempt. The other sections, we decided, could wait for a lower stage of water and other boats, and we occupied ourselves with other trips until they arrived.

The freight canoe had arrived at last. Shields and I put it into the Gunnison Delta, below the Black Canyon, and made a twelve hour run on the tamed stream, which landed us at Grand Junction. A day

Appendix F | 191

FIGURE 13.6. Inflatable canoe defeated on the Gunnison River. NAU. PH.568.6018 Cline Library, Northern Arizona University, Flagstaff, Arizona: Ellsworth Kolb photo found in Emery Kolb Collection.

later we resumed our journey and made a hundred mile run down the Grand River, to Moab, Utah. We avoided Westwater Canyon,— sometimes called Granite Canyon—close to the Utah line, by having our canoe hauled around. This twelve mile canyon had never been successfully explored by boat; several lives have been lost by those who have attempted it. It contains several dangerous rapids, two especially so, locally called "The Double Pitch" and "The Whirlpool Rapid." The last is a miniature Niagara Whirlpool, hemmed [between] steep granite sides. Two ranchmen and others living at the head of the canyon told us that it was impossible to get through these rapids and live. A favorite expression with one was "the fishes brains are spattered on the walls."

The canyon was extremely picturesque and reminded us of the Grand Canyon in Arizona, several hundred miles down this same river system, but with this difference; the granite walls—so called—are 300 feet high instead of 1000 to 1500 feet, and the sandstone walls above the inner bench or plateau on top of the granite are 500 feet high instead of 3000 or 4000. A trail runs through the canyon on the top of

FIGURE 13.7. Westwater Canyon, "The canyon is very picturesque and reminded us in a way of the Grand Canyon of Arizona." Photo from 1916, by Ellsworth Kolb. J. Willard Marriott Library, University of Utah, Salt Lake City, Utah Albert Loper Collection, P11 36 no1.13.019.

the granite. We walked through on this trail; and climbed down to the rapids at several places. The Whirlpool was bad at that stage of water but I imagined it could be run at a lower stage and expressed a determination to try it sometime later. Shortly after this trip Shields returned to his old employment.

FIGURE 13.8. "Entrance to Westwater Canyon, Utah. One man rows; the other lies on the deck, hanging to the bulkheads." Quote from reel presentation No. 2. NAU.PH.568.5969, Cline Library, Northern Arizona University, Flagstaff, Arizona: Ellsworth Kolb photo found in Emery Kolb Collection.

Bert Loper, an expert boatman, joined me two weeks after we returned from Moab, and we had another set-to with 150 miles of rapids and swift water. This included some bad water above Glenwood Springs and a run down the Grand to Grand Junction. Then we had a try at Westwater Canyon with the canoe. The two ranchers and a motion picture camera man accompanied us on horseback, keeping as near as possible on the trail. We took turns at running the rapids, the one left [ashore] helping the photographer. Loper drew the Double Pitch and had an exciting experience but came out conqueror. The Whirlpool fell to me, but in low water it was simply a straight rapid, without a whirlpool; big enough to upset me, but I righted the canoe, and climbed aboard before another rapid was reached. We landed at the end of the canyon that evening proud of our record of having been the first to shoot the rapids of Westwater Canyon. This kind of water was more like the rapids of the Colorado River and entirely to our liking. The water was big but it could be run. It was entirely different from the Black Canyon, which had water enough but so badly blocked with rocks that there was little sport in boating through it.

FIGURE 13.9. Kolb and Loper boat through the Gunnison Tunnel. NAU.PH.568.3717, Cline Library, Northern Arizona University, Flagstaff, Arizona: Ellsworth Kolb photo found in Emery Kolb Collection.

Loper planned on going with me into the Black Canyon, but he did not want to do only a part. I was hardly satisfied with my success on the first attempt, so the [sic] shipped the canoe to Cimarron and the second run was made to the tunnel, in less than two days, without trouble of any kind. The water was clear, and five feet below the stage of our first attempt. Much of the success of this trip, as well as the trip on the Grand River was due to Loper. He was the next most enthusiastic rough-water man I have ever been associated with, not excepting my brother and Mr. Stone, which is saying a good deal. Two trips through Cataract Canyon, on the Colorado River, and boating on the San Juan had given him the experience he needed for this work.

Through the kindness of the US Reclamation Service we were to have a chance of going through the Gunnison Tunnel by boat. It had never been done but we saw no reason why it shouldn't be.

Very little is known by the general public of this wonderful example of engineering. The bore is 10 feet in diameter by 11 feet high, and has a length of 30582 feet—over five and a half miles, under a mountain of rock 2100 feet high. About a fourth of the bore is cemented, the remainder is unsupported except by its granite sides and top. The bottom is cemented and has a fall of about 11 feet to the mile. The mouth opens into a valley and the waters irrigate 150,000 acres of the land in the Uncompahgre Valley, much of which would otherwise be barren. The work was authorized during ex-President Roosevelts' administration; ex-President Taft was present at the dedication.

At our suggestion, the flow of water was reduced to a three foot stage. This gave plenty of head clearance. I was amazed to learn that a bright pin-point of light somewhere ahead was the sunlight reflecting on the cement at the opposite end of the bore. Walter Tupper, the caretaker, accompanied us. Oars were replaced with paddles. Light was supplied by an oil lantern. A flashlight picture was made by Tupper and we embarked. A swift current kept us busy; a dead trolley, held by wooden hangers and fastened by drills into the roof gave us some trouble. In places, the drills had rusted, leaving the hangers afloat on the water.

There were many weird and peculiar sounds. A good current of air was passing up the stream. The direction of the air passage changes each day, we were told. When the tunnel was being constructed a number of men lost their lives by going to the windward side of some heavy blasting, but a minute afterwards the direction changed and they were suffocated. Numerous springs were piped into the tunnel; one was warm. 1900 feet inside we heard the roar of a rapid ahead. We looked

FIGURE 13.10. Two new boats arrived for Ellsworth Kolb and Bert Loper to begin the third section of the Black Canyon in 1916. NAU.PH.568.5953, Cline Library, Northern Arizona University, Flagstaff, Arizona: Ellsworth Kolb photo found in Emery Kolb Collection.

for signs of a fall of rock from the roof but saw none. The stream had been damned by something, that was certain, the canoe was bounding and slapping onto the water at a disconcerting rate. Later, when the tunnel was drained, it was found to be an upheaval of rock from underneath, caused, no doubt, by the immense pressure from above.

The journey was completed in sixty five minutes. Mr. Pyle, the chief of the project with some of his assistants were at the mouth of the tunnel to meet us. Two of these men, Mr. Foster and Mr. Funk had been through the Black Canyon below the tunnel, partly on foot and partly by boat, at a time when the tunnel diverted most of the water. All these men placed their services at our disposal and helped us in every possible way.

The new boats built by Mr. Stone had arrived, so the canoe was placed in dry dock and the flat-bottomed boats were hauled to the head of the tunnel. These boats were decked at either end, with an open cock-pit for a single oarsman. They are designed from a photographers point of view, in addition to being a most seaworthy type, as we had proved before. Their weight of 250 lbs. were the greatest objection, but we had to put up with a good deal if we were to get pictures.

Appendix F | 197

FIGURE 13.11. Bert Loper helping portage boats around Flat Rock Falls, Black Canyon. NAU.PH.568.6012, Cline Library, Northern Arizona University, Flagstaff, Arizona: Ellsworth Kolb photo found in Emery Kolb Collection. The current name from Milo's list of rapids is Day Wrecker.

We embarked on our journey into the third section of the Black Canyon on Friday, Oct. the 13th. This section was only eleven and one half miles long and ended at a side canyon named Red Rock Canyon, but Mr. Foster told us that it had a fall of 1030 feet in that short distance. The walls, too, were different from those above. Here it was more like a crack in a mountain with a torrent pouring through. Two miles below the tunnel we came to Flat Rock Falls, about fifteen feet high, and made a portage.

Somewhere in this section our trunk disappeared for good. We had put it afloat on the river, intending to picture it as it went over a cataract. Several times it had to be snaked out of whirlpools which we avoided with our boat. Finally it struck a long, clear channel and rounded a turn, floating triumphantly. We followed, expecting to catch it soon but found the Falls, instead, and the final end of the trunk is an unsolved mystery.

All went well as long as we portaged the boats, but the next day, while lining my boat through a narrow channel, it slid onto a sloping rock,

FIGURE 13.12. Bert Loper working with dynamite to dislodge boat from rocks on the Gunnison River. Boat trapped shortly after Flat Rock Falls. NAU.PH.568.5911, Cline Library, Northern Arizona University, Flagstaff, Arizona: Ellsworth Kolb photo found in Emery Kolb Collection.

the bow shot into the air and the stern settled into the water. We had overlooked the fact that most of the water ran under rocks, and the boat was trying to make a short-cut. A rope from the bow was hurriedly tied to a tree, to prevent the boat from vanishing as the trunk had. We worked an entire day with a small pulley, with ropes and poles,

FIGURE 13.13. Bert Loper looking downstream at the Narrows of the Gunnison River in the Black Canyon. NAU.PH.568.3754, Cline Library, Northern Arizona University, Flagstaff, Arizona: Ellsworth Kolb photo found in Emery Kolb Collection.

but failed to recover it. Occasionally we would look at the ledges above and ponder on a climb. The following morning I decided to make the attempt. It was not as bad as it looked and I soon gained the top. By one oclock I had descended to the tunnel. Tupper supplied me with dynamite drills and a hammer and I retraced my steps arriving after dusk.

The following morning Loper went to work. He is a miner and knows what to do with a single-jack. A hole was drilled into the small rock that held the boat, so that it reached a depth of three feet below the water. It was charged with a half stick of powder and was fired. It merely shook and slightly cracked the rock. Two more sticks finished the job and the rock was shattered. It was dark when the boat was rescued. It took another day to replace two boards that were broken near the stern. Canvass, glue and tin completed the repair and we had only lost four days.

We averaged about half a mile a day for the next four days. The rapids were unrunable; we could scarcely cross the river. Nearly all trees had disappeared, the cliffs seemed to be nearly perpendicular, the rock was granite. Our supplies had dwindled to almost nothing and we had still six miles to go, but miles should hardly be mentioned in this connection. We had reached a place banked with perpendicular walls and a little shore of boulders first on one side then on the other. This ended with a gorge with cliffs rising sheer from the river, which was only fifty two feet wide. The approach was over two dangerous rapids and swift water; a twelve foot fall, among a lot of great boulders, lay at the foot of the gorge. The river above this point had a descent of 100 feet in a fourth of a mile and we were on the right side of the river, away from Montrose; when once past a ledge there was no chance of going back.

A crack in the granite with a talus slope in the bottom appeared to be a possible avenue of escape. I prospected and got half way out before I found that it pinched and was blocked by overhanging rocks, and we returned to our work with the boats, which were at the beginning of the 100 foot descent. While lining Lopers boat it smashed on the side quite similar to the other break. The granite boulders were slippery as glass and a wet shoe would not hold. Loper fell when pulling on a rope and struck his back on a projecting rock. He was deathly pale and gave no answer but a groan to my anxious inquiry. I played nurse for two nights; our only remedy was a hot water bottle. Loper improved and helped me repair the boat but he suffered greatly. We were now on half rations.

A flimsy bridge of box elder poles and ropes was thrown across the stream at a point where great polished boulders almost hid the stream. We did not have a great deal of confidence in our engineering ability, but it got our boats and ourselves across.

FIGURE 13.14. Portage amid snow below the Narrows on the Gunnison River. NAU.PH.568.5937, Cline Library, Northern Arizona University, Flagstaff, Arizona: Ellsworth Kolb photo found in Emery Kolb Collection

That night it rained, then snowed. Our last provisions[,] excepting a half pound of sugar, were eaten that morning. This would seem to be enough, but we had neither strength nor inclination to make a portage where one was advisable, and lined instead. A boat, filled with water, shot into the stream, and overturned. One rope broke, the other was snubbed around a rock and held by Loper. I slid and fell over the icy rocks and wrestled the boat into an eddy when it swung in towards the shore. Then I found that I had wrenched my knee so that I could scarcely stand.

We drained the water from the cameras, and put them under a protecting ledge. The sugar was eaten that noon, our exposed films were divided between us and we turned to the cliffs. When I had climbed the crack or geological fault on the opposite side I had noticed that the same fault reached across the canyon, with two branches near the top. One of these branches might be an avenue of escape.

One cripple helped the other. The snow grew deeper as we climbed but, fortunately, we had no ledge work until within 300 feet of the top and it was not bad. We were soaking wet from wallowing in the snow but had managed to keep warm.

The plateau was quite flat for a mile or more, and was covered with a growth of scrub oak and sage, with snow hanging thick on the branches. I had climbed without a great deal of trouble but could make little headway in the deep snow, and fell frequently. Loper broke the trail, I followed. About dark, we saw lights in the ranch houses a few miles distant and a thousand feet below us. Loper proposed going for a horse and returning for me. Just as he was leaving he found a wood haulers road among dense juniper and piñon pine. After that I had less difficulty in following his trail, but was not sorry to see the team which was driven back from the Dunlap ranch, in Bostwick Park. The Dunlap family and the young men employed there gave us such a cordial welcome that I made this place my headquarters for subsequent trips.

A medical examination showed that Loper had broken two ribs, but the injury to his back was much more painful than the ribs. My knee needed a rest. The tendons attached to the knee-cap were loosened or strained. Somehow my good fortune was not holding out this trip. Some one said something about the advisability of starting a trip on

Friday the Thirteenth. Loper received a telegram, five days old, saying his wife was not expected to live and advising him to come home at once. He left, hoping to return, but wrote later saying that it was not possible then.

Two weeks of fine weather and a rest put me in good spirits again. Wm. Wright of Montrose had a week to spare from his business and concluded he would like to spend his vacation getting acquainted with the Black Canyon. We hauled supplies sufficient for a week to the rim of the canyon.

Before climbing into the gorge we went out onto a point at the narrowest part and looked down into the canyon. My heart almost failed me. A half mile below was a little thread of water, lashed to foam, twisting and turning among a thousand gigantic boulders. The river here has a decent [sic] of 350 feet in a mile; it disappeared entirely from sight at three points. A sullen roar rose out of the depths. The walls at this point were about 500 feet apart, on top. The cattlemen call this section, the Coffee Pot Range; possibly because the canyon is shaped like an inverted coffee-pot.

Nearly all the snow had melted and we got to the bottom by dusk. The next day was put in caulking one boat; we decided to abandon the other. One rapid was lined from the opposite side, with no worse mishap than an overturned boat. Then we had to cross again, with Wright seated on the deck behind me, hoping to catch a rock, projecting from the shore at the head of another rapid. But the rock was three times as large as it had appeared to be and holds slipped. We had all but given up, when my fingers found a crack in the rock a foot under the water, and Wright leaped out with the rope. This was undoubtedly the most difficult place in the canyon. The run through the rest of the gorge was lively and while not especially dangerous provided us with thrills enough for one day. We landed in a bay, just above the twelve foot fall.

Then it snowed and rained, and snowed again. Even on those days when the sun shone we had but twenty minutes between sunrise and sunset. The bottom of the gorge, both in and out of the river was crowded with great rounded boulders covered with a thin coating of ice. Time and again we had to lift and pull our boats on top of the rocks. We had numerous falls; twice I slipped into the river. My knee was

FIGURE 13.15. Snow and ice cover what Ellsworth Kolb described as a twelve-foot waterfall. It is known today by the kayaking community as 18' waterfall. See image 6.16. NAU.PH.568.3850, Cline Library, Northern Arizona University, Flagstaff, Arizona: Ellsworth Kolb photo found in Emery Kolb Collection.

bothering me again, provisions were dwindling, and Wright's time was about up so we hunted another crack in the granite and eased our way out of the canyon. We had only gained a quarter of a mile, but it was the most dangerous quarter in the gorge. Nothing was carried out of the canyon. Our cameras had never been thoroughly dried and ice had formed inside and had warped them badly. It was near zero weather in the canyon and all of that on top.

Lawrence Coats took Wrights' place ten days later. We were armed with boat hooks and all the supplies we could carry. Going down, we attached long ropes to our sacks of supplies and slid them down the snow covered slope ahead of us. Once they got away and we were not bothered with them for a half hour. The provisions escaped with little damage.

Coats did effective work, in our two crossings, with the boat hooks, catching into the ice at the head of a fifteen foot fall, on one occasion, and holding in rocks on another. But most of the work was portaging

FIGURE 13.16. Painted Wall as seen from the North Rim of the Black Canyon near SOB Gulch. NAU.PH.568.3790, Cline Library, Northern Arizona University, Flagstaff, Arizona: Ellsworth Kolb photo found in Emery Kolb Collection.

FIGURE 13.17. Large rapid located at the bottom of SOB Gulch currently known as either New or Next Generation Rapid. NAU.PH.568.5950, Cline Library, Northern Arizona University, Flagstaff, Arizona: Ellsworth Kolb photo found in Emery Kolb Collection.

our boat and equipment under the worst conditions I have ever seen. We soon saw that two men were helpless against the odds. We went hungry two days this trip, and failed twice, in attempted climbs, before we got out of the canyon.

Coats's brother, Adrian, and Jay Hall joined us. At last I had an adequate force. Hall couldn't swim but his 185 pounds of muscle and bone looked good to me, and I hoped to keep his feet dry. This time, we made

FIGURE 13.18. Back of photo reading, "only place where ice helped." Special Collections, J. Willard Marriott Library, University of Utah, Salt Lake City, Utah Albert Loper Collection, P11 36 no1.13.036. In July 1934, a United States Geological Survey team entered the canyon to obtain data for a topographical map and the new National Monument. They wrote of this location naming it "Underwear Pool," "where Walker lost his underwear. This black rock is 42 feet high." Through the Black Canyon, Ann Arbor, MI: Braun-Brumfield, Inc.; 1972.

a hundred mile trip around the canyon and approached it from the opposite side just to save one crossing. It was on Thanksgiving day that we climbed into the chasm. We had all the provisions we could carry. This time it was Red Rock Canyon or bust.

We got some pleasure out of the next week. Hall was a good cook and we lived high. The ice did not bother us much for we were working two hundred feet above the river much of the time, but I doubt if many boats were ever put through contortions similar to that one. Great sections of cliffs broken into rocks varying in size from forty feet to two hundred feet square had fallen in the gorge. They stood on their corners and in every position except level. At one point the boat was slipped through a crack a hundred feet above the stream, with ropes attached to either end to prevent it from being precipitated into the foam below.

This chaotic condition ended at a point where a great cliff had fallen into the gorge, completely bridging the channel with shattered rocks for a hundred yards. The rocks were of all shapes and sizes, some level with the water, while others were fifty feet high. The water disappeared in a foam under cavities and cracks left between the rocks, appearing now and then in deep whirlpools and short connected channels. There was an unscalable wall on the north side of the river, where we were; a brush covered slope of generous dimensions lay between the wall and the river bed on the other side, then this slope pinched out below the bridge, and the only shore was on the opposite side. There was a violent rapid below the bridge.

This is the point that has given rise to the mistaken idea that the Gunnison River disappears into a natural tunnel. We had no particular difficulty in getting on the rocks from the sheer wall side as the water is quiet here, and rotten ice helped us back to the same side at the lower end. Another course was used for the boat after we had looked over the ground. It was crossed in quiet water above the bridge, dragged up the slope then across the lower end of the bridge.

We made over a mile the next day and camped below Torrance [Torrence] Falls, a cascade with 100 foot descent in 500. The river, due to the freezing weather, was now very low, so that it looked as if we could wade the river in certain shallow looking places. Tiring of the constant portaging I attempted to run a rapid the next day and came to grief on

FIGURE 13.19. Portaging boat at top of Torrence Falls in the Black Canyon of Gunnison. Photo comprised R–L of NAU.PH 568.6008, 568.5945, 568.3809 and 568.5934 (flipped). Cline Library, Northern Arizona University, Flagstaff, Arizona: Ellsworth Kolb photo found in Emery Kolb Collection. The current name for this rapid is Great Falls.

the rocks. Top, bottom and sides of the boat separated near the stern. I grabbed a line in my teeth and swam for the shore, the men helping me with a pole. We saved everything but the provisions.

The boat was tied into shape with ropes, and covered with a tarpaulin from one of the beds. I wanted a boat to make the last crossing. But our work was without avail. The empty boat was being lined at a difficult point; one man on top of a rock was temporarily placed where he had the full strain and was being dragged into the water. He did the only thing possible. He turned it loose. Fortunately it was empty. For a long time it was held by the line which became tangled in the rocks, and stretched tight as a fiddle-string, as the [boat] rose and fell in the rapid. Then the rope parted, the boat crashed against a rock and it went under for the last time.

On account of the ledges we had to climb, our beds and all other equipment was left behind. We hoped to get out at Red Rock Canyon that same day. Previous to this we had seen ice across the river, at Red Rock, but a slight rise had carried the ice out. We had to get across, and Hall couldn't swim. He was game, however. Holding together with a rope, and breaking the ice with a pole as we proceeded, we pushed in to the river at what was apparently the shallowest place we could find.

Adrian Coats was giving an imitation of an old darky singing a refrain that ended with "Will the waters be chilly when I am called to die?"

When in about three feet of water, I heard Hall, who was behind, exclaim, "I'm going out of here," and he did. But he went the wrong way. He went back. Lawrence Coats, who always laughed at the wrong time, thought this was the greatest joke of the season. He was convulsed; but it looked serous to me.

We induced Hall to try it again and got two thirds of the way across, in water up to our arm-pits, and so swift we could not stand, and by mutual consent, we all retreated.

A roaring fire was built back in some cedars and we put in a miserable night drying out, with our backs against rocks and trees. Eight inches of snow fell, then it cleared and got very cold. There was no sleep for me that night; I was thinking of what we would do in the morning. Hall had stated that he would attempt a climb before he would tackle the river again, but I knew that we could not reach provisions even if we did get out, for this section is rugged back from the canyon.

The Coats boys insisted on crossing, and, as they could swim and it was only three miles to Bostwick Park, I did not worry about them. I remained with Hall and we attempted the climb, but the icy walls were unscalable and we soon returned to the river.

Another crossing was decided on at the end of a long pool, but above the swift rapid. Ice had formed for thirty feet from either shore and had to be broken as we progressed. The fresh snow had sunk and was clustered on rocks in the river bottom. Each one had a stout stick, all held together. At different times each of us, excepting Hall, were carried off our feet. Hall helped hold us together. This time we were successful.

Six mountain sheep stared at four weary, limping men making their way through the snow in Red Rock Canyon, an hour later. We had no fire-arms or the game laws of Colorado might have been broken right there. It was mid afternoon of the Eighth of Dec. when we reached the first ranch in Bostwick Park. The fourth section of the canyon would have to wait for another season.

I recovered my cameras the next week after a cold snap that froze the river in the quiet places. Some of the bedding was cached in trees, back from the river.

All Winter I planned and fussed about the last section, waiting for the snow and the Spring thaw to pass. A friend notified me when the time was ripe and I returned to the task. Many things were in my favor this time just as they were against me the season before. For various reasons I wanted to go through from the narrow gorge to the point where we had lost the boat. By swimming and walking, without a load, I made the six miles in one day. It had kept me busy for a month of the season before.

My boat, brought in at Red Rock, was a small canvass one, large enough for one man and a small load. All weight was cut to the minimum. My companion this trip was Albert Moore, of Montrose, eighteen years old, cool and careful.

For three days travel we found [the] canyon quite similar to the section below Cimarron, excepting certain sections which were quite open, with cattle trails leading down from the upper slopes. We made good progress and had little trouble. We took turns rowing the boat and

FIGURE 13.20. Ellsworth Kolb and Bert Loper with Peterborough canoe used on the Grand River and the second section of the Gunnison River. NAU. PH.568.5856, Cline Library, Northern Arizona University, Flagstaff, Arizona: Ellsworth Kolb photo found in Emery Kolb Collection.

swimming when it was necessary to cross. On the fourth day we had a different sort of canyon. The granite had given way to widely separated sandstone walls of varying hues and over 2000 feet high. An inner plateau extended for two miles away from the river or inner gorge of granite, which was about 300 feet deep, with precipitous walls, the river frequently filling the channel. Some of the rapids were violent. Two were passed by the extra man going around on the plateau and climbing in again while the other ran the boat. At another, it was necessary to swim a rapid and make a quick landing in a whirlpool. The last quarter of a mile was as quiet as a mill pond, without a shore on either side. It was my turn to swim and be towed by the boat, and I was not sorry to pull out of the numbing water at the Smith Fork, a tributary that marks the end of the Black Canyon. It took another day to row down past the North Fork to Delta. Moore entrained when we struck the railroad branch but I remained with the leaking boat until I dragged it out at the Delta bridge, and my Black Canyon exploration was no longer a dream, but an accomplished fact.

(Editors [from Ellsworth Kolb] note.) The experiences recorded in the following paragraphs occurred in the months of Aug. and Sept. 1916, but have been placed at the end in order to make the Black Canyon account a continuous one and avoid confusion regarding localities.

In the interval of time between the first attempt at the Black Canyon, which ended above the tunnel, and the second one, while waiting for the high water to recede, Shields and I proceeded with our plans for other sections, less dangerous at that stage of water. The freight canoe was put into the Gunnison River at Delta, at the very point where I finally finished the Black Canyon, and we made a twelve hour run on the tamed stream, which landed us at Grand Junction, Colo. Here we had a stream half the size of the Colorado. It is interesting to note that early maps include the Gunnison as part of the Grand River and named the larger branch above the junction, the Blue River.

A day later we resumed our journey and made a hundred mile run down the Grand River to Moab, Utah. We avoided Westwater Canyon, sometimes called Granite Canyon, just across the Utah line, by having our boats hauled around. This twelve mile canyon had never been successfully negotiated by boat; lives had been lost by those who had attempted it. Two rapids, locally known as the Double Pitch and the Whirlpool Rapid, are especially dangerous. Two ranchers, living at the head of the canyon, told us that it was impossible to go through these rapids and live.

A favorite expression with one, when describing the whirlpool, was, "the fishes brains are spattered on the walls."

The canyon is very picturesque and reminded us in a way of the Grand Canyon of Arizona, several hundred miles down this same river system. But with this difference; the granite walls, so called, are 300 feet high instead of 1500 feet, and the bright colored sandstone walls above the inner bench or plateau on top of the granite, are 500 feet high, to compare with the 3000 feet of stratified rock in the Grand Canyon. A trail runs through the canyon on top of the granite. We walked through and climbed down the steep walls to the water at several places. We could not get close to the Double Pitch but had an excellent view of it from an overhanging ledge. It lived up to its sinister reputation. It was a short but dangerous rapid. What made this section especially

FIGURE 13.21. Loper and Kolb portaging boat around Shoshone Falls on Grand River above Glenwood Springs. NAU.PH.568.9038, Cline Library, Northern Arizona University, Flagstaff, Arizona: Ellsworth Kolb photo found in Emery Kolb Collection.

dangerous was the fact that one rapid followed another altogether too close for comfort.

The Whirlpool was a miniature Niagara Whirlpool, carved out of the nearly perpendicular walls. A ten foot fountain rolled back from the edge of rock that divided the river from the whirlpool. All driftwood was smothered under tons of water, then circled for hours in the eddy. The roar was deafening. It seemed impossible, at this stage of water, to get through it in a boat, but I imagined it could be done at a lower stage and expressed a determination to try it later.[3] Shields returned to his home after the trip to Moab.

Bert Loper joined me two weeks later and we had another set-too with 150 miles of swift water and rapids. This included some bad water in Shoshone Canyon, sometimes called the Grand River Canyon, above Glenwood Springs, also a run down to Grand Junction. Then we had a try at Westwater Canyon with the canoe. The two ranchers and a photographer to operate the cineometograph accompanied us on horseback,

FIGURE 13.22. Frank E. Dean and Bert Loper filming Whirlpool Rapid aka Skull Rapid while cowboy watches the event. NAU.PH.568.5929, Cline Library, Northern Arizona University, Flagstaff, Arizona: Ellsworth Kolb photo found in Emery Kolb Collection.

FIGURE 13.23. Ellsworth Kolb photo at Whirlpool, today known as the Room of Doom in Westwater Canyon. NAU.PH.568.3827, Cline Library, Northern Arizona University, Flagstaff, Arizona: Ellsworth Kolb photo found in Emery Kolb Collection.

on the plateau, keeping as near the river as possible. Bert and I took turns at running the rapids and helping the camera-man. Bert drew the Double Pitch and had an exciting experience but came out conqueror. He was carried into the rapid before he expected it and for over an hour I did not know if he was alive or not, and was overjoyed to find him in camp, calmly eating his supper, which the ranchers had prepared.

The whirlpool fell to me, but in low water it was simply a straight rapid with quiet water in the eddy. It was big enough to upset me and I found the life-line, which I had attached to the sides of the boat, a handy thing to hold to. I was getting expert by this time, for it happened twice before. I turned the canoe upright, climbed in over the bow and had it under control before reaching another rapid 150 feet below.[4]

We landed at the end of the gorge that evening, proud of our record of having been the first to run the rapids of Westwater Canyon. This kind of water compared well with the rapids of the Colorado River and was entirely to our liking. The water was big but it could be run. It was entirely different from the Black Canyon, which had water enough at times, but was so badly blocked with rocks that there was little sport in boating through it.

APPENDIX G

COLORADO RIVER SITES—WESTWATER AREA

The following locations along the Colorado River provide a brief interpretation of human occupancy along the river in the Westwater region. Although some of the location names may have changed over the years, as a general rule mountains, hills, landmarks, creeks, sloughs, and so on originally took on names of early explorers, settlers, and incidents in the region. Some locations that are named after settlers or homesteaders are assumed to be in the vicinity of their residence or property. Most of the historical information for this guide comes from *Westwater Lost and Found* (2004) and this book.[1] The mileage is approximated based on Belknap's *Canyonlands River Guide* by Westwater books.[2]

Mile 135.3: Moore Canyon may have been named after Frank Moore, who was an area resident? Moore was arrested along with longtime resident Elwood Clark Malin in 1930 for bootlegging on "Moonshine Island" on the Colorado River upstream of the current Westwater boat launch during Prohibition.

https://doi.org/10.7330/9781646425457.c014

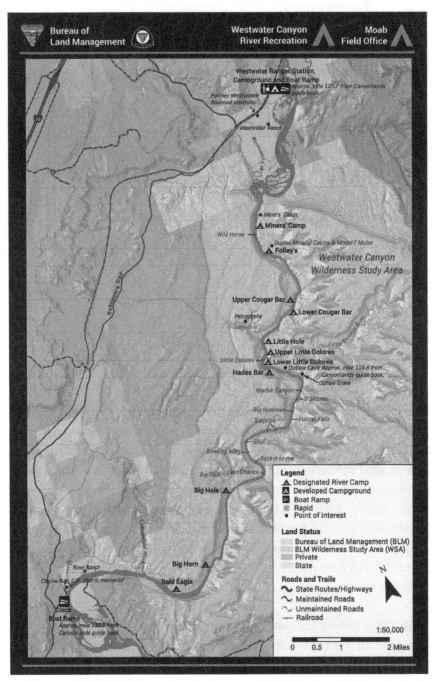

FIGURE 14.1. Modified BLM map of Westwater highlighting additional historical sites. Modified by author.

134.3: In the vicinity of McDonald Canyon, Harry McDonald built a cabin. In 1998 a group headed by John Weisheit searched the area for signs of the cabin, but none were located. Most likely the cabin was washed away by the river or removed by the railroad when it moved considerable track away from the bluffs in Ruby Canyon during the 1920s to avoid problems derived from frequent flash floods. Harry McDonald was one of the boatmen for the Brown & Stanton's Denver, Colorado Cañon and Pacific Railroad (DCC&P RR), better known as the Brown-Stanton Survey, down the Colorado River in 1889.

134.1: Knowles Canyon was possibly named after Emery Knowles, who was a cowboy in the vicinity and worked for the prominent Sieber Cattle Company at the turn of century. He later moved downstream across the river from Cisco and established the Knowles Ranch.

131: Charles Brock dugout was located river right near shore. Remains of the dugout have not been found and likely were washed away by the Colorado River. Charles Brock was shot and killed along with two of his gang members by Captain Wilson E. Davis on August 24, 1892. Davis, a sharpshooter for the Union Army in the Civil War, resided in the vicinity of Westwater Ranch. The Brock gang apparently tried to burn Davis's home while he was on business in Fruita, Colorado. After Davis discovered the attempt to burn his ranch, he followed a trail of stolen honey from his property by the culprits to the Brock dugout near the Colorado border. The following day Captain Davis shot and killed Brock and the two men. His wire to Grand Junction read: "For very good reasons, I ran against Brock and his outfit at six o'clock this morning and as a result I want three plain, cheap coffins as soon as possible."[3]

It is likely that Charles Brock was a boatman for Frank Clarence Kendrick, who surveyed the Grand River in 1889 for the DCC&P RR, aka the Brown-Stanton Survey. Shortly after the survey was completed for the Grand River, by 1890, Brock moved from Grand Junction to settle on land near the Utah-Colorado border. According to a government survey in 1894, the Brock log cabin was located in Section 29 and was still in existence and had one-half mile of fence. Brock and the two other men who were killed were buried on his claim.

FIGURE 14.2. General location along bank where Charles Brock dugout was located. Captain Wilson E. Davis's photo from approximate time of the killings, and 1915 photo from San Quentin State Prison. Prison image found at https://www.ancestry.com/search/collections/8833/. Area photo by author (2000).

Mile 130.8: May Flats was named for the John May family, owner of the Echo Ranch, which existed in the area in the early 1900s through 1920s.

Mile 129.1: Grant's Slough was a named area of Westwater and likely located near where George D. Grant settled on river right sometime in the late 1800s. One incident involving his son Frank being a witness to Captain Wilson E. Davis killing Charles Brock and two others in 1892, and the killing of his own son Royal in 1894, may have contributed to him leaving the area. His family does not appear on the 1900 US Census for Westwater.[4]

Mile 129: River left is the former Pace-Fuller Ranch. It was one of the larger ranches in Grand County. Florence Creek near McPherson Ranch on the Green River is said to have been named after the prominent co-owner, Florence Harris Fuller (1866–1930). Known as the Cattle Queen of the Colorado Plateau, at the age of nineteen or twenty,

Florence arrived in Utah Territory from Texas sometime in 1885 or 1886 with a hundred head of cattle that she claimed to have obtained from Tom Horn. She initially ran her cattle from Woodside to the Book Cliffs near Florence Creek, then later moved her herds to Westwater and Piñon Mesa.[5] After her husband, Robert Lee Fuller, died on May 4, 1902, she partnered with Joe Pace (1858–1940).

Mile 128.6: NE of the Bitter Creek area near the Colorado River, former resident Owen Malin kept a personal graveyard where he buried nine unidentified bodies that floated downriver to Westwater from Grand Junction and Fruita. On March 24, 2004, Dan O'Larie Museum's former co-curator Rusty Salmon asked me to show her where Owen's graveyard was. She had a personal interest in locating old gravesites and brought a machine with her, probably a ground-penetrating radar (GPR) for locating buried bodies. Working from a drawing that Owen's younger brother John L. "Jack" Malin drew for me, we believe that we located the gravesite but no bodies were detected. Much of the area was covered with sagebrush.

Mile 128.3: A sanitarium existed in the Bitter Creek area. Primarily for visitors with tuberculosis, it was also referred to as a hotel. Former Westwater resident Owen Malin claimed there were twenty-one rooms, and it was occupied by people who primarily came from Michigan and Chicago, because of Westwater's climate. A hotel was reported built in 1905 and was still in existence in 1912. It later burned down.

Mile 128: The house west of Bitter Creek was built in 1917 by Harvey Edward (Ed) Herbert. He was deputy sheriff and sheep inspector for a number of years for the Westwater and Cisco area. He entered the area in approximately 1898 and died in 1929. He was the stepfather of Elwood C. Malin. Herbert accompanied Ellsworth Kolb and Bert Loper when they boated through Westwater in 1916. He and cattleman William Stubbs followed along the rim of the canyon by horse in order to be available with their long ropes in case the famous river men needed help.

FIGURE 14.3. Harvey Edward Herbert's home near the confluence of Bitter Creek with the Colorado River. Herbert was a deputy sheriff of Westwater region, and he accompanied Ellsworth Kolb and Bert Loper during their historic Westwater Canyon trip in 1916. His name is inscribed near the Denis Julien inscription found in the Book Cliffs. Photo by author (1987).

Mile 127.7: SW of the river about three-quarters of a mile was the former site of the Westwater Denver & Rio Grande Western Railroad (D&RGW RR) Depot. According to a 1920 census, the small town's population reached nearly 100 residents. Mostly railroad homes existed near the depot, and numerous other ranchers spread out throughout the valley, at Bitter Creek, and along both shores of the Colorado River. In 1919, R. A. Tawney, of Grand Junction, Colorado, built a sheep-shearing plant at Westwater near the depot that could shear up to 2,500 sheep per day. The shearing of sheep during the spring was a major industry for Westwater, Cottonwood, Thompson, and Cisco during the 1920s and 1930s.

The road alongside the railroad tracks that is used to get to the Westwater Ranger Station is part of the Salt Lake Wagon Road that was expanded from a trail by the US Army in 1858 and 1860 and was a primary wagon road to travel between Salt Lake City and Colorado. The

FIGURE 14.4. Westwater water tank. Photo was likely taken between 1927 and 1929, when the contributor's mother, Myrtle Marie Anderson Holyoak, resided there with her brother William Henry "Bill" Anderson's family. He was a section foreman for the D&RGW RR. Photo courtesy of Roberta Knutson.

FIGURE 14.5. The road to Westwater Launch is part of the Old Salt Lake Wagon Road. Van parked in vicinity of former Westwater railroad station and tank. Photo by author (1987).

road was improved from preexisting North Branch of the Old Spanish Trail (OST) that converged with the Main OST near Crescent Junction. The trail was likely started from game trails and Native Americans and developed further by trappers, explorers, surveyors, settlers, and merchants traveling between New Mexico and California.[6]

Mile 127.7: Approximate location of a ford said to have been used by local ranchers and possibly Utes to cross the Colorado River during low water. An island northeast of this was named Moonshine Island by local residents. It most likely received its name because of a moonshine still that was located in a dugout built on the island south of Bitter Creek in 1930 during Prohibition. Officers had to borrow a boat from residents to reach it.

Mile 127.6: The area of the BLM Ranger Station was formerly a pasture belonging to longtime resident Elwood C. Malin. His home, also used as a boardinghouse, was across the road from the railroad depot and burned down in 1935. At the time Malin and his family were living at their new ranch near Westwater Gulch. The latter, abandoned ranch was burned down from a grass fire. According to former BLM Westwater ranger Alvin Halliday (serving 1994–2015), the Little Hole wildfire in 1999 destroyed Malin's home and other wood structures. See photo of the home on page 63 in *Westwater Lost and Found* (2004). Only a metal shed and silo remain. The 3,216-acre fire came near enough to the Westwater ranger station that Alvin remembered, "we had to load up the boats on the trailer, and park them up the road, as the fire was blowing towards the ranger station."[7]

Mile 127.4: Nearly across the Colorado River from the BLM Ranger Station and further inland stood Joe Harris's ranch and home. Joe Harris had skirmishes with his neighbor Joe Pace, one of which resulted in Harris's death in 1909.[8]

Westwater Ranch: the ranch already existed in 1889, when Frank Clarence Kendrick surveyed the area for the DCC&P RR. Westwater Ranch originally belonged to the Box X Cattle Company, which entered

FIGURE 14.6. Elwood Clark Malin and stepson Jesse Hunt at Westwater. Photo courtesy of Elwood Malin's daughter, Ila Reay.

the region from Texas in 1886.[9] The ranchers ran cattle from Thompson to Grand Junction. The ranch became the central location for industry and agricultural attempts that were made to boost recognition of Westwater as a legitimate town until 1931, when the D&RGW RR abandoned the station. Westwater Ranch was the most expensive property in Grand County in the late 1800s and early 1900s and still carries a hefty price tag. Private property.

Mile 125 to 121: Mesa SE of Colorado River was named Snyder Mesa, most likely after Daniel M. Snyder who ran a ranch on the Little Dolores

FIGURE 14.7. Old Wagon found at Westwater Ranch. Private property. Photo by author (1998).

River and appears on the 1900 US Census at Westwater. Residents and miners along the Little Dolores were frequent visitors at Westwater.

Mile 124.7: Westwater Creek drains into the Colorado River near this area. Not far from the shore is where Colonel William Wing Loring's US Army soldiers camped while they improved the Salt Lake Wagon Road to Colorado in 1858. This is also where Hallett's Pasture was located in Section 14. Charles H. Hallett was a resident from approximately 1892 until possibly 1897, or later.[10] His family would eventually move downriver to Cisco and settle property now known as Rose Ranch. Private property.

Mile 124.6: Some faint Fremont pictographs at the base of the cliffs are probably less than a one-fourth of a mile from where Westwater Creek merges with the Colorado River. Notes from a 1981 University of Utah visit indicate they were poor due to erosion. In the same approximate location are panel markings of recent visitors; a few are from the early 1900s, including former resident E.C. Malin. This site was sometimes used as a boat launch site for Westwater trips and likely explains the more recent markings. Private property.

Mile 124.5: It is still a mystery who MWJ is and how the individual chiseled their initials above the river on the cliff at the fault heading into Westwater Canyon. Possibly not related but in the same general vicinity is a chiseled date of 1915. The question is how they got there. During that year, the Colorado River ran at 1,520 cfs at its lowest level on September 10, 1915, and at its high water of 33,600 was on June 13. There is also a gazebo overlooking the river and valley that is further back and at the top of the cliff. Private property.

Mile 124.2: Wild Horse, or Miners', Cabin, was claimed to have been built by former Westwater resident Owen Madox Malin to placer mine the Colorado River. Owen arrived at Westwater to live with his father, Elwood C. Malin, in 1918 when he was ten years old.[11] BLM archeologist Richard E. Fike in 1973 dated the cabin from the 1890s to late 1920s or early 1930s.

Mile 124: Wild Horse Rapid was first recognized as the rapid immediately below Wild Horse / Miners' Cabin. The 2014 printing of *Canyonlands River Guide* by Westwater books now identifies both the rapids above and below Wild Horse / Miners' Cabin as Wild Horse Rapid.

Mile 123.6: A rock chimney exists on the slope overlooking campsite downstream of Miners' Cabin. Most likely it is the remains of a placer miner dugout.

Mile 124.5–123: Plenty of evidence still exists along this section of Westwater of placer mining activity including a Ford Model T type engine that Dee Holladay of Holiday River Expeditions reported seeing during low water for a number of years. In the fall of 2001 during a Westwater cleanup, the motor was recovered near the head of Wild Horse Rapid and kept at the Westwater Ranger yard for one year. It was

FIGURE 14.8. Miners' Cabin, fireplace, and motor used by placer miners near Wild Horse Camp. Photos 1 and 2 by author (1983, 2018), photo 3 by Bob Brennan (2021).

then returned and placed on the slope near where it was originally located and downhill from the "Duplex Miners' Cabins." The motor could not be identified by the vin number, and it was speculated to be a model especially designed for placer mining.

Mile 123.2: Dee Holladay refers to the cabins as Duplex Miners' Cabins. The cabins can be seen easily from the river during high water. Otherwise, one of them can be seen briefly while boating through Wild Horse Rapid. Newspaper sources describe numerous placer mining activities in the area beginning as early as 1883. Gold placer mining activity initially was more prominent along the upriver gravel shores near Westwater Ranch; it then moved into the canyon and up the Little Dolores River. Other reports of mining activity occurred at Outlaw Cave and Little Hole. Mining speculation seems to have diminished by the 1920s. There is a good possibility that some of the dugouts in the region may have also been used by bootleggers during Prohibition, which lasted from 1917 until 1933. The condition of the cabins has noticeably deteriorated and the roofs have collapsed since I first observed them in 1983.

Mile 123: This is the approximate location of a dam site that was proposed in the canyon in 1903–1904. Shortly afterward, this site was discarded because during high water the town at Westwater and the railroad would be flooded. The coordinates given were that it was "2

FIGURE 14.9. Remains of Duplex Miners' Cabins. See photos taken in 1983 on page 35 of *Westwater Lost and Found* (2004) to compare their deterioration. Photo is by Bob Brennan (2021).

miles below Westwater in the NE. ¼ sec.27, T. 20 S., R. 25 E., where the width between walls at the low-water line is 100 feet." The dam was proposed to return water upstream to Grand Valley for irrigation.

Mile 120.8: About the Little Hole area, two sources claim a copper mine existed here around the 1920s. Also, large bootlegging operations located at Little Hole and Big Hole were reported as having been seized and destroyed by the federal government during Prohibition. A nice petroglyph of a train of quadrupeds and an elk can be found toward the middle of the canyon on the north side. A brief survey of the petroglyphs by the University of Utah in the early 1970s speculated they were Fremont culture.

Mile 120.4: In the Little Dolores Canyon area some mining activities were reported, probably quite a bit further upstream of the falls. The

FIGURE 14.10. Quadruped Petroglyph at Little Hole. Photo by Ross Henshaw (2004).

petroglyph of an eagle and other simple figures can be found on base of the Wingate cliffs. These likely were done by Utes because one of them depicts a horse. Further up the Little Dolores River near the Colorado border there have been several significant Indigenous archaeological digs at Luster Cave beginning in 1951. James Luster purchased Florence Fuller and Joe Pace's Ranch in 1939.

Mile 119.3: Of Outlaw Cave, no concrete evidence has been uncovered regarding the story of two outlaw brothers living there. Former Westwater resident Elwood C. Malin and Cisco resident Roscoe C. Hallett identified the cave as Counterfeit Cave, claiming bogus money was produced there before the turn of the twentieth century. In 1933, Roscoe Hallett told boater Harold H. Leich that the manmade cave was chipped out possibly as early as the 1860s or 1870s.

The late Dee Holladay learned the story of two outlaw brothers living in the cave from Ray Rose, a former lessee of the Rose Ranch near the river at Cisco. Ray claimed that he had learned the story from the owner at the time, J. Perry Olsen of Grand Junction, who purchased

FIGURE 14.11. Little Dolores waterfall. Photo by author (1983)

the ranch from Roscoe Hallett in 1936. The story likely originated from Roscoe, whose family homesteaded the ranch sometime after 1900. Ray Rose was told that the source's father took supplies, sometimes by ice-skates, to a couple of outlaw brothers living in the cave.

FIGURE 14.12. Outlaw Cave collage. Dee Holladay photo by John Clark of Holiday River Expeditions, Doc Shores photo courtesy of Museums of Western Colorado, Grand Junction, Colorado, Cave entry photo in upper right corner by Bob Brennan (2021), other photos by author (2005, 2009, 2018, 1998, 2005).

The brothers supposedly robbed a bank in Vernal and avoided the law by hiding in the cave. Rose also indicated that the grave further downstream belonged to one of the brothers, who was wounded and subsequently died from his injuries.

The story may have evolved from one of two reported incidents involving outlaw brothers who were known to have been in the Westwater region. One involved two brothers, Bob, aka Ira, and Jack Smith, who with the help of two other men robbed a Denver & Rio Grande Railroad mail and express train east of Grand Junction on November 3, 1887. They escaped by boating down the Gunnison, then Grand River into Utah, where they were captured several months later. There is no concrete evidence of them boating through Westwater Canyon; however, they eventually caught a train at Cisco. One of the brothers was accidently wounded from a gunshot issued by a member of his own party. He did survive.[12]

FIGURE 14.13. Outlaw Grave. Photo by Bob Brennan (2021)

Another story from 1905 involves the Steele brothers Bob and Bill, who escaped the law crossing the Dolores River into the Dolores Triangle, where they were shot at from across the river. The brothers were wanted in Colorado and Utah for stealing horses. Perhaps one was wounded? Horse thieves were reported a number of times during the late 1800s and early 1900s escaping into the Book Cliffs and Dolores Triangle, where it was nearly impossible for the law to find them. Some stories involving the cave claim the residents were horse thieves who kept the horses near the river out of site in the Marble Canyon area to feed. For a long time, wild horses roamed on the south side of the river. A former Westwater resident, John Malin, told of an old timer who lived in the cave in the early 1930s. He trapped the wild horses and ate them. The trapper may have been L. D. (Luke) Hummel, whose name appeared in several articles in Moab's *Times Independent* for his hunting exploits, and there were letters found in the cave by the first group of kayakers that ran Westwater in 1962 addressed to "Mr. Hummell" at Westwater dated December 19, 1902.[13] See *Westwater Lost and Found* (2004) for additional stories related to Outlaw Cave.

Mile 119.4: Outlaw Grave, as mentioned above. The story is that the grave belongs to a wounded outlaw brother. Old timers didn't have any idea whose grave it is but said bodies would periodically be found floating downstream from Fruita and Grand Junction and would be buried when they could not be identified.

Mile 118.2: Big Hummer Rapid was a rapid Dee Holladay attempted to have renamed Hunters Rapid in memory of three deer hunters who lost their lives as a result of flipping their heavily loaded raft while deer hunting there on November 15, 1970.[14]

Mile 118: Funnel Falls likely was the formidable rapid known to early Westwater residents as Double Pitch Rapid, when Kolb and Loper boated Westwater Canyon in 1916. Only two rapids were named in Kolb's manuscript of the event: Double Pitch and Whirlpool Rapids.

Mile 117.3: Skull Rapid received its christened name on March 23, 1956, by Leslie "Les" Allen Jones's boating party after they capsized their raft at Funnel Falls and wound up camped in the rocks adjacent to Skull Rapid. While camping, they discovered a full skeleton tucked under one of the larger rocks near the water.[15]

In 1916, when Kolb and Loper boated Westwater, this rapid was named Whirlpool Rapid or Big Whirlpool. Of the rapid, an elderly Westwater resident told Kolb, "Fishes brains were spattered on the walls." It was also known as Cisco Bend Rapid, and Les Jones claimed it was at one time called Dead Horse Rapid.[16]

Mile 117.2: Above the Room of Doom, between Skull Rapid and Bowling Alley, is the site where Kolb and Loper camped the night before completing their historic 1916 journey through Westwater Canyon. Loper boated the first day possibly to Funnel Falls, and Kolb completed the canyon the following day.

FIGURE 14.14. Photographers awaiting Ellsworth Kolb to boat Whirlpool Rapid in 1916. NAU.PH.568.5929, Cline Library, Northern Arizona University, Flagstaff, Arizona: Ellsworth Kolb photo found in Emery Kolb Collection.

FIGURE 14.15. Room of Doom, previously known by local residents as Big Whirlpool. In 1916, Kolb and Loper camped above the Whirlpool in Westwater Canyon. See image 5.8. Photo by Ross Henshaw (2005)

Appendix G | 237

FIGURE 14.16. Second dam site proposed on Grand River below Westwater, Utah. US Congress, Geological Survey, Reclamation Service, 2d report, 1903, 58th Congress, 2nd session, 1903–1904, H. Doc. 57, no 44.

Mile 117: The approximate final proposed location of the 1903–1904 dam site was described in the Second Annual Report of Reclamation Service as being "about 6 miles below the former site (mile 123), in the SW. ¼ sec. 4, T. 21 S., R. 25 E., at a point where the river makes two sudden right-angle bends, forming a letter Z." The coordinates typed into the report are further inland, away from the river making the exact location unknown.

Mile 116.3: Trail Canyon is one of two escape routes out of the canyon, the other being at Little Hole. It was named most likely by cattlemen who grazed their cattle at Big Hole.

Mile 116: At Big Hole, according to a former resident at Westwater, was the location of one of the biggest bootlegging operations in Grand

FIGURE 14.17. Charlie Ray, C. R., Sherrill memorial. Photo by author (1983).

County. Barrel rings were located in this area by a research group headed by John Weisheit on October 30, 1998.

Mile 112: Cottonwood Wash was a former railroad stop and a temporary sheep-shearing location in the late 1920s. Petroglyphs.

Mile 111.2: Agate Wash was a former railroad stop. During Prohibition, the largest reported bootlegging operation in Grand County was accidentally discovered in this wash in 1928. Petroglyphs.

Mile 111.1: The memorial is for Charlie Ray, "C. R." Sherrill, born January 11, 1943, and lost in Westwater Canyon, November 15, 1970. Sherrill was a nephew of Ray Sherrill, who opened Ray's Tavern in Green River. C. R. Sherrill was one of three deer hunters who died in Westwater Canyon from an overturned raft on November 15, 1970. His body was found fifteen months after the accident.[17]

Mile 111: Rose Ranch was originally homesteaded by the Hallett family sometime after 1900. It is uncertain whether the husband and father,

FIGURE 14.18. Cisco post office. Photo by author (2019).

Charles H. Hallett, made it to Cisco with his family after their property at Westwater was sold. The US patent for the ranch and property was issued to his wife, Chloe A. Hallett, on February 17, 1910. The couple had two sons, Charles V. and Roscoe C. Hallett. The Halletts owned the ranch until it was sold around 1936 to J. Perry Olsen of Grand Junction.

Mile 110.5: Knowles Ranch was possibly established by Emery Knowles who was mentioned at mile 134.1. Emery Knowles once worked for the Sieber Cattle Company at the turn of the century. The Sieber Cattle Company Ranch headquarters was located in Glade Park.

Mile 110.5: Cisco Landing is located here, and like Westwater, Cisco was a railroad water stop that was farther inland. There were two other stops between them at Cottonwood and Agate; however, only Westwater and Cisco gained a reasonable population. Cisco was the larger of the two towns and at one time was said to have the largest sheep-shearing business west of the Mississippi, shearing up to 80,000 sheep annually in the spring.

NOTES

Acknowledgments

1. Mike Milligan, "Westwater Camp: Water, Wood and Grass," *Spanish Traces* 27, no. 1 (Spring 2021): 22–35.

Introduction

1. *Daily Sentinel* (Grand Junction), May 26, 1902; Don Lago, *The Powell Expedition: New Discoveries about John Wesley Powell's 1869 River Journey* (Reno: University of Nevada Press, 2018), 190–195. There is a discrepancy between Westwater and Green River, where Jack Sumner was injured.
2. Steve Allen, *Utah's Canyon Country Place Names*, vol. 1 (Durango, CO: Canyon Country Press, 2012), 264–265.
3. "On Hunt for Outlaws: Posses Are Searching Eastern and Southern Part of Utah for Slayers of Sheriff Tyler and Deputy," *Salt Lake Tribune*, May 30, 1900; "Sheriff William Preece," *Vernal Express*, September 3, 1981.
4. Smithsonian Institution Archives. record unit 7157, box 1, folder 1, Kreutzfeldt, Frederick. Frederick Kreutzfeldt Journal, 1853. The Smithsonian Institute Archives house a handwritten German and English copy of the journal that begins on June 18 and

ends on October 12, 1853. There are a typescript and an edited version made from the English translation (see appendix A). None appear to be of the original journal.
5. Mark Twain, *The Adventures of Huckleberry Finn* (Philadelphia: Courage Books an imprint of Running Press, 1986), 100.
6. "Trip through Westwater Canon Was Like Tickling Dynamite with a Lighted Match—Wow!," *Grand Junction Daily News*, September 28, 1916.
7. "E.L. Kolb and His Companion Make Long River Trip," *Grand Valley Times*, August 25, 1916.
8. *Same River Twice*, dir. Scott Featherstone, Candlelight Media Group, 1996.
9. Scott Lindgren and Thayer Walker. "After a Hard Diagnosis, One Athlete Learns to Soften Up." *Outside*, October 14, 2019, https://www.outsideonline.com/outdoor-adventure/water-activities/scott-lindgren-kayaker/. See also Rush Sturges, dir., *The River Runner* (Boone, CO: River Roots, 2021).

Chapter 1: Westwater Camp: Water, Wood, and Grass

1. *Utah Place Names: A Comprehensive Guide to the Origins of Geographic Names*, comp. John W. Van Cott (Salt Lake City: University of Utah Press, 1990), 394–395.
2. Bert J. Silliman Papers, 1951–1957, "Appropriate Names," box 1, folder 8, Utah Historical Society.
3. Jackson C. Thode, letter to author, October 2, 1987. "The original narrow gauge line out over the uplands west of Grand Junction was spiked down during January, February and March of 1883. The main line and siding at what became West Water (two words), 48.4 miles west of Grand Junction and 25.2 miles east of White House, was laid January 9, 1883. In the handwritten record the place does not show a name for the siding, but the name West Water had been assigned by the end of the year." "The water supply did not see much use because the water was alkali."
4. Lloyd Pierson and Lyle E. Jamison, "The Denver and Rio Grande Narrow Gauge Railroad across Grand County," *Canyon Legacy* 42 (Summer 2001): 14–18.
5. Bill Wolverton, "Ruby Canyon: The Railroad through It and a Brief History," *Canyon Legacy* 42 (Summer 2001): 9.
6. Helen J. Stiles, "Down the Colorado," *Colorado Magazine* 41, no. 3 (Summer 1964): 235.
7. "Is Nearly Ended. Defendants Are on the Stand," *Provo Daily Enquirer*, vol. 9, no 105. April 5, 1894.
8. "Court Filings," *Provo Daily Enquirer*, April 30, 1895. Ed Price claimed in a dispute with George H. Darrow that in "1880, he legally settled upon and improved a tract of land in Westwater valley."
9. Mike Milligan, *Westwater Lost and Found* (Logan: Utah State University Press, 2004), 29–74.
10. D. C. Collier, "Recent Explorations," *Rocky Mountain News*, September 21, 1860.
11. D. C. Collier, "Recent Explorations," *Rocky Mountain News*, September 21, September 22, September 28, September 29, October 2, October 4, October 5, October 11, October 12, and October 17, 1860.

12. Lloyd M. Pierson, "The Salt Lake Wagon Road across Grand County," *Canyon Legacy* 47 (Spring 2003): 1–8.
13. James M. Robb and William L. Chenoweth, "We Rode the Legislation Trail—from OST to NHT," *Spanish Traces* 9, no. 1 (Winter 2003): 6–7.
14. Jack William Nelson, *Forgotten Pathfinders: Along the North Branch of the Old Spanish Trail 1650–1850*, ed. Jon M. Nelson (Grand Junction, CO: Self-Published, 2016), http://northbranchost.com/wp-content/uploads/2016/11/Forgotten-Pathfinders-new-A.pdf; Lloyd M. Pierson, "The Salt Lake Wagon Road across Grand County," *Canyon Legacy* 47 (Spring 2003): 2–8; William L. Chenoweth, "A Portion of the North Branch Became the Salt Lake Wagon Road," *Spanish Traces* 15, no. 1 (Winter 2009): 10–13.
15. LeRoy R. Hafen and Ann W. Hafen, *Old Spanish Trail: Santa Fe to Los Angeles* (Lincoln: University of Nebraska Press, 1993), 19.
16. William L. Chenoweth, "Rivers of the Grand Valley," *Spanish Traces* 12 (Spring 2006): 24–26.
17. William Wolfskill may have traveled parts of the North Branch. According to his son-in-law, H. D. Barrows, "Last of Sept., 1830, the party, with Mr. Wolfskill at its head, left Taos for this then far off Territory of California. They came by a route farther north than that usually adopted by the Spaniards." LeRoy R. Hafen, "The Old Spanish Trail, Santa Fe to Los Angeles," *Huntington Library Quarterly* 11, no. 2 (1948): 155.
18. James H. Knipmeyer, *The Life and Times of Denis Julien: Fur Trader* (Chula Vista, CA: Aventine Press, 2018), 80; David J. Weber, *The Taos Trappers: The Fur Trade in the Far Southwest, 1540–1846* (Norman: University of Oklahoma Press, 1982), 84–88, 109.
19. "Letter from Mr. Benton to the People of Missouri: Central National Highway from the Mississippi River to the Pacific," *Weekly National Intelligencer*, Washington, DC, June 11, 1853.
20. Because of insufficient evidence that the West Fork of the trail through San Luis Valley was used for commercial activities between New Mexico and California during the trail's significant period (1829–1848), the West Fork of the North Branch is no longer shown on maps as part of the Old Spanish Historical Trail.
21. Jack W. Nelson, "North Branch of the Old Spanish Trail: The Trapper Variant," *Canyon Legacy* 53 (Spring 2005): 36–38.
22. The trading post was established originally as the William Reed Trading Post in 1828, with William's young nephew James and Denis Julien. It was later purchased by Antoine Robidoux in the spring of 1832. Knipmeyer, *The Life and Times of Denis Julien: Fur Trader*, 92–96; A. Reed Morrill, "The Site of Fort Robidoux," *Utah Historical Society* 9, no. 1–2 (January, April 1941): 1–11.
23. Nelson, *Forgotten Pathfinders*, 47–51; James H. Knipmeyer, "Denis Julien: New Inscription Discovery," *Canyon Legacy* 71 (Winter 2011–2012): 15–17.
24. Forbes Parkhill, *The Blazed Trail of Antoine Leroux* (Los Angeles: Westernlore Press, 1965).
25. DeWitt C. Peters., *The Life and Adventures of Kit Carson: Nestor of the Rocky Mountains* (New York: W.R.C. Clark & Co., 1858), 335.
26. Forbes Parkhill, *The Blazed Trail of Antoine Leroux*, 13–28.

27. Baldwin Möllhausen, *Diary of a journey from the Mississippi to the Coasts of the Pacific With a United States Government Expedition*, vol. 2, trans. Mrs. Percy Sinnett (London: Longman, Brown, Green, Longmans, & Roberts, 1858), 23–25, 190.
28. "Congressional: Speech of Hon. W.H. Seward, of New York," *Daily Union*, Washington, DC, February 12, 1853.
29. Forbes Parkhill, *The Blazed Trail of Antoine Leroux*, 207.
30. "Navigability of the Colorado River," *Daily Alta California*, May 31, 1857. Letter from Antoine Leroux—"I know that the river Colorado is navigable from the mouth of the Virgen [sic] down. From the mouth of the Virgen, in 1837, I constructed skin canoes until I had reached the place where timber was to be had; then I made seven wooden canoes, and continued trapping as far as the tide-waters, in which place I met with the Co-ca-pah Indians [sic]." This was a reply to a question Leroux was asked regarding the possibility of getting a steamboat up the Colorado as far as the Virgin.
31. Jacob H. Schiel, *Journey through the Rocky Mountains and the Humboldt Mountains to the Pacific Ocean* (Norman: University of Oklahoma Press, 1959), 59; Frank Schubert, *Vanguard of Expansion: Army Engineers in the Trans-Mississippi West, 1819–1879* (Washington, DC, Superintendent of Documents, US Government, August 1980): 103. According to botanist Frederick Kreutzfeldt, Leroux provided "topog directions to the Great Salt Lake."
32. Gwinn Harris Heap, *Central Route to the Pacific, From the Valley of the Mississippi to California: Journal of the Expedition of E. F. Beale, Superintendent of Indian Affairs in California, and Gwinn Harris Heap, from Missouri to California in 1853* (Philadelphia: Lippincott, Grambo, and Co., 1854), 17.
33. LeRoy R. Hafen, introduction and notes, "Colonel Loring's Expedition across Colorado in 1858," *Colorado Magazine* 23, no. 2 (March 1946):59–62; Durwood Ball, foreword to Colonel John Van Deusen Du Bois, with pencil sketches by Joseph Heger, *Campaigns in the West 1856–1861: The Journal & Letters of Colonel John Van Deusen Du Bois* (Tucson: Arizona Historical Society, 2003), 78. Second Lieutenant Du Bois may have provided the mileage to Colonel Loring. He claims in his journal that he used an odometer and Schmacalder's compass for his measurements.
34. LeRoy R. Hafen, introduction and notes, "Colonel Loring's Expedition across Colorado in 1858," *Colorado Magazine* 23, no. 2 (March 1946): 57.
35. Hafen, "Colonel Loring's Expedition across Colorado in 1858," 61.
36. Du Bois, *Campaigns in the West 1856–1861*, 78.
37. Hafen, "Colonel Loring's Expedition across Colorado in 1858," 61.
38. Lieut. E. G. Beckwith, *Report of Exploration of a Route for the Pacific Railroad Capt. Gunnison, Topography Engineers Near the 38th & 39th Parallels of Latitude, The Mouth of the Kansas River, Mo., To the Sevier Lake, In the Great Basin, Senate Reports: Explorations and Surveys, from the Mississippi River to the Pacific Ocean, 1853–4* (Washington, DC: Beverley Tucker, Printer, 1855), 58–61. https://quod.lib.umich.edu/m/moa/AFK4383.0002.001/1?rgn=full+text;view=image.
39. Beckwith, *Report of Exploration of a Route for the Pacific Railroad*.

40. Hafen, "Colonel Loring's Expedition across Colorado in 1858," 55; Nolie Mumey, "John Williams Gunnison: Centenary of His Survey and Tragic Death," *Colorado Magazine* 31 (January 1954):26n.
41. "The Central Route—Additional Testimony," *Washington Sentinel*, Washington, DC, December 8, 1853; Howard L. Conard, *"Uncle Dick" Wootton: The Pioneer Frontiersman of the Rocky Mountain Region* (Chicago: W. E. Dibble & Co, 1890), 249–262.
42. Hayden, F. V., *Ninth Annual Report of the United States Geological and Geographical Survey of the Territories embracing Colorado and parts of Adjacent Territories: being a Report of Progress of the Exploration for the year 1875* (Washington: Washington Printing Office, 1877) 349. Accessed September 4, 2023. https://www.biodiversitylibrary.org/item/124508#page/464/mode/1up.
43. Pierson, "The Salt Lake Wagon Road across Grand County," 5; Nicholas G. Morgan, "Miscellaneous Papers Pertaining to John Morgan," digitized by J. Willard Marriott Library, University of Utah, digital date 2013-04-09, 1–2; pages are from Hans Jensen Hals journal of an 1878 journey from Manti to San Luis Valley to "establish new settlements and to preside over the Saints from the Southern States that were going to emigrate to San Luis Valley." Accessed August 2, 2021, https://collections.lib.utah.edu/details?id=907246.
44. Jonathan C. Horn, Michael Prouty, Jack E. Pfertsh, and John Zachman, 2011, National Historic Trails Inventory Project, "Tasks 4, 5, and 6 Memo Report for Utah Main Route, Northern Branch, and Armijo Route of the Old Spanish Trail, Emery, Grand, Kane, Piute, San Juan, and Sevier Counties, Utah." Prepared by Alpine Archaeological Consultants, Inc., Montrose, CO. Prepared for AECOM, Fort Collins, Colorado; Jon Horn, email message and attachment of sections of the report pertaining to the Salt Lake Wagon Road through Grand County were received by author, January 21, 2020.

Chapter 2: The Outlaw Brothers

1. "A Woman Drowned Near Cisco," *Provo Daily Enquirer*, April 12, 1887.
2. Mike Milligan, *Westwater Lost and Found* (Logan; Utah State University Press, 2004), 137–138.
3. Harold H. Leich, Harold Hebert Leich papers, 1910–1985, ACCN 1973, box 1, folder 1, Special Collections, J. Willard Marriott Library, University of Utah. The quote is not found in any of the edited versions of Leich's manuscript that he initially worked with Otis Reed "Dock" Marston to have published. It is also missing from the 2019 publication of his journal *Alone on the Colorado*, with a foreword by Roy Webb.
4. "Malin Letter Clears Up Lot of Mystery of Cave History," *Times Independent*, May 24, 1956. Throughout the article the cave is referred to as "Counterfeit Cave." John L. (Jack) Malin, letter to author, March 29, 1987. In reply to a question the author asked about Outlaw Cave, John responded, "The so called outlaw cave is not correct. It is the counterfeit cave."
5. Initially, the Denver & Rio Grande Railroad was narrow gauge and established a water stop approximately ten miles inland near the Westwater Exit 227 off of I-70. In 1890, the railroad changed to standard gauge and moved the location nearer to

the river. The former railroad settlement was approximately a mile from the current Westwater boat launch.
6. The Dolores Triangle was made up of the Colorado River on the northwest, and the Dolores River to the south; the Utah/Colorado border forms the east side. "Horse Thieves in Eastern Utah," *Salt Lake Tribune*, July 18, 1888. A second article from the same issue in the miscellaneous news provides additional information about horse thieves in eastern Utah.
7. Blake and Marianna (former BLM Westwater ranger 1978–1979) Hopkins, interview by author, 1986.
8. Harold H. Leich, ACCN 1973, box 1, folder 1, Special Collections, J. Willard Marriott Library, University of Utah; "Malin Letter Clears Up Lot of Mystery of Cave History"; John L. (Jack) Malin, letter to author, March 29, 1987.
9. Larue Olsen (Mrs. J. P. Olsen), letter to author, July 17, 1987. According to Ray Rose's wife, Mary, the "Hallet Ranch" aka Rose Ranch was homesteaded by the Hallett family. Mary Rose, letter to author, February 4, 1984.
10. Milligan, *Westwater Lost and Found*, 88–96. Hallett claimed to have helped a missing California millionaire, Dr. Thomas E. Tynan, when he wandered into his mining camp in the Henry Mountains in the summer of 1893. It was suspected that Hallett made the claim to receive a $2,000 reward for any information leading to locating the missing man. Dr. Tynan left his home on October 15, 1892, and after being pronounced dead, he returned to his home on September 26, 1894. He claimed that he was in Boston the entire time. "Hallet's Prior Breaks," *Salt Lake Tribune*; September 3, 1893. "A Missing Millionaire," *Ogden Standard*, September 23, 1893; "Dr. Tynan's Estate: Hallett's Story about the Doctor in Utah," *Salt Lake Tribune*, October 27, 1893; "Doctor Tynan: A Very Lively Corpse," *Salt Lake Herald*, September 27, 1894.
11. Chloe A. Hallett received a US patent for her homestead at Cisco on February 17, 1910.
12. "Is He Innocent? The History of a Crime: John L. Campbell a Victim of Circumstances," *Grand Valley Sentinel*, July 18, 1891.
13. "A Passenger Train on the Denver & Rio Grande Robbed by Masked Men," *Gunnison Review Press*, November 3, 1887.
14. Wilson Rockwell ed., *Memoirs of a Lawman* (Denver: Sage Books, 1962), 152.
15. Rockwell, *Memoirs of a Lawman*, 158.
16. Rockwell, *Memoirs of a Lawman*, 164–165.
17. "Caught at Last: Capture of the Denver and Rio Grande Train Robbers," *Deseret News*, February 8, 1888.
18. Rockwell, *Memoirs of a Lawman*, 166.
19. Rockwell, *Memoirs of a Lawman*, 168.
20. Series 3 Manuscripts 1927–1929, box 2, Cyrus Shores Papers, WH344, Western History Collection, Denver Public 6Library.
21. Series 3 Manuscripts, 1927–1929, box 2, Cyrus Shores Papers, WH344, Western History Collection, Denver Public Library.
22. "The Train Robbers: Captured by Sheriff Shores' Deputies, Harper and Allison. They are Securely Lodged in the Gunnison County Jail," *Gunnison Review Press*, January 12, 1888.

23. "The Boyle Capture, etc.," *Gunnison Review Press*, February 4, 1888, Series 3 Manuscripts, 1927–1929, box 2, Cyrus Shores Papers, WH344, Western History Collection, Denver Public Library. The "Lone Fisherman" referred to in the news article is identified as "old man Brown" in Sheriff Wells manuscript.
24. "Capture of Two Express Robbers," *Gunnison Review Press*, December 29, 1887; "The D. & R. G. Robbers: Captured at Vernal, Utah, by Two Colorado Men," *Salt Lake Tribune*, December 28, 1887.

Chapter 3: Those Darn Woman's Shoes Found in Westwater's Cave

1. Helen J. Stiles, "Down the Colorado in 1889," *Colorado Magazine* 41 (Summer 1964): 235.
2. Harold H. Leich, ACCN 1973, box 1, folder 1. Special Collections, J. Willard Marriot Library, University of Utah; John L. Malin, mail correspondence with author, August 9, 1987. "Yes I have heard about the two men and one woman having an accident at the Whirlpool the woman drowned, if the body of the woman was recovered I don't know, or the date or who they were. If I did know I have forgotten the name or names."
3. "Sad News," *The Delta Independent*, April 12, 1887.
4. Stiles, "Down the Colorado in 1889," 235. Frank Clarence Kendrick surveyed the Grand River for the Denver, Colorado Cañon and Pacific Railroad (DCC&P RR) from Grand Junction to the confluence with the Green River. From there, his crew hauled their boat up the Green River to the town of Green River. The survey continued down the Green and Colorado Rivers under the DCC&P RR president Frank Mason Brown until his death below Soap Creek Rapid in Marble Canyon, and then his chief surveyor, Robert Brewster Stanton, completed the survey.
5. Memorandum from archaeologist Richard E. Fike to Monticello, Utah, district manager dated June 27, 1973. The memorandum includes site inventories and brief histories of the Wild Horse Cabin and Outlaw Cave in Westwater Canyon. The information is not for public use and resides with the Moab Bureau of Land Management (BLM). Moab BLM archaeologist Donald Montoya, email correspondence, March 25, 2014. "The earliest date is 1887 and the only other date is 1910 from some archival records. There was no additional dating of the artifacts."
6. John McGill, email correspondence, October 5, 2015; Dominic Massa, "Curator John Magill to Retire after 3 Decades with Historic New Orleans Collection," Nola.com, June 17, 2015, https://www.nola.com/news/article_b7c9f0dd-8a7f-5c67-9848-37f8628ff178.html.
7. Tom Mattimore, email correspondence with author, January 31, 2017, and February 2, 2017. Tom is with Mattimore Harness, a custom boots and modern footwear business in Laramie, WY. See https://www.wyomingnews.com/laramieboomerang/news/shoemaker-passes-trade-to-the-next-generation/article_0c6f940e-3cc6-5f72-bdaf-fd7b56d0a22c.html or https://senecacreekstudios.com/making-shoes-by-hand-lost-art-of-american-shoemaking-mattimore-harness-laramie-wyoming/. Tom questioned whether the boots might belong to a child. Part of his

reasoning is some photos I sent to him of the shoes included tin can artifacts that gave him a perception that they were smaller than an adult foot. Otherwise, his response centered on or around a date of 1920. "The style is post 1920. The construction is post 1870's. The heel is too low for a woman's shoe The foot also appears to be too small for five foot tall person. It is barely as big as the tin cans in the picture. Lace hooks were common by the 1880s in military shoes. The earliest example of a similar style is the 1889 Spaulding baseball company shoe. The rounded wide toe is a post 1915 example. The use of so many small parts in the pattern of a small shoe cry out cutting dies, clicker presses and assembly line sewing."

8. Mike Milligan, *Westwater Lost and Found* (Logan: Utah State University Press, 2004). 180–184.
9. *Daily Journal* (Telluride), July 25, 1908; "Three Tramps Drown by Capsizing of Boat," *Daily Sentinel* (Grand Junction), July 23, 1908.
10. Dee Holladay, interview by author, September 10, 1982.
11. "Malin Letter Clears Up Lot of Mystery of Cave History," *Times Independent*, May 24, 1956.
12. "Malin Letter Clears Up Lot of Mystery of Cave History," *Times Independent*, May 24, 1956; "Westwater Notes," *Grand Valley Times*, February 9, 1917; "Westwater Notes," *Grand Valley Times*, January 1, 1919.
13. Milligan, *Westwater Lost and Found*, 139–146.
14. Walter Kirschbaum, box 113, folder 6, Otis R. Marston Papers, Huntington Library, San Marino, California, letter from Walter Kirschbaum to John L. J. Hart, July 15, 1969.
15. As of November 1, 2021, accessing Richard Adolphus McGruder at the Ancestry.com website provides evidence of his "left arm off below shoulder" reported on US World War 1 Draft Registration Cards, 1917–1918. There is also a photo of McGruder evidencing the amputated arm.
16. As of November 1, 2021, accessing Richard Adolphus McGruder at the Ancestry.com website documents the marriage between R. A. McGruder and Ida M. Merkt on March 31, 1919, in Green River, Utah. Correspondence received as a message on ancestry.com by author on February 13, 2017, reported that a grandchild briefly described Ida as a great fisherman, a tobacco chewer, and the type of person who would not be reluctant to float the river.

Chapter 4: Dentists' Sabbatical on the Grand River in 1897

1. Roy Webb's forward to *Alone on the Colorado*, by Harold H. Leich (Salt Lake City: University of Utah Press, 2019); copies of Harold H. Leich's diary and several versions of his edited drafts are housed at the University of Utah's Marriott Library Special Collections: Harold H. Leich, ACCN 1973, box 1, folder 1. Special Collections, J. Willard Marriott Library, University of Utah.
2. Brad Dimock, *The Very Hard Way: Bert Loper and the Colorado River* (Flagstaff, AZ; Fretwater Press, 2007)

3. James H. Knipmeyer, *The Life and Times of Denis Julien: Fur Trader* (Chula Vista, CA; Aventine Press, 2018)
4. Box 2, folder 47, Robert Brewster Stanton papers, Manuscripts and Archives Division, New York Public Library, Astor, Lenox and Tilden Foundations.
5. Babcock-Miller, 1897, box 276, folder 53. Otis R. Marston Papers, Huntington Library, San Marino, CA. The note is attributed to Marston's handwriting.
6. Box 2, folder 47, Robert Brewster Stanton papers, Manuscripts and Archives Division, New York Public Library, Astor, Lenox, and Tilden Foundations. A note reads that the letter was received November 27, 1906, and that Dellenbaugh wrote back for more details. We do not have a copy of that letter. On the note he also wrote, "The point 150 miles below the mouth of the Green where he had his only danger is smooth river—no rapids—at least compared with Cataract Canyon which he found so easy. FSD."
7. Box 2, folder 47, Robert Brewster Stanton papers. Manuscripts and Archives Division. New York Public Library; Astor, Lenox, and Tilden Foundations. Dr. Miller's handwriting is not entirely legible, but he appears to have written "stomach troubles."
8. "Take a Trip down the Grand," *Glenwood Post and the Weekly Ledger*, August 14, 1897.
9. "Take a Trip down the Grand." During the nineteenth and early twentieth centuries, there were no laws governing looting of Indigenous sites. It wasn't until June 8, 1906, that Congress passed An Act for the Preservation of American Antiquities in an attempt to protect the removal of artifacts and preserve historic sites. The act did not sufficiently deter artifact collectors, and more legislation was enacted afterward until it became more strongly enforced as it is today.
10. *Avalanche*, August 11, 1897.
11. "On a Dangerous Voyage," *Colorado Weekly Chieftain*, August 19, 1897. "Crowds of people were attracted to the state bridge and other points where the start could be watched." Also, in Dr. Miller's letter to Dellenbaugh he wrote, "Made our own boat at Glenwood, the point of departure, where at least 500 people witnessed the start."
12. "Word from the Argonauts," *Avalanche*, August 16, 1897.
13. "They Have Felt the Thrill: That Comes from Dangers Narrowly Escaped—But Drs. Miller and Babcock Are Having a Good Time on the Whole—Sun Burns and Blisters," *Avalanche*, August 28, 1897.
14. *Grand Valley Times*, August 27, 1897.
15. "They Have Felt the Thrill: That Comes from Dangers Narrowly Escaped."
16. Box 2, folder 47, Robert Brewster Stanton papers, Manuscripts and Archives Division. New York Public Library, Astor, Lenox, and Tilden Foundations.
17. Box 2, folder 47, Robert Brewster Stanton papers, Manuscripts and Archives Division, New York Public Library. Astor, Lenox, and Tilden Foundations.
18. Box 2, folder 47, Robert Brewster Stanton papers, Manuscripts and Archives Division, New York Public Library, Astor, Lenox, and Tilden Foundations.
19. Box 2 Folder 47, Robert Brewster Stanton papers, Manuscripts and Archives Division, New York Public Library. Astor, Lenox, and Tilden Foundations.

250 | NOTES

20. Box 2, folder 47, Robert Brewster Stanton papers, Manuscripts and Archives Division, the New York Public Library. Astor, Lenox, and Tilden Foundations. As quoted earlier, Miller writes that they were not aware of how far they'd gone and asked a cowboy they met. The cowboy replied that they were in Buckskin Canyon. A Buckskin Gulch exists as a tributary to the Paria Canyon. It is not near enough to the Colorado River for it to be the same canyon that was named.
21. *Grand Valley Times*, September 17, 1897.

Chapter 5: Ellsworth Kolb: Losing His Boyhood

1. From part of a handwritten draft of the manuscript that was mailed by Bill Suran to the author in the mid-1980s. The incomplete handwritten copy cannot be located at Kolb Collection, Cline Library, Northern Arizona University. Copy in possession of the author.
2. E. L. Kolb, *Through the Grand Canyon from Wyoming to Mexico* (New York, Macmillan Company, 1914). Prior to the use of river maps, many early river travelers used Kolb's book, Frederick S. Dellenbaugh's, *A Canyon Voyage*, and Major John Wesley Powell's, *The Exploration of the Colorado River and Its Canyons*, as guides.
3. Ellsworth and Emery Kolb, "Experiences in the Grand Canyon," *National Geographic Magazine* 26, no. 2 (March 1914): 99–184.
4. "Old Timer Visits Grand Canyon," *Williams News*, March 29, 1917.
5. Ellsworth Kolb, NAU, MS 197, series 3, box 18, folder 1914—folder title Manuscript for Ellsworth Kolb's Gunnison River trip, ca. 1918. Emery Kolb Collection, Cline Library, Northern Arizona University.
6. William C. Suran, ed., *The Brave Ones: The Journals & Letters of the 1911–1912 Expedition down the Green & Colorado Rivers by Ellsworth L. Kolb and Emery C. Kolb, including the Journal of Hubert R. Lauzon* (Flagstaff, AZ: Fretwater Press, 2003), xiii.
7. The first successful party to run Soap Creek Rapid is attributed to Clyde Eddy in 1927.
8. Suran, William C., *The Kolb Brothers' Biography—With the Wings of an Angel: A Biography of Ellsworth and Emery Kolb, Photographers of Grand Canyon* (self-published, 1991), "The Kolb Diaries: Chapter 3, From Lodore to Bright Angel," accessed November 19, 2021, http://kaibab.org/kaibab.org/kolb/index.html.
9. C. Suran, *The Brave Ones*, 103.
10. Brad Dimock, *Sunk without a Sound* (Flagstaff, AZ: Fretwater Press, 2001), 125.
11. Suran, *The Kolb Brothers' Biography—With the Wings of an Angel*, "The Kolb Diaries: Chapter 5, 1912–1918: The Lecture Tours," accessed November 19, 2021, http://kaibab.org/kaibab.org/kolb/index.html.
12. Roger Naylor, *The Amazing Kolb Brothers of Grand Canyon* (Grand Canyon, AZ: Grand Canyon Association, 2017), 74.
13. Two members of the 1869 J. W. Powell Expedition, Jack Sumner and Andy Hall; the Brown-Stanton party in 1890; and George Flavell and Ramon Montez in 1896 boated down the Colorado River to the Gulf of California.
14. Ellsworth Kolb, box 111, folder 10, Otis R. Marston Papers, Huntington Library, San Marino, California, Letter from Ellsworth Kolb to Lewis R. Freeman, April 17, 1923.

15. "The Name of Gunnison," *Sun* 1, no. 21 (October 6, 1883), 4.
16. William L. Chenoweth, "Rivers of the Grand Valley," *Spanish Traces* 12, no. 2 (Spring 2006): 24–26.
17. Wallace B. Hansen, *The Black Canyon of the Gunnison: Today and Yesterday* (Washington, DC, US Government Printing Office, 1965), 1.
18. Hansen, *The Black Canyon of the Gunnison*, 4.
19. A 1906 or 1907 image of a crumpled *Uncompahgre Valley Colorado Topographical and Irrigation Map* (NAU.PH 568.316 and 568.5985) is located amongst the Emery Kolb Collection at the Cline Library, Northern Arizona University.
20. William C. Suran, *The Kolb Brothers of Grand Canyon* (Grand Canyon, AZ: Grand Canyon National History Association, 1991), 8.
21. Suran, ed., *The Brave Ones*, 98.
22. Brad Dimock, *The Very Hard Way* (Flagstaff, AZ: Fretwater Press, 2007), 150.
23. Ellsworth Kolb, NAU, MS 197, series 3, box, 18 folder 1914—folder title Manuscript for Ellsworth Kolb's Gunnison River trip, ca. 1918, Kolb Collection, Cline Library, Northern Arizona University, Flagstaff, AZ.
24. Otis Reed "Dock" Marston. Tom Martin ed., *From Powell to Power: A Recounting of the First One Hundred River Runners through the Grand Canyon*, ed. Tom Martin (Flagstaff, AZ: Vishnu Temple Press, 2014), 499.
25. Most likely referring to a Kapok suit.
26. Fletcher Anderson and Ann Hopkinson, *Rivers of the Southwest: A Boaters' Guide to the Rivers of Colorado, New Mexico, Utah and Arizona*. 2nd ed. (Boulder, CO: Pruett Publishing Company, 1987), 50.
27. Naylor. *The Amazing Kolb Brothers of Grand Canyon*, 77.
28. Ellsworth Kolb, box 111, folder 9, Otis R. Marston Papers, Huntington Library, San Marino, CA, letter from Ellsworth Kolb to Stanton, February 3, 1917.
29. "Ellsworth Kolb Makes Trip in Black Canon in Day Which Took Five Weeks Last Year with Boat," *Montrose Daily Press*, October 3, 1917.
30. Ellsworth Kolb, box 111, folder 12, Otis R. Marston Papers, Huntington Library, San Marino, CA, letter from Ellsworth Kolb to Lewis R. Freeman, April 17, 1923.
31. Ellsworth Kolb, box 111, folder 9, Otis R. Marston Papers, Huntington Library, San Marino, CA, correspondence between Ellsworth Kolb and Julius Stone, 12-11-16.
32. Bert Loper suffered two broken ribs and a painful back injury. Kolb twisted his knee badly.
33. Ellsworth Kolb, NAU, MS 197; series 3, box 18, folder 1914—folder title Manuscript for Ellsworth Kolb's Gunnison River trip, ca. 1918, Kolb Collection, Cline Library, Northern Arizona University, Flagstaff, AZ.
34. This was unrelated to the New York Marathon, which began on September 13, 1970.
35. "Aviator Thomas Lands in Canyon," *Williams News*, August 11, 1922. The article refers to one of the Kolb brothers. Ellsworth is recognized as paying $100 to hire Nelson to fly him into the canyon. Naylor, *The Amazing Kolb Brothers of Grand Canyon*, 82–85; Suran, *The Kolb Brothers' Biography—With the Wings of an Angel*, "The Kolb Diaries: Chapter 7, 1921–1924: The River Again," http://kaibab.org/kaibab.org/kolb/index.html; A. Gaylord, "1922-Into the Grand Canyon and Out Again by Airplane," *Grand*

252 | NOTES

Canyon Centennial Stories, Grand Canyon National Park, National Park Service. https://www.nps.gov/articles/airplaneintograndcanyon.htm#:~:text=GRCA%20IMAGE%2005235)-,R.V.,08%20AUG%201922.&text=FIRST%20AIRPLANE%20LANDING%20MADE%20IN,ARIZONA%20ON%20AUGUST%208%2C%201922.

36. Suran, *The Kolb Brothers' Biography—With the Wings of an Angel*, "The Kolb Diaries: Chapter 7, 1921–1924: The River Again," accessed November 19, 2021, http://kaibab.org/kaibab.org/kolb/index.html.
37. Suran, *The Kolb Brothers' Biography—With the Wings of an Angel*, "The Kolb Diaries: Chapter 7, 1921–1924: The River Again," accessed November 19, 2021. http://kaibab.org/kaibab.org/kolb/index.html.
38. Ellsworth Kolb, box 111, folder 10, Otis R. Marston Papers, Huntington Library, San Marino, CA. Regarding Ellsworth Kolb's marriage, his brother Emery sent a telegram to Julius F. Stone dated July 21, 2024, informing him of the marriage and wrote, "But I pity the poor girl, especially if she did not know his condition and which she had little chance to know, since she lived in Dakota." Ellsworth's Kolb's condition may be referring to the nervous breakdown.
39. Naylor, *The Amazing Kolb Brothers of Grand Canyon*, 120.
40. Suran, *The Kolb Brothers' Biography—With the Wings of an Angel*, "The Kolb Diaries: Chapter 11, The Last Years," accessed November 19, 2021, http://kaibab.org/kaibab.org/kolb/index.html
41. Ellsworth Kolb, NAU MS 197, series 2, box 17, folder/binder 19, "Ellsworth Kolb's Gunnison River Trip," n.d., Emery Kolb Collection, Cline Library, Northern Arizona University; Ellsworth Kolb, NAU MS 197, series 3, box 18, folder 1914, "Manuscript for Ellsworth Kolb's Gunnison River trip, ca 1918," Emery Kolb Collection, Cline Library, Northern Arizona University.
42. Ellsworth L. Kolb, *Through the Grand Canyon from Wyoming to Mexico* (New York: The Macmillan Company, 1914), 285.
43. Kolb, *Through the Grand Canyon from Wyoming to Mexico*, 285.
44. Ellsworth Kolb, NAU, MS 197; series 3, box 18, folder 1914—"Manuscript for Ellsworth Kolb's Gunnison River trip, ca. 1918," Kolb Collection, Cline Library, Northern Arizona University.
45. Dimock, *Sunk without a Sound*, 126.

Chapter 6: Fellows and Torrence: Overcoming the Narrows

1. NPS ranger Paul A. Zaenger, email correspondence with author, February 26, 2021.
2. "Black Canyon the Next Generation," https://vimeo.com/36298473.
3. Alvin T. Steinel, *History of Agriculture in Colorado, 1858 to 1926* (Fort Collins, CO: State of Agricultural College, August 1, 1926), 530–535. The text found in *History of Agriculture in Colorado* comes from A.L. Fellows's lectures on the Gunnison Tunnel that can be found under the title "Black Canyon of the Gunnison River: Slides and text are from the records of Mr. Fellows; they are the results of his surveys in 1901 and 1902," Black Canyon of the Gunnison National Park, NPS.

4. "Fellows on Scenery, He Tells of the Wonders of Black Canon," *Montrose Enterprise*, September 5, 1901.
5. Duane Vandenbusche, "Man against the Black Canyon," *Colorado Magazine* 50, no. 2 (Spring 1973): 126–127.
6. Wallace R. Hansen, *Black Canyon of the Gunnison: Today and Yesterday* (Washington, DC: US Government Printing Office, 1965), 2.
7. David Halpern, *A Timeless Challenge: Encounters with Colorado's Black Canyon of the Gunnison River* (Tulsa, OK: Gneissline Publishing, 2019), 7. Halpern was national park artist-in-residence twice at Black Canyon, in 1989 and 1993.
8. Vandenbusche, "Man against the Black Canyon," 125–128.
9. Steinel, *History of Agriculture in Colorado, 1858 to 1926*, 531.
10. Steinel, *History of Agriculture in Colorado*, 531.
11. Steinel, *History of Agriculture in Colorado, 1858 to 1926*, 532.
12. T. Steinel, *History of Agriculture in Colorado, 1858 to 1926*, 532.
13. Steinel, *History of Agriculture in Colorado, 1858 to 1926*, 532.
14. Steinel, *History of Agriculture in Colorado, 1858 to 1926*, 533.
15. Black Canyon (M-Box) Photo Gallery, accessed April 29, 2023. The cheat sheet of rapid names and class designations was assigned by Milo T. Wynne, who has been through the Black Canyon National Park of the Gunnison River at least fifty times, http://www.riverbrain.com/run/show/384; "Local Paddler Completes 50th Run Through the Black Canyon," *Crested Butte News*, July 3, 2012.
16. Steinel, *History of Agriculture in Colorado, 1858 to 1926*, 533.
17. Robb Magley, *Deep Black* (Montrose, CO: Western Reflections Publishing Company, 2002), 127–128.
18. Steinel, *History of Agriculture in Colorado*, 531.
19. Mark T. Warner, *Through the Black Canyon* (Ann Arbor, Michigan: Braun-Brumfield, Inc., 1972), 25. The distance getting through the Narrows was calculated by the 1934 USGS.
20. "Will's Story: W. W. Torrence Tells Our Reporter of the Trip through the Canon," *Montrose Enterprise*, August 29, 1901.
21. Steinel, *History of Agriculture in Colorado, 1858 to 1926*, 531–532.
22. Warner, *Through the Black Canyon*, 31–35. During a 1934 USGS Survey, the party measured the height of a rock at a location they named "Underwear Pool" at forty-two feet. At another location, they measured a rock that they camped on as fifty feet long by thirty feet wide. The party also discovered the oar handle from the 1916 Ellsworth Kolb attempt. On a leather band nailed to the handle of the oar was printed in large letters "KOLB."
23. Steinel, *History of Agriculture in Colorado, 1858 to 1926*, 534.
24. Steinel, *History of Agriculture in Colorado, 1858 to 1926*, 534.
25. Steinel, *History of Agriculture in Colorado, 1858 to 1926*, 534.
26. "Will's Story: W.W. Torrence Tells Our Reporter of the Trip through the Canon," *Montrose Enterprise*, August 29, 1901.
27. Fletcher Anderson and Ann Hopkinson, *Rivers of the Southwest: A Boaters' Guide to the Rivers of Colorado, New Mexico, Utah and Arizona*, 2nd 3d. (Boulder, CO: Pruett Publishing Company, 1987), 58.

254 | NOTES

28. Comments found on American Whitewater website for Gunnison 03. Crystal Dam to Chukar Trail, accessed on December 31, 2021, https://www.americanwhitewater.org/content/River/view/river-detail/401/main.
29. Comments found on American Whitewater website for Gunnison 03.
30. Tom Michael Janney, e-mail message to author, February 28, 2021.
31. Tom R. Chamberlain, e-mail message to author, January 12, 2021.
32. "Will's Story."
33. Anderson and Hopkinson, *Rivers of the Southwest*, 58.
34. Anderson and Hopkinson, *Rivers of the Southwest*, 58.
35. Paul Zaenger, email correspondence with author, February 26, 2021. Paul wrote, "The average number of kayakers, per year, over the past 15 years is 59. But the years from 2006 through 2010 (wet years) average 109 per year. The previous 10 years have been more on the dry side. We are likely to see 100 to 150 kayakers per year in wet years, 50 to 75 kayakers in dry years. The past three years we recorded 44 to 48 kayakers each year." He said his figures do not include pack rafts, which have grown in popularity, and estimates anywhere from 100 to 200 of these boaters boat the Black Canyon mostly through the Gunny Gorge section below Chukar Trail.
36. "Local Paddler Completes 50th Run through the Black Canyon."
37. Description given for Gunnison River—Black Canyon (M-Box) accessed April 29, 2023, https://www.riverbrain.com/run/show/384.
38. Whipple Yale Chester, "Ellsworth Kolb Makes Trip in Black Canon in Day Which Took Five Weeks Last Year with Boat," *Montrose Daily Press*, October 3, 1917.
39. "Kolb Will Finish Tour of Black Canyon," *Delta Independent*, September 14, 1917.
40. "Fellows on Scenery."
41. Warner, *Through the Black Canyon*, 1.
42. "Will's Story."

Epilogue

1. See appendix F.
2. Harold H. Leich, *Alone on the Colorado*, forward by Roy Webb (Salt Lake City: University of Utah Press, 2019), 185.
3. *Avalanche*, September 14, 1897.
4. Fletcher Anderson and Ann Hopkinson, *Rivers of the Southwest: A Boater's Guide to the Rivers of Colorado, New Mexico, Utah and Arizona* (Boulder, CO; Pruitt Publishing Company, 1987).
5. William John Davis, box 46, folder 8, Otis R. Marston Papers, Huntington Library, San Marino, CA, letter from William Davis to Pete Sparkes, April 16, 1956.
6. J. Frank Wright, letter to Author, November 13, 1988.
7. "River Water in his Blood," *News: The Journal of Grand Canyon River Guides, Inc.*, vol. 6, no. 3 (late summer 1993): 33, https://static1.squarespace.com/static/61d3bc4beef7c3126df06d78/t/61f73742961aef202a76aee7/1643591505677/6-3.pdf.
8. George Fuller et al., *National Geographic Guide to National Parks of the United States*, 8th ed. (Washington, DC: National Geographic Society, 2016), 207.

9. "Planes, Horses, Boats Used to Rescue Pair Lost on River after Raft Capsizes; Both Rescues by Hanksville Sheriff," *Times Independent*, June 16, 1956. Only one Cataract Canyon River Trip was scheduled on Georgie's, "Share the Expenses Plan River Trip," advertisement for June 3–13. Passengers were to meet at Green River, Utah. Georgie White 1956, box 291 folder 29, Otis R. Marston Papers, Huntington Library, San Marino, CA.
10. Music Temple Register, June 1, 1955, MSS B 108, box 1, folder 5, Colorado River Visitors' Registers Collection, 1946–1964, Utah Historical Society.
11. John L. J. Hart, "Westwater Canyon by Boat and on Foot," *Trail and Timberline*, no 544 (April 1964): 63–68.
12. Ed Hudson, box 95, folder 16, Otis R. Marston Papers, Huntington Library, San Marino CA, journal entries from May 23 to June 2, 1955.
13. Karla VanderZanden, letter to author, April 13, 1984.

Appendix A: Frederick Kreutzfeldt (Creutzfeldt)— Partial Journal Notes from 1853

Smithsonian Institution Archives, record unit 7157, box 1, folder 1, Kreutzfeldt, Frederick, Frederick Kreutzfeldt Journal, 1853. Of the four copies of Frederick Kreutzfeldt's 1853 journal held at the Smithsonian Institution Archives, two are handwritten one in German and the other in English. The remaining two copies are typescripts of the English translation, with one having been edited with handwritten additions and corrections. None appear to be of the original journal. The following text is from the edited English translation of the typescript. I retyped the manuscript, incorporating Kreutzfeldt's corrections/updates. Older or incorrect spellings, and derogatory or outdated terms, from the original have been preserved.

1. Mary Lee Spence ed., *The Expeditions of John Charles Frémont*, Vol. 3. *Travels from 1848 to 1854* (Urbana: University of Illinois Press, 1984). 54.
2. LeRoy R. Hafen and Ann Hafen eds., *Frémont's Fourth Expedition: A Documentary Account of the Disaster of 1848–1849, with Diaries, Letters, and Reports by Participants in the Tragedy* (Glendale, CA: Arthur H. Clark Company, 1960), 76.
3. Hafen and Hafen, *Frémont's Fourth Expedition*, 189–190.
4. Hafen and Hafen ed., *Frémont's Fourth Expedition*, 190. It is assumed Frémont is referring to the botanist Frederick Kreutzfeldt.
5. Spence, *The Expeditions of John Charles Frémont*, 3:128.
6. Gunnison River.
7. This word for Captain Gunnison is used several times throughout Kreutzfeldt's journal. It appears to be German and is used in a derogatory manner. The nearest English translation for *Rohrle* or *Röhrle* is "tube" or "pipe."
8. Upper Grand, or Colorado River above Grand Junction. Below the confluence of these rivers, they formed the Grand River.
9. Kreutzfeldt was well aware of the taste of "roasted greased boots" having, survived on them during the Frémont Expedition in 1848–1849.

Appendix B: Westwater Camp and Water Stop Chronology

1. Mike Milligan papers, ACCN 1441, box 2, folder 3, Special Collections, J. Willard Marriot Library, University of Utah.
2. Ron Kessler, *Old Spanish Trail North Branch and Its Travelers* (Santa Fe, NM: Sunstone Press, 1998). Kessler's book provides historical biographical sources for many of the expeditions listed in this appendix.
3. Brewerton, *Overland with Kit Carson*, 113–122. In his writings, Lt. Brewerton confused the sequence of the rivers and listed the Grand River as being the first one that they crossed and where his notebook and other valuables were lost. Without his notenotebook, there are no concrete dates provided in his writings; even so, he did note that he celebrated his birthday on the bank of the Grand (Green) River. Brewerton's birthday is June 3, 1827. It took two days for them to reach the true Grand River crossing., Kit Carson, *Kit Carson's Autobiography*, ed. Milo Milton Quaife (Lincoln: University of Nebraska Press, 196), 123–112; Mike Milligan papers, ACCN 1441, box 2, folder 3, Special Collections, J. Willard Marriot Library, University of Utah.
4. Gwinn Harris Heap, *Central Route to the Pacific, From the Valley of the Mississippi to California: Journal of the Expedition of E. F. Beale, Superintendent of Indian Affairs in California, and Gwinn Harris Heap, from Missouri to California in 1853* (Philadelphia: Lippincott, Grambo, and Co., 1854), 82.
5. Heap, *Central Route to the Pacific*, 82.
6. In his notes, Kreutzfeldt estimated that they were five to six miles from the Grand River.
7. Frank Schubert, *Vanguard of Expansion: Army Engineers in the Trans-Mississippi West, 1819–1879* (Washington, DC: US Government Printing Office, August 1980), 103. In his journal botanist Frederick Kreutzfeldt indicated that an argument broke out over Gunnison ignoring Leroux's instructions to remain camped while he reconnoitered the route ahead. Smithsonian Institution Archives, record unit 7157, box 1, folder 1, Kreutzfeldt, Frederick, Frederick Kreutzfeldt Journal, 1853.
8. Lieut. E. G. Beckwith, *Report of Exploration of a Route for the Pacific Railroad Capt. Gunnison, Topography Engineers Near the 38th & 39th Parallels of Latitude, The Mouth of the Kansas River, Mo., To the Sevier Lake, In the Great Basin*, 62.
9. Beckwith, *Report of Exploration of a Route for the Pacific Railroad Capt. Gunnison*, 63.
10. Beckwith, *Report of Exploration of a Route for the Pacific Railroad Capt. Gunnison*, 63.
11. Smithsonian Institution Archives, record unit 7157, box 1, folder 1, Kreutzfeldt, Frederick, Frederick Kreutzfeldt Journal, 1853.
12. Smithsonian Institution Archives, record unit 7157, box 1, folder 1, Kreutzfeldt, Frederick, Frederick Kreutzfeldt Journal, 1853.
13. Beckwith, *Report of Exploration of a Route for the Pacific Railroad Capt. Gunnison*, 63.
14. Smithsonian Institution Archives, record unit 7157, box 1, folder 1, Kreutzfeldt, Frederick. Frederick Kreutzfeldt Journal, 1853.
15. Solomon Nunes Carvalho, *Incidents of Travel and Adventure in the Far West with Colonel Frémont's Last Expedition* (Lincoln: University of Nebraska Press, 2004), 104.

16. LeRoy R. Hafen, "Colonel Loring's Expedition Across Colorado in 1858," *Colorado Magazine* 23, no. 2 (March 1946), 61.
17. Durwood Ball, foreword to John Van Deusen Du Bois and Joseph Heger, *Campaigns in the West 1856–1861, The Journal & Letters of Colonel John Van Deusen Du Bois* (Tucson: Arizona Historical Society, 2003), 78.
18. Ball, foreword to Du Bois Heger, *Campaigns in the West 1856–1861*, 78.
19. "Recent Explorations," *Rocky Mountain News* 1, no. 41 (October 12, 1860).
20. Lloyd M. Pierson, "The Salt Lake Wagon Road across Grand County," *Canyon Legacy* 47 (Spring 2003): 4, 8. Letter, Canby to assistant adjutant general, June 24, 1860, and "Report to Lorenzo Thomas, US Adjutant General's Office: Santa Fe: LS, 1860 July 21," CN BANC MSS P-E 235, UC Berkeley Bancroft Library, University of California.
21. Pierson, "The Salt Lake Wagon Road across Grand County," 4; Daniel W. Jones, *40 Years among the Indians* (Springville, UT: Council Press, December 1, 2004), 105. Jones records that they were "about thirty miles above the Dolores where it empties into Grand River."
22. Jones, *40 Years among the Indians*, 99–108.
23. See Sheet VIII, https://www.loc.gov/resource/g4311cm.gct00080/?st=gallery.
24. Hayden, F.V., *Ninth Annual Report of the United States Geological and Geographical Survey of the Territories embracing Colorado and parts of Adjacent Territories: being a Report of Progress of the Exploration for the year 1875* (Washington: Washington Printing Office, 1877), 349. Accessed on August 2, 2021. https://www.biodiversitylibrary.org/item/124508#page/464/mode/1up
25. Hayden, *Ninth Annual Report of the United States Geological and Geographical Survey of the Territories embracing Colorado and parts of Adjacent Territories*, 348–349.
26. Hayden, *Ninth Annual Report of the United States*, 348–349.
27. Lloyd M. Pierson, ed., "Rollin J. Reeves and the Boundary between Utah and Colorado," *Utah Historical Quarterly* 66, no. 2 (Spring 1998): 112.

Appendix C: Dr. James E. Miller's Letter to Frederick S. Dellenbaugh, November 2, 1906

Box 2, folder 47, Robert Brewster Stanton papers, Manuscripts and Archives Division, New York Public Library, Astor, Lenox, and Tilden Foundations. Dr. James E. Miller's letter to Frederick S. Dellenbaugh is handwritten and mostly legible. To be certain of my translation of his handwriting, I solicited help from Stacey Glad, whose experience comes from considerable work interpreting genealogy documents. Between us, there are only four words from the letter that may be questionable, and I have surrounded them in brackets. A note showing that Miller's letter was received on November 27, 1906, is attached to the last page of the letter and is handwritten by Frederick S. Dellenbaugh using his initials F.S.D.

Appendix D: Robert Brewster Stanton's Letter to Dr. James E. Miller, May 11, 1909

> Box 2, folder 47, Robert Brewster Stanton papers, Manuscripts and Archives Division, New York Public Library, Astor, Lenox, and Tilden Foundations. The copy of Robert Brewster Stanton's letter to Dr. James E. Miller is typed. Looking like a ransom note, the letter appears to be attached to a scrapbook page that he may have kept to help organize material for the book he intended to write, because there are other pasted images on the page, including Stanton's address and cable address, the date of the letter, and a handwritten note that reads, "Letter received by," followed by the name of the recipient whose name is mostly faded but appears to be Dellenbaugh.

Appendix E: Ellsworth L. Kolb's Newspaper Accounting of Section Three of Black Canyon of the Gunnison River

> "Kolb and Loper Have Thrilling Ride Down The Gunnison River," *Montrose Daily Press*, October 26, 1916. The Montrose newspaper article isn't entirely written by Ellsworth Kolb. The first three paragraphs are written by the editor and briefly describe what Kolb and Loper attempted to accomplish and that both men were injured and compelled to abandon their journey. The article indicates that Mr. Kolb said that it was the "worst ride" he had ever experienced, and then it reads "the graphic description, which follows, was prepared by Mr. Kolb, and is well worth reading."

1. Whipple Yale Chester, "Ellsworth Kolb Makes Trip In Black Canyon in Day Which Took Five Weeks Last Year with Boat," *Montrose Daily Press*, October 3, 1917.
2. Chester, "Ellsworth Kolb Makes Trip In Black Canyon."
3. "Kolb and Loper Have Thrilling Ride Down The Gunnison River."
4. *Merriam Webster* defines "giant powder" as "a blasting powder consisting of nitroglycerin, sodium nitrate, sulfur, rosin, and sometimes kieselguhr."

Appendix F: Ellsworth L. Kolb's 1918 Manuscript of the Grand and Gunnison Rivers

> Ellsworth Kolb, NAU, MS 197, series 3, box 18, folder 1914—folder title Manuscript for Ellsworth Kolb's Gunnison River trip, ca. 1918, Kolb Collection, Cline Library, Northern Arizona University. Ellsworth Kolb's 1918 manuscript is typewritten but includes handwritten notes throughout showing the corrections he wanted to make. I retyped the manuscript, incorporating his corrections/updates. Older or incorrect spellings and derogatory or outdated terms from the original have been preserved.

1. William C. Suran, *The Kolb Brothers of Grand Canyon* (Grand Canyon, AZ: Grand Canyon Natural History Association, 1991)

2. William C. Suran, *The Kolb Brothers Biography–With the Wings of an Angel: A Biography of Ellsworth and Emery Kolb, Photographers of Grand Canyon* (Self-published 1991), accessed July 18, 2022, http://kaibab.org/kaibab.org/kolb/index.html.
3. For August 17 and 18, 1916, the cubic feet per second (cfs) were 12,100 and 10,100 respectively.
4. On September 25, 1916, the Colorado River at Westwater ran at 3,980 cfs.

Appendix G: Colorado River Sites—Westwater Area

1. Mike Milligan, *Westwater Lost and Found* (Logan, UT: Utah State University Press, 2004)
2. Bill Belknap and Loie Belknap Evans, *Belknap's Waterproof Canyonlands River Guide* (Evergreen, CO: Westwater Books, 2014)
3. Milligan, *Westwater Lost and Found*, 77–88.
4. Milligan, *Westwater Lost and Found*, 77–96.
5. Bette Stanton, "Legends Lost: Women of the Utah-Colorado Border Country," *Canyon Legacy* 45 (Summer 2002): 18–20; Steve Allen, *Utah's Canyon Country Place Names*, vol. 1 (Durango, CO: Canyon Country Press, 2012), 264–265.
6. See chapter 1 of this book.
7. Alvin Halliday, email correspondence with author, September 13, 2023.
8. Milligan, *Westwater Lost and Found*, 107–112.
9. "Pioneers of Elgin Celebrate Golden Wedding Day," *Times Independent*, March 8, 1951.
10. On a 1900 US Census he is not listed with his wife, Chloe A., and her two sons. He did mining in the Henry Mountains and may have been away when the census was taken. On the 1910 Census for Cisco, Utah, his wife, Chloe, is listed as a widow.
11. Owen Madox Malin, interview by Dave Minor BLM, Marianna Allred (Topping) BLM Westwater ranger 1978–1979, and Blake Hopkins, April 23, 1978, Special Collections, Utah Historical Society. A transcript of the interview is also with the Mike Milligan Papers, Special Collections, J. Willard Marriott Library, University of Utah, Salt Lake City.
12. See chapter 2 of this book for details of the story.
13. Walter Kirschbaum, box 113, folder 6, Otis R. Marston Papers, Huntington Library, San Marino, California, letter from Walter Kirschbaum to John L. J. Hart, July 15, 1969.
14. Don Harris, an early Grand Canyon boater, was a distant relative of Robert Hubbs, who was one of the victims. He assisted with the search for the bodies in the inner canyon. Harris pointed out the rapid where their boat overturned to Dee Holladay. Hubbs's body was recovered two and a half miles above Dewey on May 19, 1971.
15. Milligan, *Westwater Lost and Found*, 199–215.
16. Leslie "Les" Jones, telephone interview by author, April 2, 2003.
17. Louise Sherrill and Michele Reaume, "The Memorial at Cisco," *Confluence* 4 no. 2 (Summer 1997): 25–27.

BIBLIOGRAPHY

Archives

Bancroft Library, University of California, Berkeley.
　Report to Lorenzo Thomas, U.S. Adjutant General's Office: Santa Fe: LS, 1860 July 21.

Beinecke Rare Book and Manuscript Library, Yale University, New Haven, CT.
　Abraham Lincoln Fellows Papers.
　Frederick Samuel Dellenbaugh collection of photographs and drawings of the Colorado River region.

Bureau of Land Management (BLM) Moab Field Office and Utah State Historic Preservation Office.
　Horn, Jonathan C., Michael Prouty, Jack E. Pfertsh, and John Zachman. National Historic Trails Inventory Project, "Tasks 4, 5, and 6 Memo Report for Utah Main Route, Northern Branch, and Armijo Route of the Old Spanish Trail, Emery, Grand, Kane, Piute, San Juan, and Sevier Counties,

Utah." 2011. Prepared by Alpine Archaeological Consultants, Inc., Montrose, Colorado. Prepared for AECOM, Fort Collins, CO.

Memorandum from archaeologist Richard E. Fike to Monticello, Utah, district manager, June 27, 1973. The memorandum includes site inventories and brief histories of the Wild Horse Cabin and Outlaw Cave in Westwater Canyon. The information is not for public use and resides with the Moab BLM.

Cline Library, Northern Arizona University, Flagstaff, AZ.

Emery Kolb Collection, Cline Library, Northern Arizona University, Flagstaff, AZ.

Western History Collection, Denver Public Library, Denver, CO.

Cyrus Shores Papers, Western History Collection, Denver Public Library, Denver, CO.

Will Torrence photos, Special Collections, Denver Public Library, Denver, CO.

Frontier Historical Society and Museum, Glenwood Springs, CO.

Grand Canyon National Park Museum Collection, Grand Canyon, AZ.

Harold B. Lee Library, Brigham Young University, Provo, UT.

George Edward Anderson Collection, Courtesy of L. Tom Perry Special Collections, Harold B. Lee Library, Brigham Young University, Provo, UT.

The Huntington Library, San Marino, CA.

Otis R. Marston Papers, The Huntington Library, San Marino, California. The Huntington Library houses Marston's exhaustive collection of historical documents of the people, events, and the land along the Colorado and Green Rivers. Primary files used for research include Babcock-Miller [O. D. Babcock and James E. Miller], Babcock/Miller (Glenwood Springs–Confluence–Moab), Frank "Bunny" Barnes, Jack Brennan, Bolte-Eaton [Charles Bolte and Earl Eaton] 1954, Edward R. S. Canby, Mildred Davis, William John Davis, Frederick Samuel Dellenbaugh, John Galloway, Parley Galloway, Paul Geerlings, Laphene "Don" Harris, J. E. Miller, O. D. Babcock (1897), Elmer Kane, Walter Kirschbaum, Leslie Allen Jones, Denis Julien, Ellsworth Kolb, Harold H. Leich, Antoine Leroux, Albert Loper, Ed Hudson, James P. Rigg Jr., Antoine Robidoux, Peppo [Beppo] Saeckler, Georgie White.

J. Willard Marriott Library, University of Utah, Salt Lake City, UT.

Albert (Bert) Loper Photograph Collection, Special Collections, J. Willard Marriott Library, University of Utah, Salt Lake City, UT.

Albert (Bert) Loper and Rachel Jamison Loper Papers, Special Collections, J. Willard Marriott Library, University of Utah, Salt Lake City, UT.

Chenoweth, William L. "Historic Crossings of the Colorado River in the Grand Valley." Research Article prepared for the Colorado Riverfront Foundation, funded by State Historical Fund Grant No. 94-02-065, 1998. This document and his other writings and maps are located with Mike Milligan papers, Special Collections, J. Willard Marriott Library, University of Utah, Salt Lake City, UT.

Harold Herbert Leich Papers, Special Collections, J. Willard Marriott Library, University of Utah, Salt Lake City, UT.

Harold Herbert Leich Photograph Collection, Special Collections, J. Willard Marriott Library, University of Utah, Salt Lake City, UT.

LaPhene "Don" Harris Papers, Special Collections, J. Willard Marriott Library, University of Utah, Salt Lake City, Utah.

Mike Milligan Papers, Special Collections, J. Willard Marriott Library, University of Utah, Salt Lake City, Utah.

Nicholas G. Morgan, "Miscellaneous Papers Pertaining to John Morgan," Digitized by J. Willard Marriott Library, University of Utah, Salt Lake City, UT.

Montrose Historical Society, Montrose, CO.

The New York Public Library, New York, NY.

Robert Brewster Stanton Papers, Manuscripts and Archives Division, New York Public Library, Astor, Lenox, and Tilden Foundations, New York, NY.

Smithsonian Institution Archives, Washington, DC.

Frederick Kreutzfeldt Journal, Smithsonian Institution Archives, Washington, DC.

US National Park Service, Washington, DC.

Black Canyon of the Gunnison National Park, National Park Service. Slides and text are from the records of Mr. Fellows; they are the results of his surveys in 1901 and 1902.

Utah Historical Society, Salt Lake City, UT.

Owen Malin interview, April 23, 1978, Special Collections, Utah Historical Society, Salt Lake City, UT.

Roger H. Green interview, November 8, 1986, Special Collections, Utah Historical Society, Salt Lake City, UT.

Newspapers

Chronicling America: Historic American Newspapers.
https://chroniclingamerica.loc.gov/.

Colorado Historic Newspapers Collection.
> https://www.coloradohistoricnewspapers.org/
> Colorado newspapers are less complete than those found on the Utah digital newspaper website. Primary newspapers where information was obtained:

Colorado Weekly Chieftain, Pueblo (1875–1881).
Crested Butte News, Crested Butte (1999–current).
Daily Journal, Telluride (1894–1927).
The *Daily Sentinel,* Grand Junction (1893–current).
The *Delta Independent,* Delta (1886–1923).
The *Glenwood Post and Weekly Ledger* and the *Glenwood Post,* Glenwood Springs (1897–current).
Grand Junction Daily News, Grand Valley Sentinel, and the *Avalanche,* Glenwood Springs (1891–19??).
Gunnison Review Press (1887–1890).
The *Montrose Daily Press,* Montrose (1914–current).
The *Montrose Enterprise,* Montrose (1888–19??).
The *Rocky Mountain News,* Denver (1859–2009).
The *Sun,* Gunnison, Gunnison County (1883–1884).

Daily Alta California, San Francisco.

Daily Union, Washington, DC.

Utah Digital Newspapers.
> https://newspapers.lib.utah.edu/search/advanced
> Primary Utah newspapers where information was obtained:
> *Deseret News,* Salt Lake City (1850–current).
> *Eastern Utah Advocate,* Price (1895–1915).
> *Grand Valley Times,* Moab (1896–1919).
> *Ogden Standard,* Ogden (1888–1920); afterward became the *Ogden Standard-Examiner,* which is still being published.

Provo Daily Enquirer, Provo (1891–1897).
Provo Daily Herald, Provo (1922–2009).
Salt Lake Herald, Salt Lake City (1870–1909).
Salt Lake Tribune, prev. *Salt Lake Daily Tribune*, Salt Lake City (1872–current).
Times Independent, Moab (1919–current).
The *Utah Enquirer*, Provo (1888–1895).
Vernal Express, Vernal (1891–current).

Washington Sentinel, Washington, DC (1835–1856).

Williams News, Williams, AZ (1891–1989); currently published as the *Williams–Grand Canyon News*.

Weekly National Intelligencer, Washington, DC (1800–1870).

Websites

ancestry.com: This is one of many genealogical websites where descendants of historical individuals can potentially be located. If not private, then family history charts with historical dates, photos, marriages, etc. can be obtained. Also, there is generally a messaging feature to contact surviving relatives.

American Whitewater link to the Black Canyon of the Gunnison River. https://direct.americanwhitewater.org/content/River/view/river-detail/401/main.

Arizona Archives Online. http://azarchivesonline.org/xtf/view?docId=ead/nau/kolb_emery.xml;query=kolb;brand=default; this is link to the Emery Kolb Collection, 1850–1988, Northern Arizona University (NAU), Cline Library.

"Black Canyon the Next Generation." https://vimeo.com/36298473.

Black Canyon of the Gunnison National Park (U.S. National Park Service) https://www.nps.gov/blca/index.htm.

Canyon Legacy. https://moabmuseum.org/canyon-legacy/.

Colorado Plateau River Guides. http://www.riverguides.org/search.cfm.

Description given for Gunnison River–Black Canyon (M-Box). Accessed April 29, 2023. https://www.riverbrain.com/run/show/384.

"Historic River Boats of the Grand Canyon: Chapter 13." 1960. Kirschbaum Kayak/6:02 https://vimeo.com/482381953.

Moab Museum. "Canyon Legacy: Archive." https://moabmuseum.org/canyon-legacy/.

OAC, Online Archive of California. "Otis R. Marston Papers: Finding Aid mssMarston papers." https://oac.cdlib.org/findaid/ark:/13030/tf438n99sg/entire_text/.

Old Spanish Trail Association. https://oldspanishtrail.org/. Membership required in order to access copies of *Spanish Traces*.

Utah Historical Society. https://history.utah.gov/utah-state-historical-society/utah-historical-quarterly/.

Other Sources

Alexander, Thomas G., and Leonard J. Arrington. "Camp in the Sagebrush: Camp Floyd, Utah, 1858–1861." *Utah Historical Quarterly* 34 (Winter 1966): 3–21.

Allen, Steve. *Utah's Canyon Country Place Names*. Vol. 1. Durango, CO: Canyon Country Press, 2012.

Allen, Steve. *Utah's Canyon Country Place Names*. Vol. 2. Durango, CO: Canyon Country Press, 2012.

Anderson, Fletcher, and Ann Hopkinson. *Rivers of the Southwest: A Boaters' Guide to the Rivers of Colorado, New Mexico, Utah and Arizona*. 2nd ed. Boulder, CO: Pruett Publishing Company, 1987.

Auerbach, Herbert S. "Old Trails, Old Forts, Old Trappers and Traders." *Utah Historical Society* 9 (April 1941): 13–63.

Baker, Pearl. *Trail on the Water*. Boulder, CO: Pruett Publishing Company, 1969.

Baker, Pearl. *The Wild Bunch at Robbers Roost*. Lincoln: University of Nebraska Press, 1989.

Banks, Gordon, Dave Eckhardt. *Colorado Rivers & Creeks*. 2nd ed. Hong Kong: David Eckhardt and Gordon Banks, 1995, 1999.

Barnes, F. A. "A Journey to the Rio del Tizon." *Canyon Legacy* 9 (Spring 1991): 16–22.

Barnes, F. A. "Update-Rivera's 1765 Expedition," *Canyon Legacy* 10 (Summer 1991): 31.

Beckwith, Lieut. E. G. *Report of Exploration of a Route for the Pacific Railroad Capt. Gunnison, Topography Engineers Near the 38th & 39th Parallels of Latitude, The Mouth of the Kansas River, Mo., To the Sevier Lake, In the Great Basin, Senate Reports: Explorations and Surveys, from the Mississippi River to the Pacific Ocean, 1853-4*. Washington, DC: Beverley Tucker, Printer, 1855. https://core.ac.uk/download/217216157.pdf.

Belknap, Bill, and Loie Belknap Evans. *Belknap's Waterproof Canyonlands River Guide*. Evergreen, CO: Westwater Books, 2014.

Beidleman, Richard G. "The Black Canyon of the Gunnison National Monument." *Colorado Magazine* 40 (July 1963): 161–178.

Brewerton, George Douglas. *Overland with Kit Carson: A Narrative of the Old Spanish Trail in '48*. Lincoln: University of Nebraska Press, 1993.

Bussard, Wil. "River Guide: Precambrian rocks along the Colorado River from Loma, CO to Cisco, UT: Westwater, Ruby and Horsethief Canyons Using Belknap's Canyonlands River Guide." *Confluence* 6, no. 3 (Winter 1999): 28–29.

Bussard, Wil. "Westwater Canyon: A Geologist's River Guide With a Focus on Precambrian Rocks." *Confluence* 6, no. 3 (Winter 1999): 21–27.

Carson, Kit. *Kit Carson's Autobiography*. Edited by Milo Milton Quaife. Lincoln: University of Nebraska Press, 1966.

Carter, Harvey L., and Thelma S. Guild. *Kit Carson: A Pattern for Heroes*. Lincoln: University of Nebraska Press, 1984.

Carvalho, Solomon Nunes. *Incidents of Travel and Adventure in the Far West with Colonel Frémont's Last Expedition*. Lincoln: University of Nebraska Press, 2004.

Chavez, Fray Angelico, trans. *The Dominguez-Escalante Journal: Their Expedition through Colorado, Utah, Arizona, and New Mexico in 1776*. Edited by Ted J. Warner. Salt Lake City: University of Utah Press, 1995.

Chenoweth, William L. "A Portion of the North Branch Became the Salt Lake Wagon Road." *Spanish Traces* 15, no. 1 (Winter 2009): 10–13.

Chenoweth, William L. "Gunnison's Pacific Railroad Survey." *Spanish Traces* 6 no. 2 (Spring 2000): 26–27.

Chenoweth, William L. "Rivers of the Grand Valley." *Spanish Traces* 12 (Spring 2006): 24–26.

Conard, Howard Louis. *"Uncle Dick" Wootton: The Pioneer Frontiersman of the Rocky Mountain Region*. Chicago: W.E. Dibble & Co., 1890.

Crampton, C. Gregory, and Steven K. Madsen. *In Search of the Spanish Trail: Santa Fe to Los Angeles, 1829–1848*. Salt Lake City: Gibbs-Smith Publisher, 1994.

Davis, Richard. *A Man to Cross Rivers With*. Ouray, CO.: Western Reflections Inc., 1999.

Dellenbaugh, Frederick S. *A Canyon Voyage*. New Haven, CT: Yale University Press, 1962.

Dellenbaugh, Frederick S. *The Romance of the Colorado River*. New York: Knickerbocker Press, 1902.

Dimock, Brad. *Sunk without a Sound*. Flagstaff, AZ: Fretwater Press, 2001.

Dimock, Brad. *The Very Hard Way: Bert Loper and the Colorado River*. Flagstaff, AZ: Fretwater Press, 2007.

Du Bois, Colonel John Van Deusen, and Joseph Heger. *Campaigns in the West 1856–1861: The Journal & Letters of Colonel John Van Deusen Du Bois with pencil sketches by Joseph Heger*. Foreword by Durwood Ball. Tucson: Arizona Historical Society, 2003.

Eddy, Clyde. *Down the World's Most Dangerous River*. New York: Frederick A. Stokes Company, 1929.

Farewell, R. C. *Rio Grande Secret Places*. Vol. 2, *Ruby Canyon and the Desert*. Boulder, CO.: Johnson Printing Company, 1999.

Firmage, Richard A. *A History of Grand County*. Utah Centennial County History Series. Salt Lake City: Grand County and the Utah State Historical Society, 1996.

Fuller, George, William R. Gray, Robert Earle Howells, Katheryn Knorovski, Charles Kulander, Rachael Jackson Moss, David A. Nelson, Edward Readicker-Henderson, Jenna Schnuer, Jeremy Schmidt, Mel White, and Joe Yogerst. "Canyonlands Excursions." In *National Geographic Guide to National Parks of the United States*. 8th ed., 207 Washington, DC: National Geographic Society, 2016.

Gaylord, A. "1922–Into the Grand Canyon and Out Again by Airplane," *Grand Canyon Centennial Stories*, Grand Canyon National Park, National Park Service. https://www.nps.gov/articles/airplaneintograndcanyon.htm#:~:text=GRCA%20IMAGE%2005235)-,R.V.,08%20AUG%201922.&text=FIRST%20AIRPLANE%20LANDING%20MADE%20IN,ARIZONA%20ON%20AUGUST%208%2C%201922.

Goetzmann, William H. *Army Exploration in the American West, 1803–1863*. Lincoln: University of Nebraska Press, 1979.

Hafen, LeRoy R. "Colonel Loring's Expedition across Colorado in 1858." *Colorado Magazine* 23, no. 2 (March 1946): 49–75.

Hafen, LeRoy R. "The Old Spanish Trail, Santa Fe to Los Angeles." *Huntington Library Quarterly* 11, no. 2 (1948): 155.

Hafen, LeRoy R., and Ann Hafen eds. *Frémont's Fourth Expedition: A Documentary Account of the Disaster of 1848–1849, with Diaries, Letters, and Reports by Participants in the Tragedy*. Glendale, CA: Arthur H. Clark Company, 1960.

Hafen, Leroy R., and Ann W. Hafen. *Old Spanish Trail: Santa Fe to Los Angeles*. Lincoln: University of Nebraska Press, 1993.

Halpern, David. *A Timeless Challenge: Encounters with Colorado's Black Canyon of the Gunnison River*. Tulsa, OK: Gneissline Publishing, 2019.

Hansen, Wallace R. *The Black Canyon of the Gunnison: In Depth*. Tucson, AZ: Southwest Parks and Monuments Association, 1987.

Hansen, Wallace R. *The Black Canyon of the Gunnison: Today and Yesterday*. Washington, DC: US Government Printing Office: 1965.

Hart, John L. J. "Westwater Canyon by Boat and on Foot." *Trail and Timberline*, no. 544 (April 1964): 63–68.

Hayden, F. V. *Geological and Geographical Atlas of Colorado and Portions of Adjacent Territory* (New York: Julius Bien, lith., 1877).

Hayden, F. V. *Ninth Annual Report of the United States Geological and Geographical Survey of the Territories embracing Colorado and parts of Adjacent Territories: being a Report of Progress of the Exploration for the year 1875*. Washington, DC:

Washington Printing Office, 1877. Accessed September 3, 2023. https://www.biodiversitylibrary.org/item/124508#page/464/mode/1up.

Heap, Gwinn Harris. *Central Route to the Pacific, From the Valley of the Mississippi to California: Journal of the Expedition of E. F. Beale, Superintendent of Indian Affairs in California, and Gwinn Harris Heap, from Missouri to California in 1853*. Philadelphia: Lippincott, Grambo, and Co., 1854.

Heyman, Max L., Jr. *Prudent Soldier: A Biography of Major General E.R.S. Canby 1817–1873*. Glendale, CA: Arthur H. Clark Company, 1959.

Jacobs, G. Clell. "The Phantom Pathfinder: Juan Maria Antonio de Rivera and His Expedition." *Utah Historical Quarterly* 60 (Summer 1992): 200–223.

Jessen, Ken. *Colorado Gunsmoke: True Stories of Outlaws and Lawmen on the Colorado Frontier*. Loveland, CO: J.V. Publications, 1986.

Jenkins, John. *The Essential Guide to Black Canyon of the Gunnison National Park*. Golden, CO: Colorado Mountain Club Press, 2004.

Jones, Daniel W. *40 Years among the Indians*. Springville, UT: Council Press, 2004.

Kessler, Ron. *Old Spanish Trail North Branch and Its Travelers*. Santa Fe, NM: Sunstone Press, 1998.

Kessler, Ron. *Re-tracing the Old Spanish Trail North Branch: Today's OST Travel Guide*. Monte Vista, CO: Adobe Village Press, 1995.

Knipmeyer, James H. "Denis Julien: New Inscription Discovery," *Canyon Legacy* 71 (Winter 2011–2012): 15–17.

Knipmeyer, James H. *The Life and Times of Denis Julien: Fur Trader*. Chula Vista, CA: Aventine Press, 2018.

Knipmeyer, James H. "The Old Trappers' Trail through Eastern Utah." *Canyon Legacy* 9 (Spring 1991): 10–15.

Knipmeyer, James H. "The Uncompahgre and the Fur Trade." *Canyon Legacy* 42 (Summer 2001): 6–8.

Kolb, Ellsworth L. *Through the Grand Canyon from Wyoming to Mexico*. New York: Macmillan Company, 1914.

Kolb, Ellsworth, and Emery Kolb. "Experiences in the Grand Canyon," *National Geographic Magazine* 26, no. 2 (March 1914): 99–184.

Landon, Michael N., and Brandon J. Metcalf. *The Remarkable Journey of the Mormon Battalion*. American Fork, UT: Covenant Communications Inc., 2012.

Lago, Don. *The Powell Expedition: New Discoveries about John Wesley Powell's 1869 River Journey*. Reno: University of Nevada Press, 2018.

Leich, Harold H. *Alone on the Colorado*. Forward by Roy Webb. Salt Lake City: University of Utah Press, 2019.

Lindgren, Scott, Thayer Walker. "After a Hard Diagnosis, One Athlete Learns to Soften Up." *Outside*. October 14, 2019. https://www.outsideonline.com/outdoor-adventure/water-activities/scott-lindgren-kayaker/.

Lyons, Steve. *Black Canyon of the Gunnison Explorer's Guide*. Paonia, CO: Freewheel Publications, 2001.
Magley, Robb. *Deep Black*. Montrose, CO: Western Reflections Publishing Company, 2002.
Marcy, General Randolph B. *Thirty Years of Army Life on the Border*. Big Byte Books, 2014.
Marshall, Muriel. *Red Hole in Time*. College Station: Texas A&M University Press, 1988.
Marston, Otis. "River Runners: Fast Water Navigation." *Utah Historical Quarterly* 28 (July 1960): 291–308.
Marston, Otis Reed. "Dock." *From Powell to Power: A Recounting of the First One Hundred River Runners through the Grand Canyon*, edited by Tom Martin. Flagstaff, AZ: Vishnu Temple Press, 2014.
Massa, Dominic. "Curator John Magill to Retire after 3 Decades with Historic New Orleans Collection," Nola.com, June 17, 2015. https://www.nola.com/news/article_b7c9f0dd-8a7f-5c67-9848-37f8628ff178.html.
McCarty, Florence. "A Rancher's Last Ride: Down the Road to Silverton Someone Waited—and He Wasn't a Friend." *Frontier Times* (April/May 1977): 19 and 41.
McPherson, Robert S., and Susan Rhoades Neel. *Mapping the Four Corners: Narrating the Hayden Survey of 1875*. Norman: University of Oklahoma Press; 2016.
Milligan, Mike. "Colorado River Sites Westwater Area." *Canyon Legacy* 42 (Summer 2001): 24–28.
Milligan, Mike. Letter, "The Problem with History—Continued, A Response to the Law and Lawless Issue." *Canyon Legacy*, no. 17 (Spring 1993): 32.
Milligan, Mike. "Westwater." *Canyon Legacy*, no. 12 (Winter 1991): 25–27.
Milligan, Mike. "Westwater Camp: Water, Wood and Grass." *Spanish Traces* 27 no.1 (Spring 2021): 22–35.
Milligan, Mike. "Westwater: I Guess Some Died." *Canyon Legacy* 51 (Summer 2004): 7–12.
Milligan, Mike. *Westwater Lost and Found*. Logan: Utah State University Press, 2004.
Milligan, Mike. "Westwater's Violent Beginnings." *Canyon Legacy* 42 (Summer 2001): 20–23.
Möllhausen, Baldwin. *Diary of a journey from the Mississippi to the Coasts of the Pacific With a United States Government Expedition*. Vol 2. Translated by Mrs. Percy Sinnett. London: Longman, Brown, Green, Longmans, & Roberts, 1858.
Morgan, Dale L. *Jedediah Smith and the Opening of the West*. Lincoln: University of Nebraska Press, 1964.
Morrill, Reed. "The Site of Fort Robidoux." *Utah Historical Society* 9, no. 1–2 (January, April 1941): 1–11.

Mumey, Nolie, "John William Gunnison: Centenary of His Survey and Tragic Death," *Colorado Magazine* 31 (January 1954): 19–32.

Naylor, Roger. *The Amazing Kolb Brothers of Grand Canyon*. Grand Canyon, AZ: Grand Canyon Association, 2017.

Nelson, Jack William. *Forgotten Pathfinders: Along the North Branch of the Old Spanish Trail 1650–1850*, edited by Jon M. Nelson. Grand Junction, CO: Self-Published, 2016. http://northbranchost.com/wp-content/uploads/2016/11/Forgotten-Pathfinders-new-A.pdf.

Nelson, Jack W. "North Branch of the Old Spanish Trail: The Trapper Variant." *Canyon Legacy* 53 (Spring 2005): 36–38.

Page, Charles A. *What's in a Name? In the Gunnison Country*. Gunnison, CO: B&B Printers, 1978.

Parkhill, Forbes. *The Blazed Trail of Antoine Leroux*. Los Angeles: Westernlore Press, 1965.

Peters, DeWitt C. *The Life and Adventures of Kit Carson: Nestor of the Rocky Mountains*. New York: W.R.C. Clark & Co., 1858.

Pierson, Lloyd M. "Crossing the Green at Green River, Utah." *Canyon Legacy* 44 (Spring 2002): 19–25.

Pierson, Lloyd M. ed. "Rollin J. Reeves and the Boundary between Utah and Colorado," *Utah Historical Quarterly* 66, no. 2 (Spring 1998): 100–117.

Pierson, Lloyd M. "The Salt Lake Wagon Road across Grand County." *Canyon Legacy* 47 (Spring 2003): 1–8.

Pierson, Lloyd M., and Lyle E. Jamison. "The Denver and Rio Grande Narrow Gauge Railroad across Grand County." *Canyon Legacy* 42 (Summer 2001): 14–18.

Pierson, Lloyd M. "What Happened When? A Chronology of Important Dates Relative to the Establishment of the Moab Area, 1686–1879." *Canyon Legacy* 60 (Summer 2007): 20–28. (In table of contents, the article title is listed as "Historic Events and the Ripple Effect.")

Powell, John Wesley. *The Exploration of the Colorado River and Its Canyons*. New York: Dover, 1961.

Richmond, Patricia Joy. "Trail to Disaster: John C. Frémont's Fourth Expedition into the San Juan Mountains of Southern Colorado." *Ayer Y Hoy en Taos Yesterday and Today in Taos County and Northern New Mexico* 5 (Summer 1987): 3–9.

"River Water in his Blood." *News: The Journal of Grand Canyon River Guides, Inc.*, vol. 6, no. 3 (late summer 1993): 1, 26–34. https://static1.squarespace.com/static/61d3bc4beef7c3126df06d78/t/61f73742961aef202a76aee7/1643591505677/6-3.pdf.

Robb, James M., and William L. Chenoweth. "We Rode the Legislation Trail—From OST to NHT." *Spanish Traces* 9, no. 1 (Winter 2003): 6–7.

Roberts, David. *Escalante's Dream: On the Trail of the Spanish Discovery of the Southwest*. New York: W.W. Norton and Company, 2019.

Rockwell, Wilson ed., *Memoirs of a Lawman*. Denver: Sage Books, 1962.

Rusho, W. L., ed. "River Running 1921: The Diary of E.L. Kolb." *Utah Historical Quarterly* 37 (Spring 1969): 269–283.

Same River Twice. Directed by Scott Featherstone. Candlelight Media Group, 1996.

Schiel, Jacob H. *Journey through the Rocky Mountains and the Humboldt Mountains to the Pacific Ocean*. Norman: University of Oklahoma Press, 1959.

Schubert, Frank N. *Vanguard of Expansion: Army Engineers in the Trans-Mississippi West, 1819–1879*. Washington, DC: US Government Printing Office, 1980.

Sherrill, Louise, and Michele Reame. "The Memorial at Cisco." *Confluence* 4, no. 2 (Summer 1997): 25–27.

Sides, Hampton. *Blood and Thunder: The Epic Story of Kit Carson and the Conquest of the American West*. New York: Anchor Books A Division of Random House Inc., 2007.

Sitgreaves, Captain L. *Report of an Expedition down the Zuni and Colorado Rivers*. 32d Congress 2d Session. Senate. Executive No. 59. Washington, DC: Robert Armstrong, Public Printer, 1853. https://tile.loc.gov/storage-services/public/gdcmassbookdig/reportofexpeditoounit/reportofexpeditoounit.pdf.

Sitgreaves, L. *Report of an Expedition down the Zuni and Colorado Rivers*, London: Forgotten Books&c Ltd., 2018. (Not the complete Report—see preceding.)

Smith, Dwight L., and C. Gregory Crampton, ed. *The Colorado River Survey: Robert B. Stanton and the Denver, Colorado Canyon and Pacific Railroad*. Salt Lake City: Howe Brothers, 1987.

Spence, Mary Lee, ed. *The Expeditions of John Charles Frémont*. Vol. 3, *Travels from 1848 to 1854*. Urbana: University of Illinois Press, 1984.

Stanton, Bette. "Legends Lost: Women of the Utah-Colorado Border Country" *Canyon Legacy* 45 (Summer 2002): 18–23.

Stanton, Robert Brewster. *Down the Colorado*. Edited by Dwight L. Smith. Norman: University of Oklahoma Press, 1965.

Stanton, Robert Brewster. *Colorado River Controversies*. Edited by James M. Chalfant. New York: Dodd, Mead & Company, 1932.

Steinel, Alvin T. *History of Agriculture in Colorado, 1858 to 1926*. Fort Collins, CO: State Agricultural College, 1926.

Stiles, Helen J. Stiles. "Down the Colorado in 1889." *Colorado Magazine* 41, no. 3 (Summer 1964): 225–245.

Sturges, Rush, dir. *The River Runner*. Boone, CO: River Roots, 2021.

Suran, William C., ed. and transcriber. *The Brave Ones: The Journals & Letters of the 1911–1912 Expedition down the Green & Colorado Rivers by Ellsworth L. Kolb* and Emery C. Kolb including the Journal of Hubert R. Lauzon. Flagstaff, AZ: Fretwater Press, 2003.

Suran, William C. *The Kolb Brothers of Grand Canyon.* Grand Canyon, AZ: Grand Canyon Natural History Association, 1991.

Suran, William C. *The Kolb Brothers' Biography—With the Wings of an Angel: A Biography of Ellsworth and Emery Kolb, Photographers of Grand Canyon.* Self-published 1991. Accessed July 18, 2022. http://kaibab.org/kaibab.org/kolb/index.html.

Twain, Mark. *The Adventures of Huckleberry Finn.* Philadelphia: Courage Books, an imprint of Running Press, 1986.

Utah Place Names: A Comprehensive Guide to the Origins of Geographic Names. Compiled by John W. Van Cott. Salt Lake City: The University of Utah Press, 1990.

Vandenbusche, Duane. *Images of America: The Black Canyon of the Gunnison.* Charleston, SC: Arcadia Publishing, 2009.

Vandenbusche, Duane. "Man against the Black Canyon." *Colorado Magazine* 50 (Spring 1973): 117–141.

Waller, Richard G. *Camino Norteño: Old Spanish Northern Route or On to the Wintys!* Thornton, CO: Wandering the West Books (2023).

Warner, Mark T. "Black Canyon of the Gunnison National Monument." *Colorado Magazine* 11 (May 1934): 86–97.

Warner, Mark T. "Through the Canyon." *Colorado Magazine* 40 (July 1963): 179–182.

Warner, Mark T., and Dexter B. Walker. *Through the Black Canyon.* Ann Arbor, MI: Braun-Brumfield Inc., 1972.

Warner, Ted J. ed., Fray Angelico Chavez, trans. *The Dominguez-Escalante Journal: Their Expedition through Colorado, Utah, Arizona, and New Mexico in 1776.* Salt Lake City: University of Utah Press, 1995.

Webb, Roy. *Call of the Colorado.* Moscow: University of Idaho Press, 1994.

Weber, David J. *The Taos Trappers: The Fur Trade in the Far Southwest, 1540–1846.* Norman: University of Oklahoma Press, 1971.

Weisheit, John, ed. "River Bed Case Testimony: John, Parley Galloway." *Confluence* no. 28 (Winter 2006): 11–14.

Weisheit, John, comp. "A Westwater Canyon History." *Confluence* 3, no 2 (Spring 1996): 5–6.

Weisheit, John, comp. and transcriber. "When Is a River Navigable?" *Confluence* 4 (August 1, 1997).

Wolverton, Bill. "Ruby Canyon: The Railroad Through and a Brief History." *Canyon Legacy* 42 (Summer 2001): 9.

Zaenger, Paul. *Black Canyon of the Gunnison: The Story Behind the Scenery.* Las Vegas, NV: KC Publications Inc., 2007.

INDEX

Locators with an *f* indicate a figure, and locators with an *n* indicate a footnote.

232 Mile Rapid, 107
1921 Cataract Canyon Survey, 103
1923 Grand Canyon Survey, 103

A Canyon Voyage, 68, 90
Abiquiu (N.Mex.), 25, 26
Adams, Captain Samuel, 142
Agate, 240
Agate Wash, 238
Alleghany River, 83–84
Alley, John, 15
Allison, M.L., 49–53, 55
Alone on the Colorado, 65, 141
Anderson, E.B., 114
Anderson, Fletcher, 133, 142
Anglo trappers, 25, 29
Armijo, Antonio, 25
Army Corps of Topographical Engineers, 30
Ashley, William Henry, 29
Aspen (Colo.), 71, 145

Babcock, Oro Degarmo "O.D." DDS MD, 3, 4, 8, 66–67, 69–70, 72, 76–77, 141–142, 165–167, 169–170; bio, 71; boating experience, 72, 75–76, 167
Bangs Canyon, 50–51, 56
Bar X Cattle Company, 224
Bar X Ranch (also named Box X Ranch), 19
Barnes, Frank "Bunny," 78, 142
Barrel Springs Rapid, 97
Bavarian Klepper foldboats, 145
Beale, Lt. Edward F., 32, 35, 37, 160, 162
Beckwith, Lt. E.G., 9, 33, 37, 160–161
Benikera River, 36. *See also* Colorado River
Bent's Fort, 150
Benton, Senator Thomas Hart, 30–31, 150
Best Expedition, 7
Big Drop 3 "Satan's Gut," 71, 77*f*
Big Drops, 94
Big Hole, 145–146, 148, 229, 237
Big Hummer Rapid, 139, 234
Big Salt Creek, 36. *See also* Salt Creek

276 | INDEX

Big Whirlpool, 98, 99f, 213, 234, 236f. See also Room of Doom
Birch Back Canoe, 167
Bitter Creek, 63, 221–222, 224
Bitter Water Creek, 22f, 36, 160–161. See also Westwater Creek
Black Canyon (Gunny Gorge), 136, 254n35
Black Canyon of the Gunnison National Monument, 112, 136
Black Canyon of the Gunnison National Park, 91f, 100, 109–110, 112, 119, 121f, 125, 130, 133–134; North Rim, 110, 112, 125; South Rim, 110, 125
Black Canyon of the Gunnison River, 13, 91, 100, 109–111, 122, 136, 171, 175–176
Blake, 54, 72. See also Green River
BLM, 38, 60, 218f, 247n5
Blue Mesa Reservoir, 130
Blue River, 142, 153, 212. See also Grand River
Bolte, Charles, 145
Bon Carre, 153. See also Grand River
Book Cliffs, 7, 10, 27, 221, 233
Bostwick Park, 174, 202, 210
Bowling Alley, 234
Box X Ranch, 60. See also Westwater Ranch
Boyle, Bob W., 46, 56. See also Wallace, Bob W.
Breckenridge (Colo.), 142
Breckinridge, Tom, 150–151
Brennan, Bob, 11, 146
Brennan, Jack, 143f, 144
Brewerton, Lt. George Douglas, 159, 256n3
Bridger, Jim, 29
Bright Angel Hotel, 84
Brock, Charles, 7, 219–220
Brooks, Jimmy, 107
Brown-Stanton Survey, 7, 219. See also Denver, Colorado Cañon and Pacific Railroad
Brown, Frank, 68, 76, 87, 166
Bryant, Byron, 112
Buck Mountains, 155. See also Book Cliffs
Buckskin Canyon, 76, 166, 170, 250n20
Buffalo Creek, 83, 89
Bureau of Land Management. See BLM
Bush, President George W., 22

California, 7, 15, 23–25, 30–32, 35–36, 44, 65, 89, 106, 151, 224
Cameo Dam, 73
Camp Floyd, 20, 32–33, 163
Camp Hope, 150–151
Camp Scott, 32
Campbell, John L., 46
Canby, Colonel Edward R.S., 20, 21f, 36, 163
Carbondale (Colo.), 51, 52
Carson, Kit, 25, 28, 29, 146, 159
Carvalho, Solomon Nunes, 162
Cataract Canyon, 65, 70–72, 75–76, 93–94, 103, 133, 144, 145, 166, 167, 169
Cave Camp, 133
Cedaredge (Colo.), 7, 63
central route survey, 4, 8–9, 32, 90, 111, 146, 149. See also Pacific Coast Railroad Survey; Pacific Railroad; Transcontinental Railroad
Chalifoux, Jean Baptiste, 25, 27
Chamberlain, Tom, 131
Chasm View, 90, 111f, 112
Chenoweth, William L. "Bill," 9, 16–17, 21–23, 28, 33, 35–38, 159, 161
Cheyava Falls, 103, 105
Chicago, 69, 71, 145, 221
China, 84
Christenson, Roy, 146
Chukar Trail, 131, 135
Cimarron (Colo.), 81–82, 92, 105, 107, 112, 114, 174, 179–180, 194, 210
Cimarron River (Creek), 92, 112, 115, 180–181
Cisco (Ut.), 6, 7, 10, 18, 42, 44, 54, 58–59, 75, 78, 83, 106, 146, 162, 219, 221–222, 226, 230, 232, 239–240, 246n11, 259n10
Cisco Bend Rapid, 234. See also Skull Rapid
Cisco Boat Ramp, landing, or takeout, 41, 43, 45, 240
Cisco camp on North Branch of OST, 27, 33, 164
Cisco Desert, 12, 17, 18, 36, 37f, 38, 146
Cisco Pumphouse, 42, 45, 56, 58
City of Montrose, 114
Clark, Bill, 133
Cline Library, 92, 175

Coats, Adrian, 101, 205, 209
Coats, Lawrence, 101, 204, 209
Cochetopa Pass, 27, 32, 35
Collier, D.C., 19–20, 163
Colorado Hotel, 8, 69, 166
Colorado Plateau, 221
Colorado Plateau River Guides (CPRG), 11, 15
Colorado River: above confluence, 3–7, 9, 11–12, 14, 41, 43, 45–46, 52, 57–58, 62, 65–66, 67, 69–70, 71–72, 78, 79–80, 89, 92, 93, 106, 109, 138–139, 141–142, 145, 148, 165, 217, 219, 221, 222, 224, 225, 226, 227; below confluence, 6, 25, 30–31, 52, 65, 67–68, 69–70, 71, 76, 78, 79, 81, 84–86, 89, 90, 94, 106, 107, 110, 133, 137, 140, 141, 142, 144–145, 165, 169, 176, 179, 186, 193, 195, 216, 219; confluence with Dolores River, 24; confluence with the Green River, 76, 78, 89, 110, 141; confluence with Gunnison River, 27, 49; Grand Canyon, 6, 7, 67, 78, 83, 84, 90, 94, 96, 106, 140, 141, 145, 212; North Branch of OST, 17–19, 21–22, 24, 27–28, 35, 37, 162
Church of Jesus Christ of Latter-day Saints, 37
Colorado Riverbed Case, 7, 78, 142
Colorado River Controversies, 68
Colorado Territory, 146
Comanches, 28
Confluence, the, 6, 78, 106; confluence with the Green River, 3, 24, 76, 89, 110, 141
Confluence, The, 15
Continental Divide, 27
Cooke, Colonel P. St. George, 30, 31
Corley, John, 145
Cottonwood, 222, 240
Cottonwood Wash, 140, 147, 238
Counterfeit Cave, 42, 43, 59, 62, 230, 245n4. *See also* Outlaw Cave
CPRG (Colorado Plateau River Guides)
Crescent Junction (Ut.), 146, 224
Creutzfeldt, Frederick. *See* Kreutzfeld, Frederick
Crossing of the Fathers, 24, 25
Crossing of the Grand, 24, 37

Crystal Reservoir, 130
Curry, George "Flat Nose," 7
Curtis, J.A., 114

D&RG Express Company, 48, 50
D&RG RR. *See* Denver & Rio Grande Railroad
D&RGW RR. *See* Denver & Rio Grande Western Railroad
Dallas (Colo.), 51
Dark Canyon Rapid, 93
Davis, Captain Wilson Ellis, 7, 45, 219, 220f, 220
Davis, Mildred, 145
Davis, William, 142, 145
Day Wrecker, 92, 100, 119, 197f
DCC&P. *See* Denver, Colorado Cañon and Pacific Railroad Company
De Beque Canyon, 73
Dead Horse Rapid, 234. *See also* Skull Rapid
Dean, Frank E., 49f, 98, 214f
Deep Black, 122
Defiance, 86
Dellenbaugh, Frederick S., 3–4, 8, 66–71, 68f, 76, 78, 90, 141, 148, 165–167, 170, 249n6; *A Canyon Voyage*, 68, 90; as river historian, 67–68, 106, 169; *Romance of the Colorado River*, 68–69, 76, 148, 165, 169
Delta (Colo.), 6, 47, 49, 51, 52, 59, 80, 83, 96, 105, 114, 129, 136, 180, 211, 212
Delta Station, 112
Denning, Tom, 50–51, 53
Denny, Tom (possibly Denning), 55
Denver, 19, 51, 163
Denver, Colorado Cañon and Pacific Railroad Company (DCC&P), 7, 19, 60, 67–68, 219, 224, 247n4
Denver & Rio Grande Railroad (D&RG RR), 6, 17, 18–19, 46, 48, 50, 52, 56, 107, 111, 112, 178
Denver & Rio Grande Western Railroad (D&RGW RR), 6, 17, 18–19, 38, 42–43, 146, 222, 225; narrow gauge, 17–18
D&RGW Pumphouse, 42, 58. *See also* Cisco Pumphouse
Desolation Canyon, 4, 7, 14

278 | INDEX

Dewey (Ut.), 259*n14*
Diana Temple, 105
Dillon, Asa W. "A.W.," 115–116, 119, 125, 131
Dimock, Brad, 66; *Very Hard Way: Bert Loper and the Colorado River, The*, 66
Dolores River, 24, 25, 33, 50–51, 163, 233
Dolores Triangle, 43, 233, 246*n6*
Domínguez and Escalante Expedition, 25, 110
Domínguez, Francisco Atanasio, 24, 25
Double Drop, 119
Double Pitch Rapid, 98, 139, 191, 193, 212, 215, 234. *See also* Funnel Falls
Douglas Aircraft, 104
Down the Colorado, 68
Du Bois, Lt. John Van Deusen, 33, 162, 244*n33*
Duckworth, James, 50–51
Dunn, William, 67
Duplex Miners' Cabins, 228, 229*f*
Durrance, Dick, 145
Durrance, Margaret, 145

East Portal, 100, 110, 119, 123, 130–131. *See also* Gunnison Tunnel
Eaton, Earl, 145
Echo Canyon, 100, 106, 115, 125, 136
Echo Ranch, 220
Eddy, Clyde, 4, 7, 250*n7*
Edith, 86–87
Elizondo, Emmett, 7
Escalante, Silvestre Vélez de, 24, 25, 110
Exploration of the Colorado River and Its Canyon, The, 90, 250*n2*

Falls of Sorrow, 92, 114–115, 119
Fandrich, Joe, 16
Farr, Constable, 54
Fellows, Abraham Lincoln "A.L.," 92, 106, 110, 114–117, 116*f*, 119–122, 125, 129, 131, 133, 136–137; qualifications for an assistant, 115
Ferdinand V. Hayden Survey, 21, 22*f*, 35, 111, 163
FIBArk (First in Boating the Arkansas), 142
Fifth Infantry, 163

Fike, Richard E., 60, 227, 247*n5*
Fitzpatrick, Tom, 29
Flat Rock Falls, 92, 100, 119, 197*f*, 197
Flavell, George, 4, 250*n13*
Florence Creek, 7, 220–221
Fort Garland, 20, 163
Fort Robidoux, 243*n22*
Fort Union, 32
Fort Uncompahgre, 27
Freemont Culture, 229
Frémont, Colonel John C., 9, 30, 150–152, 162
Frémont Expedition, 9, 28, 30, 150, 152
French Canadian trappers, 29
French trappers, 25
Fruita (Colo.), 7, 219, 221, 234
Fuller, Florence Harris, 7, 220–221, 230
Fuller, Robert Lee, 221
Funnel Falls, 98, 139, 234

Galloway-Stone boats, 100
Galloway, John (son), 78
Galloway, Nathaniel "Nate" (father), 7, 85, 91
Galloway, Parley (son), 7, 78
Gannett, Henry, 21, 35, 36, 37, 163–164
Gateway (Colo.), 50
Geerlings, Paul, 145
Gibson, William, 96
Gila River, 30, 151
Glade Park, 63, 240
Glass, Hugh, 29
Glen Canyon, 24, 76, 94, 95, 145
Glenwood Springs (Colo.), 6, 8, 66, 68–72, 75–78, 93, 96, 144, 145, 166, 170, 193, 213
Gore Canyon, 133, 142
Grand Canyon, 6, 7, 23, 67, 78, 80, 81, 83–89, 90, 93, 94, 96, 102–106, 110, 133, 141, 145, 171, 175, 178; South Rim, 83, 85, 89; reference to Westwater Canyon, 11–12, 140, 191, 212
Grand Canyon of the Gunnison River, 112
Grand Canyon River Expeditions, 144
Grand County, 7, 9, 17, 19, 20, 22, 28, 33, 146, 162, 163, 220, 225, 238,
Grand Junction (Colo.), 6–7, 11, 15, 17, 21, 22, 24, 27, 35, 37, 43, 46, 48, 49, 51–53, 56,

Index | 279

59, 62, 67, 75, 78, 80, 90, 97, 144, 159, 180, 190, 193, 212–213, 219, 221, 225, 232, 234; North Branch OST, 21–22, 24, 35, 43
Grand Junction/Mesa County Riverfront Commission, 21
Grand River, 3–8, 9, 14, 24, 27, 33, 36, 42, 53–54, 59, 66-67, 69, 72–73, 76–78, 89–90, 93, 96–97, 99, 102, 141–142, 146, 154, 159–161, 164, 175–176, 180, 191, 195, 212–213, 219, 232; crossing, 21, 24, 27, 35, 37, 159, 163–164. *See also* Upper Colorado River
Grand River (early name for Gunnison River), 152–153, 212
Grand River Crossing, 27, 35, 159, 163, 164, 256n3
Grand Valley, 18, 21, 112, 229
Grand Valley Diversion Dam, 73
Grand Valley Times, 5
Granite Canyon, 67, 75, 191, 212. *See also* Westwater Canyon
Grant, George D. (father), 220
Grant, Frank (son), 220
Grant, Royal (son), 45, 220
Grant's Slough, 220
Great Falls, 92, 129f, 208f. *See also* Torrence Falls
Great Fort Garland and Salt Lake City Wagon Road, 20. *See also* Salt Lake Wagon Road
Great Salt Lake, 30, 244n31
Green River, 3, 4, 7, 10, 14, 19, 24, 25, 27, 54, 67, 72–73, 76, 79, 93, 110, 141, 148, 155, 169, 220; as part of the Old Spanish Trail, 6, 16, 17, 28, 32, 33, 35–36, 39, 156–157, 162, 164
Green River (Ut.), 6, 7, 11, 15, 17, 54, 67, 72, 76, 93, 94, 238
Green River (Wy.), 85
Green River Crossing, 6, 16, 32, 43
Green River Station, 93
Grubb, H.W., 48
Guest, Doug, 138
Gulf of California, 6, 68, 79, 89, 106, 250n13
Gunnison (Colo.), 6, 42, 48, 50, 55
Gunnison, Captain John W., 6, 8–9, 32, 33, 35, 36, 111, 146, 151–152, 160–162; death, 9, 90, 149
Gunnison Gorge "Gunny Gorge," 136, 254n35
Gunnison River, 4, 6, 13, 25, 27, 46, 49–52, 56, 66, 75, 78, 79–81, 89–90, 92–94, 100, 102, 106–107, 109–112, 114–116, 121–122, 125, 130–133, 136, 141, 160, 172, 176, 178, 181, 207, 212; confluence with Cimarron River, 92, 115; confluence with Uncompahgre River, 25, 27, 112
Gunnison Survey, 152, 162. *See* also central route survey
Gunnison Tunnel, 8, 63, 81, 83, 92–93, 100, 114, 122, 129–130, 172, 180, 185, 188, 194f, 195. *See also* East Portal

Hades Canyon, 57, 60, 67, 75, 145
Haemmerle, Beatrice, 145
Haemmerle, Florian, 145
Hafen, Ann W., 23
Hafen, Ann W. & Leroy R., *Old Spanish Trail*, 23
Hafen, Leroy R., 23
Hall, Andy, 250n13
Hall, Jay, 101, 205
Hallett, Charles H. (father), 44, 226, 239, 246n10
Hallett, Charles V. (son), 45, 239
Hallett, Chloe A. (mother), 44, 239
Hallett, Roscoe C. (son), 42, 45, 58–59, 230–231, 239
Hallett family, 45, 56, 238, 246n9
Hallett's Pasture, 226
Halliday, Alvin, 60, 224
Harper, Sam W., 55
Harris, Joe, 62, 224
Harris, Laphene "Don," 96, 143f, 143–144, 259n14
Hart, John L.J. "Jerry," 145
Harvey, Fred, 87
Hay Canyon, 27
Heap, Gwinn Harris, 32, 37, 160
Henry, Andrew, 29
Henry Mountains, 246n10, 259n10
Herbert, Harvey Edward "Ed," 98, 221, 222f
Hite, 94, 144

Holiday River Expeditions, 12, 41, 43, 60, 144, 227
Holladay, Dee, 12, 40–41, 43–44, 44f, 46, 56, 60, 139, 144, 227, 228, 230, 234, 259n14. *See also* Holiday River Expeditions
Hoover Dam, 6
Horn, Tom, 221
Hovey, M.V. "Frank," 114
Howlands (Oramel G. and Seneca), 67
Hubbs, Robert, 259n14
Huckleberry Finn, 10
Hudson, Ed, 143–145
Hummel, L.D. "Luke," 63, 233–234
Hunt, Jesse (Elwood Clark Malin's stepson), 225f
Hunter's Rapid, 139, 234
Huntington Library, 65, 66
Huntoon, Dr. Peter, 11
Hyde, Bessie, 103, 107–108
Hyde, Glen, 103, 107

J. Willard Marriott Library, 176
Jacques, Maria Roselia, 28
Janney, Tom Michael, 131, 132f, 135f
John C. Bell, 114
Johnstone, Colonel Albert Sydney, 32
Jones, Dan, 163
Jones, Lesley Allen "Les," 146, 234
Jones, Sam, 46
Julien, Denis, 25, 27, 66, 222f, 243n22

Kanab Creek, 67
Kane, Elmer, 7, 78, 142
Kendrick, Frank Clarence, 7, 19, 60, 67, 219, 224
Kern, Dr. Benmamin J. (brother), 152
Kern, Chuck, 13, 133
Kern, Edward M. (brother), 152
Kern, Richard H. (brother), 152
King, Henry, 150–151
Kirschbaum, Walter, 63, 130, 133, 134f, 134, 140, 142
Klevin, Chester, 96
Knipmeyer, James H., 66; *Life and Times of Denis Julien: Fur Trader, The*, 66
Knowles Canyon, 219
Knowles, Emery, 219, 240

Knowles Ranch, 219, 240
Kolb Brothers, 84, 86, 102, 175
Kolb Studios, 87, 102
Kolb, Blanche (Emery Kolb's wife), 88, 104
Kolb, Edward (father), 83
Kolb, Ella Nelson (mother), 83
Kolb, Ellsworth Leonardson, 4, 6, 11, 58, 66, 78, 79–96, 98, 100–108, 109–110, 114, 125, 130, 131, 133, 136–137, 140, 141, 142, 145, 171–172, 175–176, 215f, 221; with Bert Loper, 59, 78, 94, 96–98, 100, 106, 146, 172, 234; and brother Emery, 80–81, 83–89, 90, 94, 96, 103–104, 105, 107, 176, 195; mental breakdown, 104; photographic business, 84–85, 88; *Through the Grand Canyon from Wyoming to Mexico*, 81, 104; unpublished manuscript, 79, 102, 141, 176; youth, 83–84
Kolb, Emery (brother), 80–81, 83–89, 94, 103–105, 107
Kolb, Eric (brother), 104, 105
Kreutzfeldt, Frederick, 4, 8–9, 146, 149–152, 160–161

Labyrinth Canyon, 93
Lacy, Joe M., 63, 133, 140
Lake Fork, 92, 107, 111, 116, 176–178, 177f, 180
Lake Powell, 24
Lake San Cristobal, 177
La Roux, 152, 155, 161. *See also* Leroux, Joaquin Antoine
La Sal Mountains, 33, 34, 161, 163. *See also* Salt Mountains
Lauzon, F.C., 114
Leadville (Colo.), 71
Lee's Ferry, 7, 94
Leich, Harold H., 4–5, 42, 46, 58–59, 65, 78, 142, 230, 245n3; *Alone on the Colorado*, 65, 141
Leroux, Joaquin Antoine (aka Watkins), 25, 26, 27, 28–33, 35–36, 146, 160–162, 244n30, 244n31, 256n7; bio, 28–29; *Life and Times of Denis Julien: Fur Trader, The*, 66
Lindgren, Scott, 13
Little Colorado River, 31

Little Dolores Canyon, 226, 229
Little Dolores Rapid, 139
Little Dolores River, 43, 225, 228, 230
Little Dolores waterfall, 231*f*
Little Gold Dust, 72
Little Hole, 139, 228–229, 230*f*, 237
Little Hole Wildfire, 224
Little Salt Creek, 36
Loper, Albert "Bert," 6, 58, 59, 66, 78, 95*f*, 96–100, 106, 130, 142, 143*f*, 146, 171–174, 176, 193–195, 197*f*, 198*f*, 200, 202–203, 211*f*, 213, 221, 234; with Charles Russell and Ed Monett, 93–94, 95, 171; Grand Old Man of the Colorado River, 66, 93, 96; reputation 93–95, 171
Loper, Rachel Jamison, 93
Loring's Trail, 20, 163. *See also* Salt Lake Wagon Road
Loring, Colonel William Wing, 16*f*, 32–33, 34*f*, 35, 36, 37, 146, 162–163, 226
Los Angeles (Calif.), 23–24, 88, 104, 107
Louisiana Purchase, 25, 28
Lower Intestine, 119
Luster, James, 230
Luster Cave, 230

Magill, John, 60
Magley, Robb, 122; *Deep Black*, 122
Malin, Elwood Clark (father), 42, 62–63, 217, 221, 224, 225*f*, 227, 230
Malin, John L. "Jack" (son), 221, 233, 245*n*4, 247*n*2
Malin, Owen Madox (son), 221, 227
Malloy, Ed, 47
Marble Canyon (Grand Canyon), 86
Marble Canyon (Westwater), 43, 233
Marcy, Captain Randolph B., 32
Marston, Otis Reed "Dock," 65–67, 70, 78, 93, 106
Martins, Ulrich, 133, 140, 142
Mattimore, Tom, 247*n*7
Mason, Ron, 133
May, John, 220
May Flats, 220
McDonald, Harry, 6–7, 219
McDonald Canyon, 219
McGraw Bottom, 27, 33

McGruder, Richard Adolphus "Rich," 8, 62–64, 248*n*15
McPherson Ranch, 220
Merkt, Ida, 64, 248*n*16
Mesa County, 21, 51, 55
Mexican-American War, 31
Mexican Hat Expeditions, 143
Mexico, 25, 29
Michigan, 221
Midland Railroad, 51
Mile Long Rapids, 93
Miller, Albert, 105, 136
Miller, James Edwin DDS, 3–4, 8, 66–67, 69–73, 69*f*, 75–76, 78, 141, 142, 165–167, 169; bio, 71; boating experience, 72, 75–76, 167; pictures, 8, 70, 76, 141, 167
Milligan, Lindsi, 138
Miners' Cabin, 60, 227, 228*f*. *See also* Wild Horse Cabin
Mississippi River, 25, 30, 240
Missouri River, 25, 29
Moab (Ut.), 6–7, 11, 15, 57, 59, 63, 73, 76–77, 78, 80, 83, 93, 96, 97, 106, 141, 191, 193, 212, 213; Old Spanish Trail, 16, 24
Moab Crossing, 16, 24
Moab Library, 5
Moccasin Bill, 122
Möllhausen, Baldwin, 29
Monett, Ed, 93–94, 95, 171
Montoya, Don, 60, 247*n*5
Montrose (Colo.), 6, 37, 51, 63, 101, 105, 115, 136, 174, 180, 185, 188, 200
Montrose Daily Press, 171–172
Moonshine Island, 217, 224
Moore, Frank, 217
Moore Canyon, 217
Mormon Battalion, 29, 30, 31, 37
Morrow Reservoir, 130
Mount Leroux, 35
Mountain Man Rendezvous, 27
Mt. Ouray, 178
Music Temple, 145

Narrows, the, 92, 100–101, 102, 105, 109, 112, 114, 119–125, 123*f*, 124*f*, 130, 131, 133, 136–137, 199*f*; physical measurement, 90, 122

National Geographic Magazine, 79, 81, 102, 144, 176
National Park Service (NPS), 87
National Trails System Act, 22
Native American, 14, 17, 24, 28, 29, 224
Navajos, 24, 163
Needles (Calif.), 7, 89, 106
Nelson, Ed, 133
Nelson, Jack, 17, 23, 37
Nelson, Katherine, 37
New Generation Rapid (also called Next Generation Rapid), 126f, 132f
New Mexico, 15, 20, 23–24, 28–29, 30–32, 66, 150, 224
New York, 62, 69, 102, 105, 178
New York Public Library, 8, 66
Next Generation Rapid. *See* New Generation Rapid
Nichols, Ed, 144
North Branch of the Old Spanish Trail, 3, 6, 14, 15–17, 22–24, 25–26, 28, 30, 31f, 32–33, 37–38, 41, 66, 110, 141, 149, 224; preceding Salt Lake Wagon Road, 19, 22, 23, 35–37, 146
North Branch of the Old Spanish Historical Trail, 31f
North Rim of the Black Canyon, 110, 111f, 112, 125
Northern Arizona University (NAU), 92, 175–176
Nottingham, D.M., 34f
Nottingham Point, 34f
NPS. *See* National Park Service
Nunes Carvalho, Solomon, 162

Ohkay Owingeh (current name for San Juan Pubelo), 26
Old Salt Lake Wagon Road, 19, 20, 36, 164, 223f. *See also* North Branch of the Old Spanish Trail; Salt Lake Wagon Road
Old Spanish Trail (OST), 17, 23f, 24, 25, 27–28, 32–33, 35, 36, 146, 151, 156–157, 160, 162, 224
Old Spanish Trail Association (OSTA), 17
Olsen, J. Perry, 43, 230, 239
Osborne, Jos., 59
Osborne, Mary, 59–60, 62, 64

OST. *See* Old Spanish Trail
Ouray (Colo.), 106, 164, 178
Ouray Indian Reservation, 112
Outlaw Cave, 3, 8, 12, 14, 40–43, 45, 53f, 56, 57, 58f, 60, 62–64, 141, 147, 228, 230, 234
Outlaw Grave, 44, 45f, 232, 234

Pace-Fuller Ranch, 7, 220, 230
Pace, Joe, 221, 224, 230
Pacific Coast Railroad Survey, 30
Pacific Ocean, 30, 84, 106, 149
Pacific Railroad, 4, 8, 9, 90, 111
Pahvant Utes, 9, 90, 149
Painted Wall, 111f, 125, 205f
Pawnees, 28
Peach Springs, 107
Pearl Harbor, 104
Peterborough canoe, 80, 81, 83, 96, 98, 100, 211f
Palisade, 53, 73, 75
Palisade Wine Country, 73
Palmer, General William Jackson, 112
Paria Canyon, 250n20
Paris, Roger, 142
Pattie, James Ohio, 25
Pelton, John, 92, 114
Pelton Survey, 92, 115, 119, 122, 131
Peter's Point, 10
Pierson, Lloyd M., 17, 23, 28, 36, 37, 38, 159, 163
Pike's Peak, 84
Piñon Mesa, 221
Pioneer's Cemetery, 105
Placerville (Colo.), 51
Pope, William, 35
Posada, Alonso de, 24
Powell, Major John Wesley, 4, 8, 69–70, 76, 77, 81, 84, 89, 166; *Exploration of the Colorado River and Its Canyon, The*, 90, 250n2; Powell's 1869 Survey, 67, 85, 90, 142
Principals Office, 119
Provost, Etienne, 25

Ramp w/S-Turn, 118f, 119
Raven's Beak, 53
Ray's Tavern, 238

Razor Rock, 11, 139
Red Rock Canyon, 92, 100, 102, 105, 106, 110, 115, 129, 136, 131, 173, 197, 207, 209–210
Reeves, Rollen J., 164
Rhoades, Ed, 46, 51
Rifle (Colo.), 6, 71, 73
Rigg, James P. Jr. "Jim," 143
Rio Grande River, 19, 150
Rivera, Juan Maria de Antonio, 25
River Runner, The, 13
RMFC. *See* Rocky Mountain Fur Company
Road to Colorado, 20. *See also* Salt Lake Wagon Road
Road to Salt Lake, 20. *See also* Salt Lake Wagon Road
Roan Mountains, 27, 160
Roaring Fork River, 145
Robb, Judge James M., 21–23, 33, 35, 37, 38
Robidoux brothers, 25, 28
Robidoux, Antoine, 25, 26f, 27
Robidoux, Francois, 25
Robidoux, Louis, 25, 27
Robidoux, Miguel, 25
Rock Creek, 4
Rocky Mountain Fur Company (RMFC), 29
Rocky Mountains, 25, 66, 111, 150, 178
Romance of the Colorado River, The, 68–69, 76, 148, 165, 169
Ron Smith's Grand Canyon River Expeditions, 144
Room of Doom, 98, 139, 215f, 234, 236f
Roosevelt, Theodore, 195
Rose Ranch, 41, 43, 44, 226, 230, 238, 246n9
Rose, Mary, 41, 43
Rose, Ray, 41, 43, 56, 230–231
Ruby Canyon, 17–19, 38, 164, 219
Russell, Charles, 93–94, 95, 171
Rust, Dave, 86
Ruwitch, Tom, 133

Saeckler, Beppo (Peppo), 7, 78, 142
Saguache (Colo.), 27
St. Louis (Mo.), 28, 149

Salida (Colo.), 142
Salina (Ut.), 37
Salmon, Rusty, 221
Salt Creek, 27, 35, 36, 154, 160, 164
Salt Lake City (Ut.), 10, 17, 19, 20, 47, 63, 222
Salt Lake Wagon Road, 20f, 20–22, 23, 35–36, 37, 146, 163, 222, 226; followed the North Branch of the OST, 19, 22, 23, 35–37, 146. *See also* Old Salt Lake Wagon Road
Salt Mountain, 34, 155, 157. *See also* La Sal Mountains
San Diego (Calif.), 30
San Francisco (Calif.), 45, 84
San Juan Mining District, 178
San Juan Mountains, 37
San Juan Pueblo (N.Mex.). *See* Ohkay Owingeh
San Juan River, 93, 195
San Luis Valley, 27, 31f, 37, 243n20, 245n43
San Miguel River, 33, 51
Santa Fe (N.Mex.), 23–24, 25–26, 159, 163, 178
Santa Fe Railroad, 84
Santa Fe Trail, 32
Sapinero (Colo.), 112
Schiel, Dr. James, 9
Schmacalder's compass, 244n33
Section Four—Red Rock Canyon to Smith's Fork, 92, 102, 105
Section One—Lake Fork to Cimarron, 92, 107
Section Three—Gunnison Tunnel to Red Rock Canyon, 92, 100–102, 130, 136, 171, 172
Section Two—Cimarron to Gunnison Tunnel, 92, 93, 100, 107, 130
Sellinger, Fred, 47
Separation Rapid, 67
Sherrill, Charlie Ray "C.R.," 238, 238f
Sherill, Ray, 238
Shields, John W., 78, 80–81, 82f, 83, 93, 98, 130, 178, 182f, 183–185, 187f, 187–190, 192, 212–213
Shonsbye, Ella J., 104, 252n38

Shores, Sheriff Cyrus Wells "Doc," 42, 48–56, 49f
Shoshone Canyon, 213
Shoshone Falls, 93, 96–97, 96f, 213f
Sieber Cattle Company, 219, 240
Silverton (Colo.), 46, 178
Sinbad Valley, 50
Sitgreaves, Captain Lorenzo, 31
Skull Rapid, 11, 12, 74f, 75, 83, 98, 139, 140, 148, 214f, 234. See also Whirlpool Rapid
Slide Draw, 122
Slover, Isaac, 35
Spanish Valley, 24
Smith Fork, 211
Smith brothers, 42, 51–52, 54
Smith, Bob, 6, 42, 46, 56, 232
Smith, Ira, 42, 46, 232. See also Bob Smith
Smith, Jack, 6, 46, 52, 56, 232
Smith, James H., 45
Smith, Jedediah, 24, 29
Smith, Thomas Long "Peg Leg," 25
Smithsonian Institute, 8–9, 149
Smithton (Penn.), 83
Snyder, Daniel M., 225
Snyder Mesa, 225
Soap Creek Rapid, 86–87, 107, 250n6
SOB Gulch, 205f
Sockdolager Rapid, 105
Sock-It-To-Me Rapid, 139
Sokol, Filip, 133
Sonora River, 151
South Rim of the Black Canyon, 110, 125
South Rim of the Grand Canyon, 83, 85, 89
southern route survey, 29. See also Pacific Coast Railroad
Southwest, 23, 28–29, 35, 36, 146
Staircase, 139
Stanton, Robert Brewster, 8, 66–68, 68f, 70–71, 76, 78, 106, 169–170; *Colorado River Controversies*, 68; *Down the Colorado*, 68; as river historian, 67–68, 106, 169
Steele, Bill, 233
Steele, Bob, 233
Steinway, Theodore, 145
Stern, Nathan B. "N.B.," 81–83, 82f, 83, 130, 178, 182f, 183–184, 186–188, 187f
Stillwater Canyon, 93

Stith, Lt. Donald C., 163
Stone, Julius F., 4, 81–83, 82f, 86, 90, 95, 96, 130, 131, 178–180, 182f, 183–187, 187f, 195; credits Ellsworth Kolb for saving his life, 83; financed boats, 100, 174, 188, 196
Stubbs, William, 98, 221
Sublette, William, 29
Sumner, John Colton "Jack," 6, 241n1, 250n13
Suran, William C. "Bill," 84, 92, 104, 105, 175–176,
Surprise Rapid, 139

Tabeguache Utes. See Uncompahgre Utes
Taft, William Howard, 195
Taos (N.Mex.), 15, 24, 25–26, 28, 29, 32, 35–36, 66, 159, 162, 243n17
Tawney, R.A., 222
Telluride (Colo.), 71
Tenth Infantry, 163
Thirty-eighth parallel, 4, 9, 30, 149
Thirty-fifth parallel, 29, 32
Thirty-ninth parallel, 4, 9, 30, 149
Thode, Jackson, 18, 242n3
Thomas, Royal V., 103, 251n35
Thompson (Ut.), 18, 55, 222, 225
Thompson Cattle Ranch, 188
Three Spanish Crosses, 5f, 146–148, 147f
Through the Grand Canyon from Wyoming to Mexico, 81, 104
Times Independent, 5
Torrence Falls, 92, 102, 128f, 129, 129f, 208f
Torrence, William W. "Will," 92, 106, 110, 116, 116f, 120–122, 125, 128–129, 131, 133, 136–137; with Pelton Survey, 114, 115
Torrey, John, 151
Trail Canyon, 237
Trail/Nyswonger Gulch, 115
Transcontinental Railroad, 30, 149. See also central route survey
Trapper Trail, 27, 66, 110, 146
Triple Drop, 119
Twain, Mark, 10
Tyler, Jesse, 7
Tynan, Dr. Thomas E., 45, 246n10

Uintah Basin, 27
Uintah Indian Reservation, 112
"Ultima Thule," 119
Unaweep Canyon, 46, 50–51
Unaweep Switch, 46–48, 52–53
Uncompahgre River, 25, 27, 112, 114, 152, 180
Uncompahgre Trading Post, 27
Uncompahgre Utes, 43
Uncompahgre Valley, 111–112, 114, 122, 129, 195
University of Minnesota, 71
University of Oregon, 71
University of Utah, 145, 176, 226, 229
Upper Colorado River, 4–6, 9, 14, 41, 65–66, 67, 78, 79, 109, 141–142, 145, 148. *See also* Grand River
Upper Death, 97
Uravan (Colo.), 51
USGS. *See* U.S. Geological Survey
U.S. Geological Survey (USGS), 114
U.S. Reclamation Service, 114, 130, 195, 237
Utah Digital Newspapers, 41
Utah Lake, 24, 25
Utah Line, 46, 191, 212
Utah Territory, 90, 146, 149, 162, 164, 221
Utes, 12, 19, 22, 24, 37, 43, 59, 112, 150, 152, 163, 224, 230

VanderZanden, Karla, 12, 148
Vernal (Ut.), 42–43, 45, 46, 56, 232
Vernal bank robbers, 45, 46, 56
Vernal Mesa, 114
Very Hard Way: Bert Loper and the Colorado River, The, 66
Virgin River, 31, 244n30
Virginia, 69

Wallace, Bob W. (alias of Bob W. Boyle), 46, 51–52. *See also* Boyle, Bob W.
Warner, Reverend Mark T., 136
Warren, John, 62
Webb, Roy, 65, 141; *Alone on the Colorado*, 65, 141
Weisheit, John, 15, 219, 238
West Creek area of Unaweep Canyon, 46

West Fork of the North Branch OST, 31*f*, 243n20
West Palm Beach (Florida), 167
West Water, 18, 43, 242n3
Westwater (Ut.), 6, 12, 58, 78, 80–81, 222, 225, 228, 240
Westwater camp, 9, 15–17, 28, 33–35, 34*f*, 36–39, 41, 141, 159–163, 226
Westwater Canyon, 4–5, 7, 8, 11–12, 14, 41–43, 44–45, 54, 57–58, 60, 62, 64, 67, 73, 75, 78, 80, 83, 93, 97–99, 109, 110, 133, 138–146, 148, 175, 191, 192*f*, 193, 212–213, 215–216, 227, 232, 234, 238; historical significance of location, 14, 145–146
Westwater Creek, 6, 18, 22*f*, 27, 36, 37, 44, 160–161, 226
Westwater Gulch, 224
Westwater launch, 38*f*
Westwater Railroad Station, 17, 39, 223*f*
Westwater Ranch, 7, 16, 18*f*, 19, 20*f*, 60, 62, 139, 219, 224–225, 228
Westwater Ranger Station, 7, 12, 19, 33, 138, 140, 222, 224, 227
Westwater town, 6, 12, 18*f*, 58, 78, 80–81, 97, 222, 225, 228, 240
Westwater Valley, 19, 60; significance of location, 14, 146
Whipple, Lt. Amiel Weeks, 29, 32, 160
Whirlpool Rapid, 11, 75, 81, 83, 98, 139, 191–193, 212, 213, 214*f*, 215, 234, 235*f*. *See also* Skull Rapid
White, Georgie, 143, 144, 255n9
White, James, 67
White River, 19
Whitewater (Colo.), 50, 52
Wild Bunch, 4, 7
Wild Horse Cabin, 60, 247n5. *See also* Miners' Cabin
Wild Horse Rapid, 227, 228
William Reed Trading Post, 243n22
Williams (Ariz.), 85
Williams, Dick, 48
Williams, William Sherley "Old Bill," 25, 150–152
Willow Creek Canyon, 27
Winty, 27
Wolfskill, John, 35

Wolfskill, William, 24, 25, 35, 243*n17*
Woodside (Ut.), 54, 221
Wootton, Richens Lacy "Uncle Dick," 36
World War I, 64, 102, 105
World War II, 104
Wright, J. Frank, 143–144
Wright, William "Billie," 101, 203–204
Wynne, Milo (aka Captain Black), 120*f*, 135

Yampa (Colo.), 70, 165, 169
Yellowstone Park, 84
Yosemite Park, 84
Young, George C., 24
Young, Ted, 133, 140

Zaenger, Paul, 135, 254*n35*
Zuni River, 31